K

THE PSYCHOLOGY OF QUALITY OF LIFE

Social Indicators Research Series

Volume 12

This new series aims to provide a public forum for single treatises and collections of papers on social indicators research that are too long to be published in our journal *Social Indicators Research*. Like the journal, the book series deals with statistical assessments of the quality of life from a broad perspective. It welcomes the research on a wide variety of substantive areas, including health, crime, housing, education, family life, leisure activities, transportation, mobility, economics, work, religion and environmental issues. These areas of research will focus on the impact of key issues such as health on the overall quality of life and vice versa. An international review board, consisting of Ruut Veenhoven, Joachim Vogel, Ed Diener, Torbjorn Moum and Wolfgang Glatzer, will ensure the high quality of the series as a whole.

The titles published in this series are listed at the end of this volume.

THE PSYCHOLOGY OF QUALITY OF LIFE

by

M. JOSEPH SIRGY

Virginia Polytechnic Institute and State University,
Blacksburg, Virginia, U.S.A.

KLUWER ACADEMIC PUBLISHERS
DORDRECHT / BOSTON / LONDON

A C.I.P. Catalogue record for this book is available from the Library of Congress.

ISBN 1-4020-0800-7

Published by Kluwer Academic Publishers,
P.O. Box 17, 3300 AA Dordrecht, The Netherlands.

Sold and distributed in North, Central and South America
by Kluwer Academic Publishers,
101 Philip Drive, Norwell, MA 02061, U.S.A.

In all other countries, sold and distributed
by Kluwer Academic Publishers,
P.O. Box 322, 3300 AH Dordrecht, The Netherlands.

Printed on acid-free paper

Printed and bound in the Netherlands.

LIFE IS LIKE

AN ARTICHOKE.

YOU STRIP AWAY

A FEW YEARS.

YOU PEEL OFF

AN ILLUSION OR TWO,

AND WHAT REMAINS

IS ESSENTIAL . . .

<u>THE HEART</u>.

ANONYMOUS

ACKNOWLEDGEMENTS

There are many people who helped me directly and indirectly write this book. Quality-of-life researchers who made their contributions to the literature should have the greatest credit. Those who helped me directly by commenting and critiquing the entire book include Alex Michalos (editor of the Social Indicators Research book series) and Pamela Ann Jackson (who is an experimental psychologist and an associate Professor of Psychology at Radford University). Others have commented on certain parts of the book include Michael Frisch (a clinical psychologist, Professor of Psychology at Baylor University, and whose work on quality-of-life therapy is highly regarded), and Dong-Jin Lee (an assistant professor of marketing at SUNY-Binghamton, one of my ex-doctoral students who shares my passion in quality-of-life research). I extend my many thanks to them too. Finally, I like to express my appreciation to the editorial staff at Kluwer Academic Publishers. They include Sabine Wesseldjik, Renee de Boo, Peter de Liefde, and Evelien Bakker. I owe them my gratitude and deep appreciation for their caring attitude and helpfulness.

CONTENTS

Preface   xi

Part I: Introduction   1
   Chapter 1: Definitions and Distinctions   3
   Chapter 2: Examples of Measures of Subjective Well Being   17
   Chapter 3: Motives Underlying Subjective Well Being   33

Part II: Inter-domain Strategies   51
   Chapter 4: Bottom-up Spillover   53
   Chapter 5: Top-down Spillover   69
   Chapter 6: Horizontal Spillover   77
   Chapter 7: Compensation   89

Part III: Intra-domain Strategies   101
   Chapter 8: Re-evaluation Based on Personal History   103
   Chapter 9: Re-evaluation Based on Self-concept   117
   Chapter 10: Re-evaluation Based on Social Comparison   135
   Chapter 11: Goal Selection   149
   Chapter 12: Goal Implementation and Attainment   177
   Chapter 13: Re-appraisal   187

Part IV: Inter- and Intra-domain Strategies   199
   Chapter 14: Balance   201

References   215

Appendix   249

Index   263
About the Author   279

PREFACE

The purpose of this book is to make an effort to bring together a body of research on the subjective aspects of quality of life ("subjective well being", "happiness", "life satisfaction", "perceived quality of life") by starting out with Wilson's (1968) theory of avowed happiness. I build on Wilson's theory by applying diverse but selected findings from the ever-burgeoning quality-of-life literature. Wilson's theory of happiness can be captured by two key postulates. These were summarised by Diener, Suh, Lucas, and Smith (1999). They stated that fulfilment of needs causes happiness, whereas the persistence of unfulfilled needs causes unhappiness. The degree of need fulfillment required to produce satisfaction depends on the adaptation level of the needs, which is influenced by past experience, comparisons with others, personal values, among others.

Well, the literature on the subjective aspects of quality of life has grown by leaps and bounds since 1967. Diener (1984) and Diener et al. (1999) did a great job reviewing a small part of this voluminous and growing literature. But the literature remains quite fragmented. It needs synthesis and integration. Furthermore, the literature needs to answer the "so what" question. I make an attempt in this book to pull the literature together. I do so by providing a common theoretical language that serves to establish a nomological network. Most importantly, I make a strong attempt to answer the "so what" question by showing how people can use this massive literature to enhance their own subjective well being and the well being of others. Specifically, I show the reader that there are 11 strategies that people can use to optimise subjective well being. These are:
1. Bottom-up spillover,
2. Top-down spillover,
3. Horizontal spillover,
4. Compensation,
5. Re-evaluation based on personal history,
6. Re-evaluation based on the self-concept,
7. Re-evaluation based on social comparison,
8. Goal selection,
9. Goal implementation and attainment,
10. Re-appraisal, and
11. Balance.

These personal growth strategies can be categorised in terms of their focus on inter versus intra domain dynamics. There are strategies that focus on the interrelationships among life domains in a hierarchy of domains. These particular strategies are bottom-up spillover, top-down spillover, horizontal spillover, and compensation. We call these "inter-domain strategies". In contrast, other personal growth strategies focus on manipulating aspects within a given life domain. These are re-evaluation based on personal history, re-evaluation based on the self-concept, re-evaluation based on social comparison, goal selection, goal implementation and attainment, and re-appraisal. These are "intra-domain strategies". There is also a strategy that involves the manipulation of psychological aspects within a given life domain and across various life domains. This particular strategy is balance.

Why is subjective well being an important concept to study? The answer to this question is twofold: *Subjective well being leads to prosocial behaviour, a prerequisite to civilised society.* Are there any empirical studies to substantiate the link between prosocial behaviour and subjective well being? Yes. Here is an example of a recent study providing evidence of that link. Magen (1996) conducted a study to investigate the relationship between adolescents' experience of happiness and altruism and prosocial behaviour. The findings of the study showed that those who experience happiness in greater depth and intensity tend to be more altruistic and prosocial in their behaviour than those who experience less are happiness. Examples of excerpts from youths who scored high on happiness include:

I would like to help people who need help, to make them happy, to make them feel good. I want to be a psychologist because I want to understand the heart of each person, to help him in life, so that nothing will weigh heavy on him or interfere with his living his life in peace (p. 261).

I volunteered at an old age home where we helped the elderly . . . to eat, to get dressed, and sometimes we told them stories that warmed their hearts. It was a wonderful week. I went to an institution for the blind before the holidays, where we students sang and cheered them up . . .. When we left I felt that we had really made a contribution to them, and this deed and the happiness we sparked in those people gave me a feeling that life is really wonderful (p. 261).

How can we explain this finding? Subjective well being can be construed *a la* Maslow as need satiation. When needs are satisfied and satiated, the individual is released to focus on higher-order needs. The greater the need satiation the greater the propensity to move into the higher stages of cognitive moral development. Thus, increased happiness enhances people's disposition to become more moral and altruistic in their behaviour. The more people become happy with their lives the more they contribute positively and significantly to society. Hence, to promote social and societal development we to need to enhance people's quality of life, i.e., to enhance their subjective well being (cf. Diener, 2000).

Ruut Veenhoven, a renowned quality-of-life researcher, has made this argument repeatedly (Veenhoven, 1991b). He argues that happy people have identity integrity, ego strength, mental maturity, inner control, social ability, activity, and perceptual openness. Happiness leads people to become actively involved in society; it frees them to be creative; and it fosters better personal relations with people in general. Happiness enhances health and promotes longevity. Ultimately, happiness has survival value for the human species. Enjoyment of life fosters activity, strengthens social bonds, and preserves health.

The second answer to the question (about why the study of subjective aspects of quality of life is important) involves *values*. Milton Rokeach (1972), a renowned social psychologist, once made the distinction between instrumental and terminal values. Terminal values are goals in life that are end states, not means to ends. Examples of terminal values include happiness, a comfortable life, a meaningful life, peace, equality, freedom, wisdom, true friendship, and salvation, among others. Instrumental values are highly valued goals because we believe that by pursuing these goals we will be able to experience those cherished terminal values. Examples of instrumental values include hard work, respect for others, co-operation, competition, loyalty, fidelity, commitment, gratitude, and respect for the environment, among others. This distinction between terminal and instrumental values is helpful because it informs us that there are certain values in life that give meaning to our existence. We live to experience those terminal values. One of those terminal values is the *quality of life*. Quality of life, as a terminal value, is captured by common-language terms such as *happiness*, *meaningful life*, and a *comfortable life*. Quality of life is an end goal for the human species, and society organises its many institutions to strive to attain a better quality of life for all.

Philosophers and scholars advice us that sometimes we act confused. Our current values are out of synch with the notion of the good life. Many of us pursue material consumption as if it were an end goal, a terminal value. Social critics maintain that material consumption is an instrumental value, *not* a terminal one. We consume material goods to achieve happiness in life. We should not consume material goods for the sake of consumption. Many of our social ills (e.g., crime, environmental degradation, and immorality) are symptomatic of a society that has confused instrumental values with terminal ones. Materialism should be a means to a higher end, namely the quality of life. If excessive materialism denigrates the quality of life, then we should find ways to realign it with quality of life. We should be focusing on quality of life, not materialism. Materialism should serve this higher end, not work against it.

Over the last several centuries so much effort and good works have been focused on the "quantity of life," not necessarily the "quality of life". Efforts at eradicating poverty, hunger, and disease are directed to the *quantity of life*, not quality of life. These efforts prolong life. They may not enhance the quality of life. Programs designed to enhance economic development are attempts to enhance the quantity of life, not necessarily the quality of life. Quantity of life has its focus on meeting basic human needs, extending life expectancy, and sustaining the survival of an exploding population worldwide. Of course, efforts at enhancing the quantity of life are extremely important, and some may argue are more important than efforts directed to enhance the quality of life. But as human civilisation grows and as we make satisfactory progress to deal with issues of the quantity of life, our attention shifts to tackle issues of quality of life. The study of quality of life is becoming increasingly more important, and I suspect that it will play an increasingly important role in the years and centuries to come.

This book is about the *psychology* of quality of life. The focus here is on the subjective aspects of quality of life. Psychologists (particularly social, personality, and developmental psychologists) and quality-of-life researchers refer to the subjective aspects of quality of life as happiness, life satisfaction, subjective well being, and perceived quality of life. I will use the term *subjective well being* throughout this book to mean the subjective aspects of quality of life. Quality-of-life studies is a growing field of study that subsumes subjective well being. Quality-of-life researchers study both subjective and objective aspects of quality of life. Many quality-of-life economists, for example, focus on measuring the quality of life using objective indicators such as life expectancy, educational attainment, health status, food and nutrition, expenditures on consumer goods, energy consumption, etc. The focus of the quality-of-life economist is society at large. Quality-of-life psychologists focus on the subjective aspects of quality of life, and we work with the *individual in a social context*. They usually do not work with groups such as families and communities. Quality-of-life sociologists do that. Quality-of-life psychologists, sociologists, and economists are not all housed in the traditional disciplines of psychology, sociology, and economics. Many of us are spread across many disciplines. You will find us doing quality-of-life research in travel and tourism, leisure studies, family and child development, gerontology, architecture and design, urban planning, marketing, management, social work, clothing and textiles, environmental studies, pharmacology, health sciences, public administration, religious studies, food and nutrition, and many others. Most of us are *applied social/behavioural scientists*.

The problems and issues of quality of life are so varied. I do not pretend that this book comes anywhere close to dealing with the full spectrum of this growing field of study. This book has a very narrow focus. It deals only with subjective well being. The focus is to find out how people successfully use personal strategies to enhance their subjective well being and communicate this information to readers in a way that can be useful. These strategies are discussed in terms principles that capture the essence of the research in the field. Here is a list of the quality-of-life strateges and their unlining principles.

The Bottom-Up Spillover Strategy
o   The Bottom-Up Spillover Principle
o   The Means-End Chain Principle of Bottom-up Spillover
o   The Multi-domain Satisfaction Principle of Bottom-up Spillover
o   The Abstractness of Life Domain Principle of Bottom-up Spillover
o   The Self-proximity Principle of Bottom-up Spillover

The Top-Down Spillover Strategy
o   The Principle of Top-Down Spillover
o   The Personality Principle of Top-down Spillover
o   The Very Happy and the Depressed Principle of Top-down Spillover

The Horizontal Spillover Strategy
o   The Horizontal-Spillover Principle
o   The Overlap Principle of Horizontal Spillover
o   The High Involvement Principle of Horizontal Spillover
o   The Skills Principle of Horizontal Spillover
o   The Cultural Pressures Principle of Horizontal Spillover

The Compensation Strategy
o   The Compensation Principle
o   The Repeated Failure Principle of Compensation
o   The Low-versus-High-Status Principle of Compensation
o   The Personal Crisis Principle of Compensation
o   The Public Condition Principle of Compensation
o   The Fixed-Sum-of-Resources Principle of Compensation
o   The Needs Principle of Compensation

The Re-Evaluation Based on Personal History Strategy
o   The Personal History Principle of Re-evaluation

    o   The Adaptation-Level Principle of Re-evaluation
    o   The Range-Frequency Principle of Re-evaluation
    o   The Adaptation-over-time Principle of Re-evaluation
    o   The Sensitisation-over-time Principle of Re-evaluation

The Re-Evaluation Based on Self-Concept Strategy
    o   The Self-concept Principle of Re-evaluation
    o   The Ideal Self Principle of Re-evaluation
    o   The Social Self Principle of Re-evaluation
    o   The Deserved-self Principle of Re-evaluation
    o   The Minimum-needs Principle of Re-evaluation
    o   The Predicted Self Principle of Re-evaluation
    o   The Competent Self Principle of Re-evaluation
    o   The Aspired Self-Principle of Re-evaluation
    o   The Principle of Self-concept Integration of Re-evaluation

The Re-Evaluation Based on Social Comparison Strategy
    o   The Principle of Social Comparison of Re-evaluation
    o   The Self-enhancement Principle of Re-evaluation
    o   The Self-improvement Principle of Re-evaluation
    o   The Self-identification Principle of Re-evaluation
    o   The Principle of What Might Have Been of Re-evaluation.
    o   The Principle of Integrated Social Comparisons

The Goal Selection Strategy
    o   The Goal Selection Principle
    o   The Meaningfulness Principle of Goal Selection
    o   The Intrinsicness Principle of Goal Selection
    o   The High-Level Goal Principle of Goal Selection
    o   The Growth Needs Principle of Goal Selection
    o   The Approach Principle of Goal Selection
    o   The Frequency Principle of Goal Selection
    o   The Cultural Norms Principle of Goal Selection
    o   The Need Deprivation Principle of Goal Selection
    o   The Achievement Principle of Goal Selection
    o   The Autonomy Principle of Goal Selection
    o   The Flow Principle of Goal Selection
    o   The Skilful Winning Principle of Goal Selection
    o   The Adaptation Principle of Goal Selection
    o   The Feedfoward Principle of Goal Selection
    o   The Motive Congruence Principle of Goal Selection

o   The Cultural Value Congruence Principle of Goal Selection
o   The Resources Congruence Principle of Goal Selection
o   The Realism Principle of Goal Selection
o   The Conflict Principle of Goal Selection

The Goal Implementation and Attainment Strategy
o   The Principle of Goal Implementation and Attainment
o   The Principle of Recognition of Goal Attainment
o   The Concreteness Principle of Goal Attainment
o   The Progress Principle of Goal Attainment
o   The Commitment Principle of Goal Implementation
o   The Feedback Principle of Goal Implementation

The Re-appraisal Strategy
o   The Re-appraisal Principle
o   The Teaching Principle of Re-appraisal.
o   The Spiritual Principle of Re-appraisal
o   The Social Support Principle of Re-appraisal
o   The Time Principle of Re-appraisal

The Balance Strategy
o   The Principle of Balance Within Life Domains
o   The Principle of Balance Between Life Domains
o   The Quota Principle of Balance
o   The Aggregation Principle of Balance
o   The Satisfaction Efficiency Principle of Balance

The book has 14 chapters. The first three chapters serve to introduce the reader to concepts and distinctions in the psychology of quality of life, concepts such as happiness, life satisfaction, positive and negative affect, and subjective well being (Chapter 1). The reader is exposed to traditional measures of subjective well being (Chapter 2). Chapter 3 describes the motivational dynamics underlying subjective well being.

Specifically, the first chapter focuses on basic definitions of subjective quality of life. Distinctions are made among related concepts of subjective well being, life satisfaction, happiness, and positive and negative affect. I describe studies showing distinctions among these concepts and show how the literature leads us to believe that subjective well being may be an umbrella concept capturing experiences and evaluations related to happiness and depression. Subjective well being involves both positive and negative affect as well as affective and cognitive experiences.

The second chapter focuses on measures of subjective well being. The chapter allows the reader to appreciate the concept of subjective well being by understanding how quality-of-life researchers have measured it over the past several decades. I group these measures into two camps, namely reflective and formative indicators of subjective well being. Reflective indicators are measures designed to capture subjective well being globally, totally, and holistically. In contrast, formative indicators of subjective well being capture the behavioural phenomenon by measuring its "causes" or "determinants".

Chapter 3 is an attempt to provide the reader with an understanding of the motivational dynamics underlying subjective well being. To do so an attempt was made to establish a theoretical framework of subjective well and to show why people are motivated to optimise their subjective well being. I start out the chapter with a definition of subjective well being as satisfaction of developmental needs through participation in salient life domains. Participation in salient life domains translate into a value-laden belief about the totality of one's life. Thus, I assume that those who are more successful in satisfying their developmental needs are likely to experience greater happiness and life satisfaction than those who are less successful. Happy people tend to be successful in organising their lives in manageable domains. They participate actively in these domains to generate satisfaction within those domains. The underlying motive is to increase positive affect but not to exceed an upper threshold and prevent negative affect from sliding below an intolerable lower level. Therefore, people tend to optimise subjective well being, not maximise it. In optimising subjective well being, they use different *inter-domain* strategies (bottom-up spillover, top-down spillover, horizontal spillover, and compensation), different *intra-domain* strategies (re-evaluation based on personal history, re-evaluation based on the self-concept, re-evaluation based on social comparison, goal selection, goal implementation and attainment, and re-appraisal), and a strategy that combine inter- and intra-domains aspects (balance).

The second part of the book focuses on inter-domain strategies--these are personal growth strategies that focus on manipulating psychological aspects dealing with the inter-relationships among life domains. Again, these strategies are bottom-up spillover, top-down spillover, horizontal spillover, and compensation.

Specifically, Chapter 4 covers *bottom-up spillover*. The strategy refers to the influence of affect in subordinate domains (e.g., family life) on superordinate domains (e.g., overall life). That is affect travels up the hierarchy of life domains. This is done in a compensatory manner, in that the negative affect in one life domain is offset by the positive affect invested in other life domains.

Top-down spillover (Chapter 5) refers to the influence of affect of superordinate domains (e.g., overall life) on subordinate domains (e.g., family, work, leisure, social, and health). It is used as a strategy to enhance subjective well being given that the most superordinate life domain (i.e., overall life) contains more positive than negative affect. The positive affect is allowed to spillover downward the domain hierarchy to increase the positive valence of the subordinate life domains, which in turn feeds back to overall life.

Horizontal spillover (Chapter 6) refers to the influence of affect in a life domain on another life domain that is neither subordinate nor superordinate to it (e.g., influence of work satisfaction on family satisfaction). Horizontal spillover focuses on a positive life domain and allows the positive affect associated with that domain to reduce the negative valence of another domain.

With respect to *compensation* (Chapter 7), this strategy involves making life domains in which the person feels good more important and other domains in which he feels bad less important. Doing so multiplies his good feelings invested in that domain; and these feelings are allowed to spill over to the most superordinate domain--overall life. By the same token, increasing the salience of the positive life domain serves to decrease the salience of the negative life domain, which in turn serves to decrease the negative spillover from that domain to overall life.

The third part of the book focuses on intra-domain strategies--these are personal growth strategies that focus on manipulating psychological aspects dealing with the intra-relationships within life domains. Again, these strategies are re-evaluation based on personal history, re-evaluation based on the self-concept, re-evaluation based on social comparisons, goal selection, goal implementation and attainment, and re-appraisal.

With respect to *re-evaluation based on personal history* (Chapter 8), this strategy to enhance subjective well being refers to the manipulation of expectancies (based on one's personal history) used in judging one's well being in a given domain. For example, if a person is dissatisfied in a particular life domain, he or she may re-evaluate this domain by noting progress toward goal attainment based on his or her history of activities. With respect to *re-evaluation based on self-concept* (Chapter 9), this strategy to enhance subjective well being refers to the use of the self-concept in making judgements about well being in a given domain. The self-concept involves expectancies such as the ideal self, the social self, the deserved self, the aspired self, the competent self, etc. Thus, a person dissatisfied in a particular life domain may re-evaluate this domain by comparing his actual self with another type of self-concept that would ensure positive evaluation. With respect to *re-evaluation based on social comparison* (Chapter 10), this strategy to enhance subjective well being refers to the manipulation of the standard of comparison (based on significant others) used in judging one's well being in a given domain.

With respect to *goal selection* (Chapter 11), this strategy to enhance subjective well being refers to the selection of personal goals that should be capable of generating a great deal of positive affect. Another strategy that will be discussed in some length is *goal implementation and attainment* (Chapter 12). The focus of this strategy is direct action designed to complete a set of tasks that would ensure goal attainment. Chapter 13 (*re-appraisal*) refers to the strategy of re-interpreting significant negative events in such a way to generate positive affect and diffuse the negative affect. Doing so serves to decrease dissatisfaction with that domain housing the experience of these events. Conversely, re-interpreting significant positive events can enhance the positive valence of the events, thereby increasing satisfaction in the domain housing these events.

Finally the *balance* chapter (Chapter 14) constitutes the fourth part of the book and serves to tie things together. This is because the chapter focuses on combining inter- and intra-psychological dynamics of the previous chapters (chapters 4 through 13) to show how subjective well being can be optimised through balance--balance within life domains and balance between and among domains. Specifically, the balance strategy refers to how people engage in events to generate both positive and negative affect within a given life domain and how they compensate across life domains. Positive affect in a domain serves to enhance subjective well being in the here and now. Negative affect serves to motivate the individual to plan ahead to correct past mistakes and to take advantage of new opportunities. Negative affect is the basis of motivation to strive to attain future goals. People look forward to future joy.

I hope you learn much from reading this book. I hope that you can use the advice from the many principles I spell out throughout this book. These principles are practical guides to help people help themselves and others enhance their quality of life. I wish you, my readers, best wishes and happiness, especially the kind of happiness you can create by applying the principles fleshed out in this book.

Happy reading,

Joe Sirgy

PART I:

INTRODUCTION

Part I involves three chapters. The first chapter serves to introduce the reader to concepts and distinctions in the psychology of quality of life, concepts such as happiness, life satisfaction, positive and negative affect, and subjective well being. Specifically, the first chapter focuses on basic definitions of subjective quality of life. Distinctions are made among related concepts of subjective well being, life satisfaction, happiness, and positive and negative affect. I describe studies showing distinctions among these concepts and show how the literature leads us to believe that subjective well being may be an umbrella concept capturing experiences and evaluations related to happiness and depression. That subjective well being involves both positive and negative affect as well as affective and cognitive experiences.

The second chapter focuses on measures of subjective well being. The chapter allows the reader to appreciate the concept of subjective well being by understanding how quality-of-life researchers have measured it over the past several decades. I group these measures into two camps, namely reflective and formative indicators of subjective well being. Reflective indicators are measures designed to capture subjective well being globally, totally, and holistically. In contrast, formative indicators of subjective well being capture the behavioural phenomenon by capturing its "causes" or "determinants".

Chapter 3 is an attempt to provide the reader with an understanding of the motives underlying subjective well being. I have tried to show why people are motivated to optimise their subjective well being. I started out the chapter with a definition of subjective well being as satisfaction of developmental needs through participation in salient life domains. This satisfaction is reflected in a value-laden belief about the totality of one's life. Thus, those who are more successful in satisfying their developmental needs are likely to experience greater happiness and life satisfaction than those who are less successful. Happy people tend to be successful in organising their lives in manageable domains. They participate actively in these domains to generate satisfaction within those domains. The underlying motive is to increase positive affect but not to exceed an upper threshold and prevent negative affect from sliding below an intolerable lower level. Therefore, people tend to enhance subjective well being, not maximise it. In optimising subjective well being, they use different *inter-domain* strategies (bottom-up spillover, top-down spillover, horizontal spillover, and compensation), different *intra-domain* strategies (re-evaluation based on personal history, re-evaluation based on the self-concept, re-evaluation based on social comparison, goal selection, goal implementation and attainment, and re-appraisal), and a strategy that combine inter- and intra-domains aspects (balance).

DEFINITIONS AND DISTINCTIONS

In this chapter, I will make an attempt to sensitise the reader to the study of subjective aspects of quality of life by making references to the concepts of happiness, positive and negative affect, life satisfaction, subjective well being, and perceived quality of life. In Chapter 2, I will use the term subjective well being to mean subjective aspects of quality of life (happiness, life satisfaction, and perceived quality of life). I will highlight certain distinctions as discussed in the literature. In Chapter 3, I will present the reader with examples of common measures of subjective well being. This coverage should provide the reader with sufficient background to follow the logic of the concepts, principles, and strategies designed to enhance subjective well being starting from Chapter 3. Readers who are only interested in understanding how those strategies may be applied to enhance subjective well being may skip chapters 1-3 and jump right into Chapter 4.

1. HAPPINESS

The famous and most renowned Greek philosophers--Plato, Socrates, and Aristotle--associated happiness with virtue (e.g., Aristotle, 340 BC/1986; Plato, 360 BC/1892). For example, in Plato's dialogue "Gorgias", Socrates tells Polus, "The men and women who are gentle and good are also happy, as I maintain, and the unjust and evil are miserable" (Plato, 360 BC/1892 translated, p. 529). They believed that people become happy through wisdom and choosing wisely. People do not act irresponsibly towards themselves or others when they choose wisely.

Bentham (1789/1969), the founder of the moral philosophy of utilitarianism, viewed happiness as a consequence of choice among alternative courses of action. His famous moral dictum of *choosing the action that leads to the greatest happiness of the greatest number* illustrates his view of happiness. Happiness is a state of being that people experience as a result of action by oneself or others. Russell (1930/1975), another utilitarian philosopher and ethicist, asserted that people who experience pleasure from seeing others happy become happy too.

It is important to note that many philosophers have addressed the issue of happiness. Happiness to most philosophers is not simply a psychological matter; it is an evaluative matter. It concerns the conditions of leading a good and moral life. Therefore, it is not a psychological phenomenon but a phenomenon of ethics (Haybron, 2000). Happiness to philosophers such as Aristotle and Thomas Jefferson require more than a state of mind. People can be deluded to be happy by religion. Many religions promise happiness in the here and now as well as in the "afterlife". Do people who "discover" religious find true happiness? A man lives in dire poverty and wretched material conditions, finds solace in religion. Is this man happy? Not according to some philosophers. For example, Aristotle viewed happiness as living in a manner that actively expresses excellence of character or virtue (Aristotle, 1962). Thus, one can be happy by expressing excellence of character (the essence of the good and moral life), not by being cheerful and serene (feeling happy).

Haybron (2000) makes the distinction among three philosophical concepts of happiness--psychological happiness, prudential happiness, and perfectionist happiness. *Psychological happiness,* and to some extent *prudential happiness*, is what this book is all about.

According to Haybron, psychological happiness is indeed a state of mind. It amounts to feelings of joy, serenity, and affection. Psychological happiness is the experience of positive emotions over time. Philosophers who address happiness in psychological terms include Benditt (1974, 1978), Carson (1978a, 1978b, 1979, 1981), Davis (1981a, 1981b), Gauthier (1967), Griffin (1986), Mayerfeld (1996, 1999), Montague (1967), Nozick (1989), Rescher (1972), Sen (1987), Sumner (1996), Von Wright (1963), Wilson (1968), and Wolf (1997).

An illustrative conceptualisation of the psychological happiness concept is Parducci's theory of happiness (Parducci, 1995). Parducci, a renowned psychologist who is well known for his range-frequency theory of satisfaction, defined happiness as a theoretical summation of separate momentary pleasures and pains. Although happiness can refer to a particular moment, the term is frequently used to describe our state of affect over much longer periods such as one's life. However, within any period, happiness can be viewed as a conceptual summation of separate hedonic values, positive and negative, divided by the duration of that period.

Prudential happiness, on the other hand, refers to a state of well being. Psychological happiness may be a necessary but not sufficient condition of prudential happiness. Prudential happiness is achieved when a person achieves a high state of well being, both mentally and physically (cf. Veenhoven, 2000). Therefore, prudential happiness is leading a good life. It involves both the feelings of happiness and the action that generates personal growth.

Haybron illustrates this condition by describing a brain in a vat. The brain in a vat may experience perfect bliss (psychological happiness), but physically it is not leading a good life as a person (prudential happiness). In other words, happiness is more than feelings of joy. It necessitates engagement in life to realize one's potentiality. It is what people do in life to achieve personal fulfilment. It is leading the good life.

Philosophers who talk about prudential happiness include Almeder (2000), Annas (1993, 1998), Cottingham (1998), Edwards (1979), Gert (1988), Hill (1999), Jacobs (1985), Kekes (1982, 1988, 1992), Kenny (1966), Kraut (1979), Luper (1996), Mill (1979), Rawls (1971), Scrutton (1975), Simpson (1975), Tatarkiewicz (1976), Thomas (1968), and Warner (1987).

The well-known psychologist who introduced us to the concept of "flow" (Mihaly Csikszentmihalyi), has argued repeatedly that a happy life is not an excellent life. To lead an excellent life is to engage in activities that help us grow and fulfil our potential (Csikszentmihalyi, 1975, 1982, 1990, & 1997). In his book *Finding Flow*, he states:

> The quality of life does not depend on happiness alone, but also on what one does to be happy. If one fails to develop goals that give meaning to one's existence, if one does not use the mind to its fullest, then good feelings fulfil just a fraction of the potential we possess. A person who achieves contentment by withdrawing from the world "to cultivate his own garden," like Voltaire's *Candide*, cannot be said to lead an excellent life. Without dreams, without risks, only a trivial semblance of living can be achieved (Csikszentmihalyi, 1997, p. 22).

An example of a measure of prudential happiness is the *ComQuality of life-A5* (Cummins, 1993, 1996, Cummins, McCabe, Romeo, & Gullone, 1994). Quality of life is captured in both subjective and objective terms. Each subjective and objective axis is composed of seven life domains-- material well being, health, productivity, intimacy, safety, place in community, and emotional well being.

In contrast, *perfectionist happiness* refers to a life that is good in all respects, including a *moral* life. It is a life that is desirable without qualification, both enviable and admirable. Perfectionist happiness is achieved when a person achieves a state of well being plus leading a moral life (Haybron, 2000). Haybron illustrates the concept of perfectionist happiness by describing an evil person. This person may be psychologically happy (high on psychological happiness), is well off in every way (high on prudential happiness), but is a parasite to society (low on perfectionist happiness). Philosophers who talk about happiness in the perfectionist sense include Austin (1968), Goldstein (1973), and McFall (1989).

An example of a theory of quality of life based on this notion of perfectionist happiness is Lane (1991, 2000). He defines quality of life (QOL) as the relation between a person's subjective and objective sets of circumstances. The *subjective* set of a person reflecting a high QOL involves nine elements: (1) capacity for enjoying life, (2) cognitive complexity, (3) a sense of autonomy and effectiveness, (4) self-knowledge, (5) self-esteem, (6) ease of interpersonal relations, (7) an ethical orientation, (8) personality integration, and (9) a productivity orientation. Lane believes that these nine elements describing the psychological makeup of a person are the hallmark of mental health and social responsibility. These elements combined are responsible for a sense of subjective well being and societal development. This subjective set makes up what Lane calls the "quality of the person" (or QP). The objective set reflects the quality of the environmental conditions (QC) representing opportunities for the person to achieve QP. Lane specified nine opportunities and assets comprising a high quality of environmental conditions. These are: (1) adequate material support, (2) physical safety and security, (3) available friends and social support, (4) opportunities for the expression and receipt of love, (5) opportunities for intrinsically challenging work, (6) leisure opportunities that have elements of skill, creativity, and relaxation, (7) available set of moral values that can give meaning to life, (8) opportunities for self-development, and (9) a justice system that is managed by disinterested and competent parties. Therefore, QOL = f (QP, QC) or the quality of life (QOL) of a person is a function of both the quality of his character (QP) and the environmental conditions surrounding him (QC).

The reason for making reference to Haybron's distinctions among psychological, prudential, and perfectionist happiness is to provide the reader with a sense of conceptual boundaries for this book. This book deals mostly with psychological happiness. It deals with prudential happiness to a lesser extent and perfectionist happiness the least extent. I do not make any claims on perfectionist happiness. The concept of perfectionist happiness is outside the scope of this book. Readers interested in understanding the full scope of quality-of-life research should consult my other work entitled *Handbook of Quality-of-Life Research* (Sirgy, 2001). Nevertheless, I like to emphasize the fact that many quality-of-life researchers realize that these three happiness concepts are interrelated. How? Psychological happiness influences the objective circumstances of people. Thus, psychological happiness increases the likelihood of actions leading to a good life, i.e., the experience of prudential happiness. In turn, prudential happiness (leading a good life) makes it more likely to lead a moral life. Leading a good plus moral life is what perfectionist happiness is all about.

2. LIFE SATISFACTION

A great majority of quality-of-life researchers view life satisfaction as self-avowals of happiness (see Diener, 1984; and Veenhoven, 1984a, 1984b; Veenhoven and coworkers, 1994 for literature reviews).   Thus, life satisfaction is viewed as a "cognitive" conceptualisation of happiness or subjective well being.   It may involve judgements of fulfillment of one's needs, goals, and wishes (e.g., Campbell et al., 1976; Cantril, 1965; Michalos, 1985).   Diener et al. (1985) defined life satisfaction as "a cognitive judgmental process dependent upon a comparison of one's circumstances with what is thought to be an appropriate standard" (p. 71). Thus the lower the discrepancy between the perception of life achievements and some standard the higher the life satisfaction. Frisch (1998, 1999, 2000, and 2001) equates quality of life with life satisfaction and defines life satisfaction also in cognitive terms. He assumes that the affective correlates of subjective well being are determined by cognitively based life satisfaction judgements.

Typical studies of life satisfaction use surveys in which respondents are asked to assess how their lives have been going over some period, such as the last few weeks, months, or years.   A typical way of measuring life satisfaction is a single item with a three-point scale: "Taken all together, how would you say things are these days—would you say that you are very happy (1), pretty happy (2), or not happy (3)?" (Andrews & Robinson, 1991). Andrews and Withey (1976) asked the following questions about global evaluations of, or feelings toward, life: "How satisfied are you with your life these days?" and "How do you feel about how happy you are?"

3. HAPPINESS AND LIFE SATISFACTION MAY BE DIFFERENT BUT RELATED CONSTRUCTS

It has been argued that happiness and life satisfaction are two different constructs (Chamberlain, 1988).   Happiness is an affective construct, whereas life satisfaction is a cognitive one (Andrews & McKennell, 1980; Brief & Roberson, 1989; Campbell, 1976; Crooker & Near, 1995; McKennell, 1978; McKennell & Andrews, 1980; Organ & Near, 1985). Measures of happiness and life satisfaction share a maximum 50-60 percent common variance (Cameron et al., 1973; Diener, Smith, & Fujita, 1995; Kozma, 1996; Kozma, et al., 1990). That is, the meaning happiness and life satisfaction (as operationlised by the measures used in the studies) overlap significantly.   Other studies have found yet lower or nonsignificant correlations (e.g., Balatsky & Diener, 1993; Friedman, 1993).   Life satisfaction involves one's evaluation of one's life or life accomplishments against some standard, e.g., the achievements of significant others. Happiness, on the other hand, is more emotional. People simply report they are happy. This is an emotional response, a gut reaction, without knowing why they feel the way they do.

Therefore, some quality-of-life researchers have viewed life satisfaction as the cognitive element of subjective well being, whereas happiness is regarded as the affective element. Studies have shown that the cognitive (life satisfaction) and affective (happiness) elements tend to be correlated with absolutes values ranging from .25 to .50 (e.g., Lucas, Diener, & Suh, 1996; Diener & Fujita, 1995),

4. HAPPINESS AND LIFE SATISFACTION MAY HAVE DIFFERENT CAUSES AND CORRELATES

The results of a national survey (Andrews & Withey, 1976) revealed that fun and family contribute more to happiness than life satisfaction. In contrast, money, economic security, one's house, and the goods and services bought in the market contribute to life satisfaction more than happiness (cf. Saris & Andreenkova, 2001). Similarly, Michalos (1980) showed that evaluations of all ten measured domains (health, financial security, family life, and self-esteem, etc.) were more closely related to life satisfaction than to happiness. Financial security was an important factor here. Veenhoven (1991a) suggested that the extent to which one's income meets one's material norm has a stronger influence on life satisfaction than happiness (cf. Diener & Fujita, 1995). This seems to contradict earlier findings. For example, Bradburn (1969) has shown that happiness-oriented people are less pleased with the market than satisfaction-oriented people, and money seems to be less of an important contribution to well being for young than old people.

Furthermore, Inglehart and Rabier (1986) reported that substantial income increments increase happiness but not satisfaction, while substantial income decrements increase dissatisfaction much more than unhappiness. Thus, the authors conclude that happiness, but not satisfaction, applies to substantial gains, but dissatisfaction and not unhappiness, applies to substantial losses.

Consider the following example that helps illustrate the distinction between happiness and life satisfaction. A Catholic priest dedicates his life to the service of God and the Catholic Church. His life is characterized by many bodily and material sacrifices. He does not feel happy because he has deprived himself from the pleasures of life; yet he evaluates his life positively. Note that life satisfaction is derived from goal attainment, even if these goals lead him to experience pain, agony, and material deprivation. The priest has a goal to serve God and the Church. He does this successfully and feels good about his life. Yet he may not experience the simple pleasures of life as other people do--therefore, his unhappiness (cf. Rehberg, 2000).

5. POSITIVE AND NEGATIVE AFFECT

Many quality-of-life researchers have captured the concept of subjective well being by measuring two types of affect--positive and negative--and then summing up the scores to derive an index of subjective well being (e.g., Bradburn, 1969; Chamberlain, 1988; Diener & Emmons, 1984; Diener et al., 1993; Diener, Smith, & Fujita, 1995; Headey, Kelly, & Wearing, 1993; Kim & Mueller, 2001; Lucas, Diener, & Suh, 1996; Watson, Clark, & Tellegen, 1988). That is, a person who has a high level of subjective well being is one who has a preponderance of positive affect (such as joy, contentment, or pleasure) over negative affect (such as sadness, depression, anxiety, or anger).

Quality-of-life researchers using this definition of subjective well being formulated measures of subjective well being that capture both intensity and frequency of positive and negative affect. This is because studies have found that both frequency and intensity of affect contribute significantly to subjective well being--with frequency contributing more than intensity (Diener & Larsen, 1994).

Furthermore, quality-of-life researchers have shown that depression and other measures of psychopathology are negatively correlated with measures of subjective well being (e.g., Lewinsohn, Redner, & Seeley, 1991; Mechanic, 1979; Reich & Zautra, 1981; Tanaka & Huba, 1984). Lewinsohn et al. explained this relationship as follows: Those who become dissatisfied with life may become depressed. In other words, life dissatisfaction may be a precursor to depression.[1]

6. SUBJECTIVE WELL BEING AS AN UMBRELLA CONCEPT

In a recent review of the literature on subjective well being, Diener et al. (1999) defined subjective well being as a broad category of phenomena that

---

[1] One can argue that the reverse may be equally true. That is, those who become clinically depressed may end up feeling dissatisfied with life. This may be due to the fact that depression causes a great deal of negative affect above and beyond what the individual can experience in positive affect. Experiencing prolonged negative affect (unhappiness) may be a precursor to life dissatisfaction.

includes people's emotional responses, domain satisfactions, and global judgements of life satisfaction (p. 2). They added that each of these concepts should be studied individually. However, measures of these constructs often correlate substantially, suggesting the need for a higher-order factor.

Kozma and Stones (1992) have theorised that happiness is a direct function of two psychological states, one short term and the other long term. The short-term state is an affective state that involves positive and negative affect mostly influenced by environmental factors. The long-term state is also an affective state involving both positive and negative affect. The long-term component is dispositional and is less affected by environmental factors (cf. Kozma, 1996).

Based on these distinctions, an attempt is made here to reconstruct these concepts in a framework that integrates these disparate concepts. It is my opinion that this framework may reflect a semblance of consensus among quality-of-life researchers working in the area of subjective well being.

6.1 Subjective Well Being

The concept of subjective well being used throughout this book is essentially defined as:

Subjective well being is an enduring (long-term) affective state that is made of a composite of three components: (a) actual experience of happiness or cumulative positive affect (joy, affection, pride, etc.) in salient life domains, (b) actual experience of depression or cumulative negative affect (sadness, anger, guilt, shame, anxiety, etc.) in salient life domains, and (c) evaluations of one's overall life or evaluations of salient life domains.

Figure 1 shows how these three components make up the construct of subjective well being. The figure also shows the determinants of the components. Specifically, one's actual experience of *happiness* is determined by an aggregation of pleasant feelings (e.g., joy, affection, pride) over time in salient life domains, in which each pleasant feeling is determined by a positive life event. Similarly, one's actual experience of *depression* is determined by an aggregation of unpleasant feelings (e.g., sadness, anger, guilt, anxiety, shame) over time in salient life domains, in which each unpleasant feeling is determined by a negative life event. The third component, *life satisfaction*, deals, not with the actual emotional experiences (e.g., joy, affection, pride, depression, sadness, anger, guilt, anxiety, and shame) but with cognitive evaluations of life overall and salient life domains.   One's evaluation of one's own life is determined by an aggregation of evaluations of positive and negative events of important life domains (e.g., leisure life, work life, family life, community life, social life, and sex life) or recall of those evaluations made in the past from memory. The evaluation of each life domain is determined by a host of evaluations of life events in that domain or simply one's assessment of positive and negative affect in that domain.

The three components and their interrelationships as well as their determinants capture three distinctions made in the literature: (1) the distinction between the cognitive and affective aspects of subjective well being, (2) the distinction between positive and negative affect of subjective well being, and (3) the distinction between short-term and long-term affective states of subjective well being Furthermore, throughout the book we will make reference of satisfaction of human developmental needs. This is an important point and the reader needs to be sensitised to the notion that people experience positive and negative affect as a direct function of the extent to which life events satisfy human developmental needs (e.g., biological, safety, social, esteem, actualisation needs). The satisfaction of needs also influence and guide people's cognitive evaluation of life events.

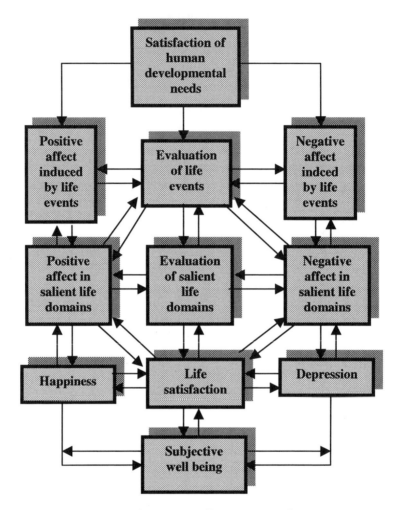

Figure 1. [Subjective Well Being: Its Elements]

Table 1 captures the underlying constructs of thes three components of subjective well being. The table shows the three distinctions: (1) cognitive versus affective, (2) and positive versus negative affect, and (3) short-term versus long-term.

Table 1. [The Underlying Constructs of the Various Components of Subjective Well Being]

	Affective	**Cognitive**
Positive	Cumulative pleasant emotions (**short-term**) and feelings of happiness (**long-term**)	Positive evaluation of life events (**short-term**) and life domains (**long-term**)
Negative	Cumulative unpleasant emotions (**short-term**) and feelings of depression (**long-term**)	Negative evaluation of life events (**short-term**) and life domains (**long-term**)

6.2 Cognitive versus Affective

To reiterate, the distinction between cognitive and affective is important in quality-of-life research. High profile quality-of-life researchers such as Parducci (1995) and Kahneman (1999) have argued strongly that subjective well being can be captured directly and objectively[2], rather than subjectively. Thus, subjective well being of any period of time is a conceptual summation of these separate hedonic values, positive and negative, divided by the duration of that period. This is an "affective" conceptualisation of subjective well being. It is not identified with the global assessments that people make when asked to rate their overall happiness. The latter is a "cognitive" conceptualisation of subjective well being. This is because it is an evaluation made by thinking and judging the major elements of one's life. Many quality-of-life researchers have made the distinction between cognitive and affective aspects of subjective well being. For example, Andrews and McKennell (1980), Brief and Roberson (1989), Campbell

---

[2] An example of an objective measure of subjective well being is to have subjects carry with them a beeper. The experimenter would then beep subjects randomly and ask them to report on their subjective well being during the last few hours or so.

(1976), Crooker and Near (1995), McKennell (1978), McKennell and Andrews (1980), Organ and Near (1985) have all argued that happiness and life satisfaction are two different constructs. That happiness is an affective construct, whereas life satisfaction is a cognitive one. That life satisfaction involves one's evaluation of one's life or life domains. In contrast, happiness is an emotional phenomenon. People simply report they are happy. This is an emotional response, a gut reaction, not knowing always why they feel they way they do.

6.3 Positive versus Negative

To reiterate, the distinction between positive and negative affect also is highly consistent with quality-of-life research. Many quality-of-life researchers have measured subjective well being by a composite index made up of positive and negative affect (e.g., Bradburn, 1969; Diener & Emmons, 1984; Diener et al., 1993; Diener, Smith, & Fujita, 1995; Headey, Kelly, & Wearing, 1993; Lucas, Diener, & Suh, 1996; Watson, Clark, & Tellegen, 1988). The impetus for this distinction is the realisation by many quality-of-life researchers that the factors that cause positive affect are not the same as those that cause negative affect. For example, experiencing culture and the arts may be a factor that may enhance happiness (or positive affect); the lack of culture and the arts may not influence depression (or negative affect). Marital abuse may cause a spouse to feel depressed (negative affect), but the absence of marital abuse does not lead to happiness (or positive affect).

Similarly, when people evaluate their life, they focus on their evaluation of salient life domains. Certain life domains tend to generate more satisfaction than dissatisfaction, and vice versa. For example, in the area of income and standard of living, a person who evaluates that life domain positively may experience little satisfaction. In contrast, a person evaluating the same domain negatively may experience high level of dissatisfaction. Now let's focus on another life domain, let's say leisure life. Evaluating one's leisure life positively may produce high levels of satisfaction. Conversely, evaluating the same domain negatively may produce little dissatisfaction (cf. Herzberg, 1966; Herzberg, et al., 1957).

6.4 Short-term versus Long-term

Note that the model shows that the three components of subjective well being are not momentary, transient, and ephemeral affective states. They are enduring and relatively stable affective states. They are long-term affective states determined by an aggregation of short-term affect experienced over time. This distinction between short-term and long-term subjective well being is consistent with the research conducted by Kozma and Stones (1992).

7. CONCLUSION

The reader should keep in mind the aforementioned definitions and distinctions of happiness, life satisfaction, and subjective well being as he or she reads the remaining chapters of this book. There are many places in the book in which I describe how satisfaction accrues in certain life domains differently from dissatisfaction. Therefore, the distinction between positive and negative affect is important.

Equally important is the distinction between cognitive and affective. Life events within certain life domains can lead to positive and negative affective experiences (e.g., joy, pride, affection, sadness, guilt, anxiety, anger, and shame). We will address the many factors that cause people to experience happiness and depression in the context of life domains and how these feelings spill over from one domain to the next contributing to subjective well being. These affective dynamics may operate at a subconscious level. This affective system operates somewhat independently from the cognitive system. That is not to say that the cognitive system has very little to do with the experience of happiness and depression in the various life domains. The cognitive system does indeed play an important role. In many parts of this book I will describe how people make certain evaluations and arrive at certain judgements. These "cognitive" behaviours do play an important role in the experience of satisfaction and dissatisfaction. Therefore, the reader is likely to find the distinction between cognitive and affective helpful in understanding and appreciating the cognitive and affective dynamics involving the strategies people use to enhance their subjective well being.

Most importantly is the element of time. There is substantial agreement among quality-of-life researchers that subjective well being is not a momentary behavioural phenomenon. It is an enduring phenomenon that is significantly affected by a great deal of cognitive and affective dynamics over time. On the other hand, subjective well being is not an enduring behavioural phenomenon to the point where we can call it a personality trait or disposition. It is far from that too. Although quality-of-life researchers talk about happy and unhappy people, they do not address it in personality terms. Personality traits and dispositions are hard to change. The other extreme involves ephemeral behavioural phenomena, such as mood, which are easily influenced by situational factors. Subjective well being is neither a situational nor a dispositional concept. It is somewhere in-between.

Affect in certain life domains accrues over time. The element of time is important here. The reader should keep this in mind while reading about the various strategies people use in enhancing their subjective well being.

EXAMPLES OF MEASURES OF SUBJECTIVE WELL BEING

Readers who are not interested in research issues pertaining to subjective well being may skip this chapter. This chapter is written to help those not familiar with subjective well-being measures become familiar with a variety of methodological and research issues. Readers who are reading this book exclusively to help them understand what strategies people use to enhance their subjective well being can skip this chapter and the next chapter too. Those personal growth strategies are discussed starting Chapter 4.

There are many measures of subjective well being (e.g., happiness, life satisfaction, positive and negative affect, and perceived quality of life). One possible way of organising them is through the distinction between reflective and formative indicators of this construct. *Reflective indicators* of subjective well being are measures designed to capture the construct directly, whereas *formative indicators* capture it indirectly through other constructs believed to play a significant role in the formation of the construct in question. The examples provided here are very cursory. The goal is not to provide the reader with a detailed or comprehensive review of the measures of subjective well being, but merely enough to get the reader to appreciate the concept (see Table 2). Readers who are interested in using specific measurement instruments of subjective well being should not rely on this chapter. I do not necessarily recommend nor endorse the measures covered in this chapter. They are selected to help the reader understand and build an appreciation for how quality-of-life researchers typically measure subjective well being. At the end of the chapter, I will discuss measurement caveats raised by quality-of-life researchers. Doing so should further help the reader build an appreciation for the measurement complexities involving subjective well being.

Table 2. [Examples of Reflective and Formative Measures of Subjective Well Being]

Examples of reflective indicators of subjective well being	Examples of formative indicators of subjective well being
• The Neugarten et al.'s (1961) *Life Satisfaction Rating* (LSR), • The *Cantril Ladder* (Cantril, 1965), • The *Reflective Life Satisfaction* (RLS) measure (Wood, Wylie, & Shaefer, 1969), • The Andrews and Withey's (1976) *Delighted-Terrible* (D-T) Scale, • The *Eurobarometer* (Inglehart, 1977), • The Spreitzer and Snyder's (1974) measure of life satisfaction, • The Diener et al.'s (1985) *Satisfaction with Life Scale* (SWLS), and • The *Congruity Life Satisfaction* (CLS) measure (Meadow et al., 1992; Sirgy et al., 1995a).	• The *Quality-of-Life Index* (Ferrans & Powers,1985), • The *Quality-of-Life Inventory* (Frisch, 1992, 1993, 1994a, 1994b, 1998), • The *ComQuality of life-A5* (Cummins, McCabe, Romeo, & Gullone, 1994), • The *Need Hierarchy Measure of Life Satisfaction* (Sirgy et al. 1995b). • The *Quality-of-Life Questionnaire* (Greenley, Greenberg, & Brown, 1997),

8. EXAMPLES OF REFLECTIVE INDICATORS OF SUBJECTIVE WELL BEING

Table 2 shows examples of measures representative of reflective indicators of subjective well being. I will briefly describe these.

8.1 The Neugarten et al.'s Life Satisfaction Rating (LSR)

The Neugarten et al. (1961) *Life Satisfaction Rating* (LSR) is a widely used measure of life satisfaction among the elderly. The measure involves a complex interviewer schedule. A trained interviewer rates life satisfaction of an elderly respondent on five dimensions using a 5-point scale. The dimensions are:

1. Zest for life,
2. Resolution to fate,
3. Goal achievement desire,
4. Level of self-concept, and
5. General mood tone.

Instead of this interview schedule, two short self-rated scales, can be substituted. These are the *Life Satisfaction Index-A* (LSIA) and the *Life Satisfaction Index-B* (LSIB). Wood *et al.* (1969) modified the LSIA measure, which was referred to as LSIZ (Adams, 1969; Larsen, 1978; Meadow & Cooper, 1990).

8.2 The Cantril Ladder

The *Cantril Ladder* (Cantril, 1965) measures life satisfaction using the following instructions:

> The respondent is first asked to describe wishes and hopes for his or her future, and then describe what would be the most unhappy life for him or her. The respondent is then presented with a picture of a ladder numbered from zero on the bottom rung to nine on the top rung. The respondent is then asked to suppose that the top of the ladder represents the best possible life for him or her, and the bottom represents the worst possible life. The respondent is then asked: "Where on the ladder do you feel you stand at the present time?"

> "Here is a picture of a ladder. Suppose the top of the ladder represents the best possible life for you and the bottom of the ladder the worst possible life. Where on the ladder do you feel you personally stand at the present time? (0-10 rating scale using a picture of a ladder)

8.3 The Reflective Life Satisfaction (RLS) Measure

The *Reflective Life Satisfaction* (RLS) measure (Wood, Wylie, & Shaefer, 1969) involves the following items:
- "As I look back on my life I am fairly well satisfied."
- "I've gotten pretty much what I expected out of my life."
- "When I think back over my life, I did not get most of the important things I wanted." (reverse coded)
- "I've gotten more of the breaks in life than most of the people I know."
- "In spite of what people say, the lot of the average man is getting worse, not better." (reverse coded)

- "Most of the things I do are boring or monotonous." (reverse coded)
- "These are the better years of my life."
- "The things I do are as interesting to me as they ever were."
- "I am just as happy as when I was younger."

Responses to these items are recorded on a 5-point Likert scale. A study by Barak and Rahtz (1990) has shown that this measure is somewhat reliable.

8.4 The Spreitzer and Snyder's Measure of Life Satisfaction

The Spreitzer and Snyder's (1974) measure of life satisfaction is a single indicator measure of life satisfaction designed for the elderly. The measure contains the following response cue: "Taking things all together, how would you say things are these days—would you say that you are very happy, pretty happy, or not too happy." The rating scale is essentially three response categories--"not too happy" scored as 1, "pretty happy" scored as 2, and "very happy" scored as 3.

8.5 Andrews and Withey's Delighted-Terrible (D-T) Scale

Andrews and Withey's (1976) D-T measure involves a straightforward repeated[3] question: "How do you feel about your life as a whole?" Responses are coded on a scale: "delighted," "pleased," "mostly satisfied," "about equally satisfied and dissatisfied," "mostly dissatisfied," "unhappy," and "terrible." Andrews and Withey conducted a national study to measure subjective well being at the societal level. The study employed a number of samples totalling around 5,000 respondents for obtaining self-reported assessments about a factor analysed list of life domains, as well as a global question about satisfaction with life in general. The developed measure was guided by the theoretical notion that quality of life is an overall sense of well being reflecting affective responses to various life domains.[4] The resulting instrument containing global measures of satisfaction and the domains were found to have high convergent and predictive validity, and repeated samplings produced reliability coefficients between .7 and .8. This effort generated a linear additive indicator of well being called the *Index of Overall Life Quality*.

---

[3] Repeated in the sense that the item appears in different part of the questionnaire to allow the testing of internal consistency-type of reliability.

[4] Examples of life domains include leisure life, work life, family life, social life, and community life, among others.

8.6 *Eurobarometer*

The *Eurobarmoter* is a good example of a subjective indicator used to assess subjective well at the country level (Saris & Kaase, 1997). The *Eurobarameter* is mostly due to the work of Ronald Inglehart (Inglehart, 1977, 1990, 1997; Reif & Inglehart, 1991). Inglehart was able to influence the content of a regular survey financed by the Commission of the European Communities in Brussels since its inception in the early 1970s. The *Eurobarameter* survey has been conducted twice a year since 1973 in all members of the European Union (EU). A large number of adults (sampled from the in the various EU countries) are surveyed. Part of the survey is the question concerning life satisfaction. The exact question is as follows: "On the whole, are you very satisfied, fairly satisfied, not very satisfied, or not at all satisfied with the life you lead? Would you say: very satisfied, fairly satisfied, not very satisfied, or not at all satisfied."

8.7 *Diener* et al.*'s Satisfaction with Life Scale (SWLS)*

Diener et al. (1985) developed a measure involving five questions, rated on a 7-point Likert scale. The measure is called the *Satisfaction with Life Scale* or SWLS. The items are:
- "In most ways my life is close to ideal."
- "The conditions of my life are excellent."
- "I am satisfied with my life."
- "So far I have gotten the important things I want in life."
- "If I could live my life over, I would change almost nothing."

8.8 *The Congruity Life Satisfaction (CLS) Measure*

The *Congruity Life Satisfaction* (Meadow et al. 1992; Sirgy et al. 1995a) is based on the theoretical notion that life satisfaction is a function of comparison between perceived life accomplishments and a set of standards used to evaluate these accomplishments. These standards are classified as a direct function of their derivative sources (e.g., the life accomplishments of relatives, friends, associates, past experience, self-concepts of strengths and weaknesses, and average person in a similar position) and different forms (e.g., standards based on ideal, expected, deserved minimum tolerable, and predicted outcomes). Responses are recorded on a 6-point scale from "very dissatisfied" to "very satisfied." The items are as follows:
- "Compared to your lifetime goals, ideals, and what you had ideally hoped to become, how satisfied are you?"

- "Compared to what you feel you deserve to have happened to you considering all that you've worked for, how satisfied are you?"
- "Compared to the accomplishments of our relatives (parents, brother, sister, etc.), how satisfied are you?"
- "Compared to the accomplishments of your friends and associates, how satisfied are you?"
- "Compared to the accomplishments of most people in your position, how satisfied are you?"
- "Compared to what you've been and how far you have come along (the progress you have made, the changes you have gone through, or the level of growth you have experienced), how satisfied are you?"
- "Compared to what you have expected from your self all along considering your resources, strengths, and weaknesses, how satisfied are you?"
- "Compared to what you may have predicted about yourself becoming, how satisfied are you?"
- "Compared to what you feel you should have accomplished so far, how satisfied are you?"
- "Compared to what you feel is the minimum of what anyone in your position should have accomplished (and be able to accomplish), how satisfied are you?"

9. EXAMPLES OF FORMATIVE INDICATORS OF SUBJECTIVE WELL BEING

- Table 2 shows five formative indicators quality-of-life measures of individuals. These will be briefly described here.

9.1 *The Quality-of-Life Index*

The *Quality of Life Index* was developed by Ferrans and Powers (1985) and used in a number of studies (e.g., Lewellyn & Wibker, 1990). This index involves asking respondents to report their degree of satisfaction ("How satisfied are you with?") with the following life domains and experiences:
- "Your relationship with your spouse,"
- "Your friends,"
- "Your standard of living,"
- "Your ability to meet non-financial family responsibilities,"
- "Your usefulness to others,"

- "Amount of non-job stress or worries in your life,"
- "Your financial independence,"
- "Your leisure time activities,"
- "Your achievement of personal goals,"
- "Your happiness in general,"
- "Your health,"
- "Size of the city in which you live in,"
- "Your religious life,"
- "Your family's happiness,"

Responses are recorded on a six-point scale varying from "very dissatisfied" to "very satisfied."

9.2 The Quality-of-Life Inventory

The *Quality-of-Life Inventory* (Frisch, 1992, 1993, 1994a, 1994b, 1998) has 16 dimensions of life satisfaction:

1. Health,
2. Self-esteem,
3. Goals-and-values,
4. Money,
5. Work,
6. Play,
7. Learning,
8. Creativity,
9. Helping,
10. Love,
11. Friends,
12. Children,
13. Relatives,
14. Home,
15. Neighbourhood, and
16. Community.

Life satisfaction is defined as how one feels one's most important needs, goals, and wishes are being met in important life domains. Operationally speaking, an overall life satisfaction is computed as the sum of satisfactions in important life domains. That is, for each domain the satisfaction score is multiplied by an importance weight. The weighted domain satisfaction scores are then summed and divided by the sum of the weights.

9.3 *The ComQuality of life-A5*

The *ComQuality of life-A5* (Cummins, 1993, 1996, 1997a, 1997b; Cummins, McCabe, Romeo, & Gullone, 1994) is a self-report instrument designed to capture individual's quality of life in a comprehensive manner. Quality of life is described in both subjective and objective terms. Each subjective and objective axis is composed of seven life domains. These are:

1. Material well being,
2. Health,
3. Productivity,
4. Intimacy,
5. Safety,
6. Place in community, and
7. Emotional well being.

The measurement of each subjective well being domain is accomplished through a composite satisfaction score of that domain weighted by the perceived importance of that domain. Thus, a total subjective summing the product of domain satisfaction scores weighted by perceived importance. Internal consistency tests have shown that the objective, importance, and satisfaction subscales have satisfactory reliability. Test-retest correlations (5-month interval) have been reported to be satisfactory too.

9.4 *The Need Hierarchy Measure of Life Satisfaction*

Sirgy et al. (1995b) have developed a measure of overall quality of life based on Maslow's need-hierarchy theory. Four need categories were used (survival needs, social needs, ego needs, and self-actualisation needs (cf. Kosenko, Sirgy, & Efraty, 1990). The items were as follows:

- "The feeling of having been secure."
- "The feeling of having given to (and having received help from) others."
- "The feeling of having developed close friendships."
- "The feeling of having been 'in the know'."
- "The feeling of self-esteem (pride) a person has about oneself."
- "The feeling of prestige (reputation) one person has about oneself."
- "The feeling of having experienced independent thought and action."
- "The feeling of having determined my life course."
- "The feeling of having experienced personal growth and development."
- "The feeling of having experienced self-fulfilment."
- "The feeling of having had worthwhile accomplishments."

The following scales are used to record responses for each of the 11 items:

How much is there now?   Minimum 1 2 3 4 5 6 7 Maximum
How much should there be? Minimum 1 2 3 4 5 6 7 Maximum

The overall score of life satisfaction of a particular respondent is computed by taking the absolute difference score (between "how much is there now" and "how much should there be") for each item and deriving an average score. The lower the resultant average score, the higher the overall life satisfaction.

9.5 The Quality-of-Life Questionnaire

The *Quality-of-Life Questionnaire,* developed by Greenley, Greenberg, and Brown (1997), is a short-form questionnaire containing seven dimensions of quality of life with each dimension captured through several items in which respondents indicate their extent of satisfaction. These dimensions are:

- Living situation (e.g., "The living arrangements where you live."),
- Finances (e.g., "The amount of money you get."),
- Leisure (e.g., "The way you spend your spare time."),
- Family (e.g., "Your family in general."),
- Social life (e.g., "The things you do with other people."),
- Health (e.g., "Your health in general."), and
- Access to medical care (e.g., "The medical care available to you if you need it.").

10. WHEN TO USE REFLECTIVE VERSUS FORMATIVE INDICATORS?

The reader should have noted by now that reflective indicators of subjective well being attempt to capture the behavioural phenomenon holistically and globally.   These measures capture manifestations of subjective well being. For example, the Andrews and Withey D-T Scale is a single item measure ("How do you feel about your life as a whole?" Responses are coded on a scale: "delighted," "pleased," "mostly satisfied," "about equally satisfied and dissatisfied," "mostly dissatisfied," "unhappy," and "terrible."). In contrast, formative indicators capture subjective well being by tapping its "causes." For example, the Greenley, Greenberg, and

Brown *Quality-of-Life Questionnaire* is based on the notion that overall life satisfaction can be captured by measuring satisfaction of seven life domains (financial life, leisure life, family life, social life, and health and health care). Formative indicators of subjective well being are more diagnostic because they give the researcher an understanding of the "causes" of overall life satisfaction.   The   "causes"   are   implicit   in   the   definition   and operationalisation of the construct.

The caveat, of course, is whether the conceptualisation of the "causes" of subjective well being is in line with the research objectives. Thus, if the researcher desires a measure of subjective well being without having to buy into the "causes" of subjective well being that are implicit in the measure, then he or she may opt for a reflective indicator. This may be because the researcher may be testing the effect of certain "causes" of subjective well being. Therefore, he or she may not want to confound the operationalisation of subjective well being with the implicit "causes" that are part of the "baggage" inherent in the formative indicators' measure.

Selecting a reflective indicator measure of subjective well being to avoid the theoretical baggage that comes along with all formative indicators type of measures should not be considered a panacea to this problem. The best it can do is decrease possible conceptual confounds. This is because all reflective measures also are grounded in some theoretical framework. Although the dimensions and/or items used in the reflective indicators type measure tend to be "manifestations" of subjective well being rather than "causes", these manifestations can reflect a conceptualisation of subjective well being quite foreign to the researcher. Here, the researcher is advised to select the reflective measure that, again, should be consistent with an overall nomological network of concepts grounded in one theory (or theories consistent with one another at a meta-conceptual level).

11. MEASUREMENT CAVEATS

Many of the measures described in this chapter are based on several assumptions. The first assumption is that people have the ability to add their day-to-day affective experiences into a composite reflective of global feelings about life or a particular domain of life. A second assumption is that these global feelings are relatively stable over time. Yet another assumption is that people can describe these feelings accurately and honestly (Campbell, 1981, p. 23). These assumptions have been challenged by a number of quality-of-life researchers. Below are selected examples of criticisms. For comprehensive review of methodological issues of subjective well being measures, see Andrews and Robinson (1992), Diener et al. (1999,

Larsen, Diener, and Emmons (1985), and Schwarz and Strack (1999). Highlights of these caveats are summarised in Table 3.

Table 3. [Measurement Caveats]

Measurement caveats related to global subjective well-being measures that are based on self-report

---

- Memory biases
- Biases related to situational influences
- Biases related to interview or questionnaire format
- Biases related to standard of comparison
- Biases related to scaling effects
- Biases related to mood
- Temporal stability problems
- Biases related to social desirability

11.1 Memory Biases

Schwarz, Strack, and colleagues (e.g., Schwarz & Strack, 1991; Strack, Martin, & Schwarz, 1988; Strack, Schwarz, & Gschneidinger, 1985) have demonstrated that responses to global measures of subjective well being are strongly influenced by information accessibility from memory, which in turn is strongly influenced by frequency and recency of the information. In other words, affective experiences in certain life domains that have occurred recently and with greater frequency are more likely to be retrieved from memory and used in responding to the well being question than less-recent and less-frequent affective experiences in other life domains. Kahneman (1999) also has strongly criticised measures of global happiness, life satisfaction, and subjective well being. He argued that these global measures are subject to many confounds. One such confound is retrospective evaluations of life tend to be biased because they mostly reflect peak and recent affective experiences. Alternatively, Kahneman suggested that satisfaction should be measured using a dense record of experience at each "point-instant utility" (i.e., during or right after the experience of an affective episode). Thus, "objective happiness" can be derived by an average of utility over a period of time.

Parducci (1995) also argued that happiness can be determined by a theoretical summation over separate momentary pleasures and pains as coded in memory. The period may be a moment, a day, or a longer period in one's life. Therefore, domain satisfaction of any period is a conceptual summation of these separate hedonic values, positive and negative, divided by the duration of that period. Also Csikszentmihalyi (1997) has long advocated the use of the *experience sampling method* (ESM) to measure concepts such as happiness, flow, contentment, joy, etc. The ESM entails the use of a pager or programmable watch to signal people to fill out two pages in a booklet they carry with them. Signals are programmed to go off at random times within two-hour intervals throughout the day. The subject responds by writing down the activity he or she is engaging in, the situation, and his or feelings at that time (e.g., how happy, degree of concentration, level of motivation, level of self-esteem, and so on).

11.2 Biases Related to Situational Influences

Ross, Eyman, and Kishchuck (1986) studied how subjects arrived at a judgement of subjective well being. They found that 41-53 percent of the reason subjects used to explain their judgements of subjective well being reflect references to one's momentary affective state, followed by future expectations (22-40 percent), past events (5-20 percent), and social comparisons (5-13 percent). Schwarz, Strack, Kommer, and Wagner (1987, Exp. 2) found support for the hypothesis that a situational cue may affect the respondent's mood, which in turn may influence that person's report of global well being. By the same token, the same situational cue may serve as a standard of comparison to judge the person's condition in a specific domain, thus affecting his report of satisfaction in that domain. For example, subjects were tested in two conditions: (a) a small, dirty laboratory that was overheated, noisy, with flickering lights, and a foul odour, and (b) a friendly office. Subjects reported lower levels of subjective well being in the unpleasant environment than the pleasant one. However, when asked to report how satisfied they were with their housing conditions, subjects in the unpleasant environment reported higher levels of housing satisfaction than those in the pleasant environment. The authors explained that the same stimulus acted as a standard of reference for the subjects in judging their housing conditions. Thus, the same stimulus influencing global well being reports may serve to influence reports of domain satisfaction in the opposite direction.

11.3 Biases Related to Interview or Questionnaire Format

Schuman and Presser (1981) have shown that the measures are quite sensitive to influences from preceding questions in a questionnaire or in an interview (cf. Smith, 1979). For example, Strack, Martin, and Schwarz (1987, 1988) have demonstrated that highly accessible information is not likely to be used in responding to well being questions if the information is perceived by the respondent to have been already provided in an earlier part of the questionnaire (or interview). For example, if the interviewer asks a subject "How is your wife?" in one part of the interview, then follows up this question by "How is your family?" in another part of the interview, the subject is not likely to provide information about the wife's well being by responding to the latter question. This is because the subject may feel that he already provided that information by responding to the former question (Schwarz & Strack, 1991).

11.4 Biases Related to Standard of Comparison

Strack, Schwarz, and Gschneidinger (1985) were able to demonstrate that events recalled from the past may lead to different social judgements of subjective well being. Specifically, a subject, thinking about a negative past event, may report higher levels of subjective well being than a person thinking about a positive event may. This is because the subject uses the negative past event as a standard of reference to compare his present situation. Using a negative standard of reference enhances the likelihood that the person will judge his present circumstance to be better than the past, thus generating feelings of well being. This finding can be further illustrated by results showing that senior US citizens who lived through the depression years (past negative event) report higher levels of subjective well being than those who did not live through the depression years (Elder, 1974). The reverse may be true. In other words, those who are asked to think of a positive past event report lower levels of subjective well being (than those who think of a negative past event). This is because the standard of reference is high and the chances are not good that the present circumstance is better than the past, thus generating lower levels of subjective well being (Schwarz & Strack, 1991).

11.5 Biases Related to Scaling Effects

Schwarz and colleagues (e.g., Schwarz, 1988; Schwarz & Hippler, 1987; Schwarz & Strack, 1991) have shown that respondents assume that the mid-point of the scale of a subjective well being measure reflect "an average," i.e., the level where most people are. Thus, they compare themselves against the average to indicate their own level of subjective well being--relative to the average. The problem, of course, is that the mid-point is not necessarily the average.

11.6 Biases Related to Mood

In answering questions related to subjective well being, respondents are influenced by their mood at the time of their response. A positive mood biases responses toward reporting higher levels of subjective well being, and vice versa. Much evidence has been amassed by Schwarz, Strack, and colleagues demonstrating the effect of mood on responses to subjective well being questions (e.g., Munkel, Strack, & Schwarz, 1987; Schwarz, 1983; Schwarz & Clore, 1983; Schwarz, Strack, Kommer, & Wagner, 1987).

11.7 Temporal Stability Problems

Measures of subjective well being have been shown to have low test-retest reliability, between .40 and .60 within an hour interval, i.e., the same question is asked in different places in the same questionnaire or within a 1-hour interview (Glatzer, 1984). In contrast, Diener (1984) reported more satisfactory reliability results. Specifically, he reported that most studies with long-term reliabilities show values ranging from .55 to .70.

11.8 Biases Related to Social Desirability

Much evidence suggests that higher subjective well being ratings are reported in a face-to-face interview than through a mail questionnaire (Smith, 1979). The effect reflects social desirability confounds prevalent in social science research (Schwarz & Strack, 1991). That is, subjects interviewed face-to-face tend to report inflated satisfaction ratings--inflated relative to their "true" feelings. They do this because they do not want to look "bad" in the "eyes" of the interviewer. The severity of this problem is significantly diminished using mail questionnaires in which respondents complete the questionnaires privately.

12. IN DEFENCE OF SELF-REPORTS AND GLOBAL MEASURES OF SUBJECTIVE WELL BEING

Veenhoven (1991b has argued that such criticisms are not wholly justified. Self-reports of happiness tend to be prompt, non-response is low, and temporal stability is high. Furthermore, there is little evidence to indicate that self-reports of happiness are confounded by stereotypical responses (evidence reviewed in Veenhoven, 1984b pp. 40-42). The criticism of overstatement (that people overstate their state of happiness) is also unjustified (evidence reviewed in Veenhoven, 1984b pp. 44-51). Andrews and Withey (1976, p. 216) estimated that error accounts for half the variance in life satisfaction (cf. Kammann, 1982). Veenhoven (1991b explains the causes for the error. He asserted:

> Several reasons for this vulnerability seem to be involved. Firstly, some people may not have a definite opinion in mind and engage in an instant (re)assessment which is then influenced by situational characteristics. . . . Secondly, those who do have a definite opinion will mostly hold a rather global idea of how happy they are and will not think in terms of a ten-point scale. Hence, their precise score may vary. Thirdly, the process of retrieval involves some uncertainty as well (p. 12).

Kammann (1983) and Kammann et al. (1979) presented evidence that counters the criticism that subjective well being measures are influenced by the questions immediately preceding their administration. Diener (1984), based on a literature review, has asserted that none of the measures reviewed shows high social desirability effects. Most of the measures correlate as expected with personality measures and show high convergent validity. Furthermore, the measures correlate as expected with non-self-report data involving demographic variables. Diener concluded:

> Thus, the SWB measures seem to contain substantial amounts of valid variance. However, this does not imply that some distortions do not occur. The topic of distortion, bias, and encoding of SWB is a valuable direction for future research. Thus, although there is certainly sufficient validity in the measures to build theories of SWB, one part of these theories should be how these subjective reports are formed (including various forms of distortion). Theories of encoding one's affect should be integrated with the bottom-up versus top-down approaches to happiness. . . (p. 551).

More recently, Diener and Suh (1999) have defended the use of subjective well being surveys in measuring concepts such as life satisfaction, hedonic balance, and positive and negative affect by arguing that most of these measures show a good deal of convergent validity. For example, global subjective well being measures based on self-reports were found to covary with ratings made by family and friends, with interviewer ratings, with amount of smiling in an interview, and with the number of positive versus negative memories people recall. The validity of the global subjective well being measures based on self-report has also been demonstrated by significant correlations with other measures as predicted by theory and past research. For example, the subjective well being measures were found to correlate with measures of self-esteem, optimism, self-efficacy, and depression, as predicted by theory and past research. Furthermore, there is good evidence of temporal reliability of the global subjective well being measures based on self-reports. Finally, the authors made a strong case for the fact that the global subjective well being measures (based on self-reports) are not significantly influenced by methodological artefacts such as subject's mood, habitual use of numbers in responding to scales, propensity to be humble, and tendency to avoid extremes on the scale. Thus, they concluded as follows:

> Our broad conclusion about the assessment of SWB is that although the SWB measures have a degree of validity and are often not as contaminated as popular lore might suggest, they can be influenced by measurement artefacts and momentary situational factors. Thus, strong conclusions can be gained only when measurement artefacts are assessed and controlled, and when several types of measurement methods are employed and lead to the same conclusion (p. 438).

THE MOTIVES UNDERLYING SUBJECTIVE WELL BEING

This chapter describes the various motivational states underlying subjective well being. To do this we start out by providing the reader with a framework or a language to help understand the underlying motives of subjective well being and why people do whatever it takes to enhance their subjective well being. Again, the focus here is on the "why" question. I will describe also the available evidence providing support for these motives. The chapter closes by outlining and highlighting 11 subjective well being strategies that are the subject of the remainder of the book.

13. WHAT IS SUBJECTIVE WELL BEING?

Based on the works of Andrew and Withey (1976), Campbell and colleagues (Campbell, 1976, 1981; Campbell, Converse, & Rodgers, 1976), I define subjective well being as *satisfaction of developmental needs through participation in salient life domains and reflected in a value-laden belief about the totality of one's life.* This definition of subjective well being necessitates the further definition of four key concepts, namely "value-laden belief about the totality of one's life," "satisfaction of developmental needs," "life domains," and "domain salience."

13.1 Value-laden Belief about the Totality of One's Life

Rice, McFarlin, Hunt, and Near (1985) defined perceived quality of life as a variable reflecting a psychological state—feeling and cognition—of pleasure, happiness, well being, or satisfaction directed to overall life. In the previous chapter on measurement, I described many reflective measures of perceived quality of life or what is referred to in this book as subjective well being. A popular measure of subjective well being is Andrews and Withey's (1976) D-T measure. It involves a straightforward question: "How do you feel about your life as a whole?" Responses are coded on a scale: delighted, pleased, mostly satisfied, about equally satisfied and dissatisfied, mostly dissatisfied, unhappy, and terrible.

13.2   Satisfaction of Developmental Needs

The *need satisfaction* approach to subjective well being is based on the needs-satisfaction models developed by Maslow (1954, 1970), Mclelland (1961), Herzberg (1966), and Alderfer (1972).[5]   The basic tenet of this approach to subjective well being is that people have a variety of needs they seek to fulfil, and the more they satisfy these needs the more they feel good about their lives.   To reiterate, *the assumption is that those who are more successful in satisfying their developmental needs are likely to experience greater happiness and life satisfaction than those who are less successful.* Those who are more successful, they do so because they are effective in organising their lives in manageable domains and participate actively in these domains.   Doing so generates satisfaction in the life domains in the here and now as well as into the future.   Examples of life domains include work, family, leisure, health, community, social, cultural, and so on.[6]

Let us examine some of the developmental needs and see how people organise their lives to fulfill these needs.   Let us focus on biological needs as an example.   To satisfy their biological needs, people engage in a variety of activities such as eating right, exercising regularly, having regular medical check-ups, having regular sex, and so on.   The events related to those activities and their outcomes generate a certain amount of satisfaction and dissatisfaction.   These affective experiences are organised and stored in memory in certain life domains such as health, love, residential, and family (see Table 4).   So when a person is asked how he feels about his health life, it is very likely that he will reflect on his affective experiences in relation to health-related activities such as eating right, exercising regularly, having regular check-ups, and so on.   When the same person is asked about his sex life, he reflects about his affective experiences related to having sex regularly.   When asked about his residential life, he reflects on those experiences related to the use of his residence, his neighbourhood, and community. And so on.

Note that although most life domains are organised and structured around one focal set of needs (biological, safety, social, etc.), they reflect affective experiences related to satisfaction of other needs.   For example, many think

---

[5] I am aware that need-based theories have been criticised in relation to the need prepotency notion, i.e., the assumption that lower-order needs have a stronger prepotency than higher-order needs (e.g., O'Brien, 1986; Roberts & Glick, 1981; Salanick & Pfeffer, 1977).   The view in this book is partly based on Maslow's taxonomy of needs, not his notion of need prepotency.

[6] Seeman (1967) has argued that people segment their life experiences in life domains that closely correspond to the major institutions in modern society.

leisure life involves a set of activities dealing with one's social needs. Those activities serve not only to satisfy one's social needs but also a variety of other needs such as the need for aesthetics and creativity (see Table 4).

The point here is that people are driven to satisfy their developmental needs. The more they are able to satisfy their developmental needs the happier they are in life. The way they satisfy their developmental needs is by engaging in various activities. These activities result in positive and/or negative affect encoded in memory related to particular life domains. Cognition related to these affective responses are organised in memory in terms of life domains (health life, leisure life, family life, work life, spiritual life, etc.). In addition to the positive and negative affect generated directly from those domain-specific actions and activities, people evaluate their current state of affairs within their life domains. These cognitive evaluations reflect their feelings of satisfaction or dissatisfaction in those domains.

Table 4. [Developmental Needs Satisfied through Activities Organised in terms of Life Domains]

	Health life	Love life	Residential life	Family life	Social life	Leisure life	Work life	Education al life	Spiritual life
Biological needs	Most	Most	Most	Most	Some	Some	Most	Least	Least
Safety needs	Most	Most	Most	Some	Some	Some	Some	Least	Some
Social Needs	Some	Most	Some	Some	Most	Most	Some	Some	Some
Esteem needs	Least	Some	Some	Least	Some	Some	Most	Some	Some
Self-actualisation needs	Least	Some	Least	Least	Least	Some	Some	Most	Most
Knowledge needs	Least	Least	Least	Least	Least	Some	Some	Most	Most
Aesthetics needs	Least	Least	Least	Least	Some	Most	Some	Most	Most

NOTES: Developmental needs (biological, safety, social, etc.) are satisfied through activities engaged in certain life domains. The life domains shown in the table are for illustrative purposes only. They are not meant to capture all life domains. It should be noted that different people segment their affective experiences differently. For example, a person actively engaged in political activities may have a "political life", which may be absent for many others. "Most", "some", and "least" indicate the extent to which those activities in a specific life domain are successful in satisfying a specific developmental need. For example, the table shows that safety needs can be "most" satisfied through the health, love, and residential life domains and "least" satisfied in the educational life domain.

13.3 Life Domains

From organisational psychology, Danna and Griffin (1999) have advanced the view that quality of work life involves a hierarchy of concepts that includes life satisfaction (top of the hierarchy), job satisfaction (middle of the hierarchy), and work-specific facet satisfaction such as satisfaction with pay, co-workers, supervisor, among others (cf. Seeman, 1967). To further understand how satisfaction in a given life domain such as work contributes to overall life satisfaction, one needs to understand the concept of *life domains* and how these domains are cognitively structured. Social psychologists such as Kurt Lewin (1951) have long recognised that affective experiences are segmented in life spheres or what quality-of-life researchers refer to as *life domains*. Thus, a person may have affective experiences segmented in relation to education, family, health, job, friends, and romantic relationships, among others. Memory (conscious, subconscious, and unconscious) is likely to be divided into life domains, and within each life domain the person has deep-seated cognitions reflecting affective experiences in that domain (cf. Meadow, 1988; Rice, McFarlin, Hunt, and Near, 1985).

These life domains are organised in memory in terms of an overall hierarchy. The hierarchy is shown in Figure 2. Feelings about life overall or happiness are at the top of the hierarchy. Underneath this life sphere reflecting feelings about life at large, there are subordinate domains, such as work, family, leisure, health, community, social, etc. Each of these life domains houses affective experiences concerning that domain. Thus, one may have overall good feelings about their work but bad feelings concerning their family, social life, and leisure. Also, each life domain is subdivided in terms of major life events within the domain, and again people segment affective experiences regarding these life events[7] within each domain. To

---

[7] Diener (1984) reviewed much of the evidence up to the early 1980s dealing with the effect of life events on subjective well being and concluded " . . . life events have shown a consistent, but modest, relationship to SWB . . ." (p. 558). To illustrate the effect of life events on subjective well being, let us turn to a large-scale study conducted by Headey and Wearing (1991). The authors conducted a major study referred to as the Victorian Quality-of-Life Study. They found that favourable and unfavourable life events accounted for a significant portion of the variance in life satisfaction, positive affect, and negative affect above and beyond stock variables. Stock variables are social background factors such as socio-economic status, personality factors such as extraversion, neuroticism, openness,

reiterate, much of life experiences is organised in memory in terms of life domains involving a hierarchical structure in which the superordinate domain is life overall. The subordinate level in that hierarchy involves major life domains such as family, work, community, health, leisure, etc. Within each life domain, affective experiences (emotional responses to domain outcome--positive emotions such as joy, affection, and pride, and negative emotions such as sadness, anger, fear, shame, and guilt) are further segmented into life events. Each life domain houses affective experiences reflecting one's overall feelings about one's positive and negative outcomes in that domain.

Besides the cognitions related to positive and negative affect, other cognitions related to domain evaluations are housed within their respective domains. An example of a cognitive evaluation of a particular life domain such as family life is the person asking the question, "how is my family life?" The answer generated to this question (e.g., "I feel pretty good about my family life.") represents a cognitive evaluation of that life domain and is stored in memory. Note that cognitive evaluations of a life domain are different from the cognitions that capture positive and negative affect (joy, affection, pride, anger, fear, shame, guilt, etc.) generated from outcomes related to domain activities. Both sets of cognitions related to positive/negative affect and evaluations play an important role determining one's overall level of satisfaction/dissatisfaction of a life domain. Domain satisfaction/dissatisfaction, in turn, play an important role in determining satisfaction/dissatisfaction with life overall.

The concept of domain hierarchy is very important to understand the strategies people use to enhance their subjective well being. We will continuously make reference to how affective experiences in memory are segmented in a hierarchy reflecting a set of superordinate and subordinate domains, and how these life domains and sub domains (events) are segmented.

---

and social support as in intimate attachments and friendship network. Favourable event scores were positively correlated with positive affect; adverse event scores were negatively correlated with life satisfaction and positively correlated with negative affect. Life events, as a concept, was measured using items such as "You made lots of new friends"; "you experienced a religious conversion or a great deepening of faith", etc.

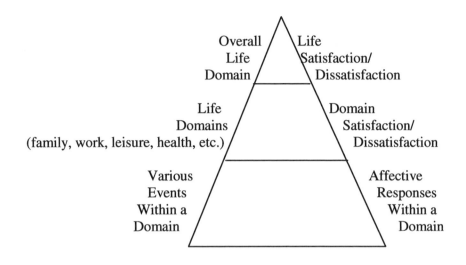

Figure 2. [The Domain Hierarchy]

13.4 Domain Salience

It is also important to understand that the domain hierarchy reflects a salience hierarchy of sorts. That is, domains in which a person has invested considerable effort to attain positive affect (or eliminate negative affect) are likely to be more hierarchically elevated than those in which there is less emotional investment are. We can explain the concept of domain salience in another way. People have value-laden beliefs directly related to particular life domains, such as material, health, job, family, friends, community, among others. All life domains vary in *salience*. That is, some life domains may be more important than others may. A number of prominent social psychologists (e.g., McCall and Simmons 1978; Rosenberg 1978; Stryker 1968) suggested that various identities (self-concepts reflective of certain life domains) are organised in hierarchies of salience that influence self-evaluations. For example, in the mind of one person, the job life domain may be the most superordinate domain, i.e., his job is most important relative to other things in life. For another person, family may be the most important domain; yet for another person, the material domain may be most important (see Figure 3).

Consider an example of a materialistic person. He considers the world of material goods and possessions to be very important relative to other things in life. He considers the material life domain to be more important than other domains such as family, leisure, social, community, and so on. This is reflected in his enduring involvement in that domain—a condition that reflects greater cognitive effort and heightened emotional reactions in relation to material stimuli. He is more involved (cognitively and emotionally) in the material life domain. He regards wealth as an important life goal. He feels that activities related to the accumulation of wealth are very important. He judges people's life accomplishments based on material possessions, and so on.

The concept of domain salience is well known among industrial/organizational psychologists. For example, Dubin (1956) addressed the issue of the extent to which work life is of 'central life interest." Many industrial/organizational psychologists have investigated the concept of central life interest or job involvement (for a dated review see Dubin, Headley, & Traveggia, 1976; Rabinowitz & Hall, 1977). A review of studies of work/nonwork relationship by Near, Rice, and Hunt (1980) has documented the following findings:

- Work seems to be of average importance relative to other life domains;
- The importance of work life has declined from earlier times;
- The importance of work life varies with occupation;
- The importance of work increases when working conditions are good, organizational climate is positive, and when the skill level of the job is high;
- Those who consider work as very important in their life belong to occupational communities, which influence their self-image, their choice of reference groups, and their choice of friends.

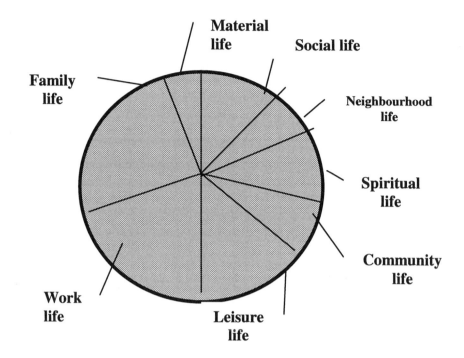

Figure 3. [A Graphic Representation of Domain Salience]

13.5 *The Motive to Optimise Subjective Well being*

Do people optimise or maximise their satisfaction with life? The immediate and most instantaneous response I get from students when I ask them is, "Maximise, of course!" I respond, "Optimise, not maximise!" The motivation is to *increase positive affect but not to exceed an upper threshold, and prevent negative affect from sliding below an intolerable lower threshold.* This assertion begs two questions: why do people seek to increase positive affect only up to some upper threshold? And why do people seek to prevent negative affect from sliding below an intolerable threshold? See an illustration of this motivational tendency in Figure 4.

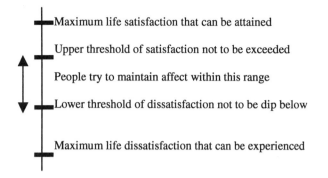

Figure 4. [The Motivational Tendency to Optimise Subjective Well Being]

Cummins (1998) has examined life satisfaction data from countries representing all major geographic regions of the globe and found that these data yield a more inclusive standard of 70 + or − 5 percentage of scale maximum. He concluded that the narrow range of the scores suggest that life satisfaction is held under homeostatic control. A homeostatic model of life satisfaction implies two motivational tendencies: (1) a tendency to increase positive affect not to exceed an upper threshold and (2) a tendency to prevent negative affect from sliding below an intolerable threshold.

My notion of homeostasis is based Heckhausen and Schultz's (1995) theory of *primary and secondary control*. Primary control refers to action taken to control the self or the environment for the purpose of generating positive affect. In contrast, secondary control refers to behaviours designed to control damage. Examples of damage control include devaluation of the goal (the goal that the person failed to attain) and the refocus on outcomes that are non-contingent on the person's behaviour. Doing so serves to minimise the experience of negative affect and ill being.

This notion of homeostasis is also consistent with Wilson's (2000) research on "affective allostasis". Wilson's research has shown that feelings of extreme happiness tend to be short-lived. People tend to keep their emotions within a limited range, in order to maintain a predicable range of responses to life events.

13.5.1 The Tendency to Experience Subjective Well Being
There is an inherent motivational tendency to increase positive affect in everyday life. People are motivated to feel good about themselves and their lives. We are genetically wired to do what we can to experience positive feelings and avoid negative ones. Lykken (1999) has argued in his book,

Happiness: The Nature and Nurture of Joy and Contentment, that we are genetically motivated (i.e., by nature) to pursue and experience happiness. He identified several human motives and abilities that propel us toward the experience of subjective well being. These motives and abilities include effectance, nurturance, self-concept, future perspective, vicarious thought, and aesthetics.

Human beings, as well as other social animals, are born with an *effectance motive*. Effectance motivation refers to the tendency to control one's environment. Thus, we do things to control our lives, the people around us, and our destiny in life. Experiencing the fruits of our labour gives us pleasure, which serves an adaptive function for the human species at large. We are also genetically wired to *nurture* others. Nurturance such as feeding children, fondling infants, and taking care of others is inherently satisfying for humans, as well as other social animals. Nature dictates nurturance. The goal is to preserve the species.

In contrast to all other living organisms, including other social animals, humans have the ability to form, maintain, and change *self-conceptions*. The ability to see oneself in certain ways allows people to make judgements about themselves and experience positive self-evaluations. Positive self-evaluations are a major source of subjective well being. For example, we compare our actual self with our image of ourselves from the past and realize that we made much progress over time. This type of judgement enhances subjective well being. Other living species do not have self-concepts and therefore lack in the ability to make judgments about themselves that can enhance their subjective well being. Also, particular to the human species are distinct abilities of *anticipating* the future and experience events *vicariously*. These two human abilities allow humans to experience joy and happiness--abilities lacking in other species. By anticipating the future, people set goals and experience positive affect in planning and anticipating goal attainment. They plan action guided by the vicarious feelings of goal consumption. Imagining how it would feel attaining a particular goal does make a contribution to subjective well being in its own right.

Another ability that is unique to the human species is the ability to experience *aesthetic pleasures*. People have the ability to take delight from the small as well as big things in life. Imagine hiking in the woods and observing the beauty of the trees, the flowers, the shrubbery, the rolling hills, the meadows, the sunset, the little animals that roam the forest. And so on. Seeing beauty in ordinary things is ability relegated to the human species only. Experiencing beauty contributes to one's subjective well being.

Other suggestive evidence of the tendency to experience subjective well being include:

- Greenwald (1980) reviewed much of the research literature on the self-concept and declared that most people possess a very positive view of their self. That is positive self-evaluation is motivated by ego defence mechanisms. For example, when people are asked to describe themselves, most subjects describe themselves in positive than negative terms.

- Research on the self-serving bias in causal attribution shows that most people attribute more success than failure outcomes to themselves (see Bradley, 1978; Miller & Ross, 1975; Ross & Fletcher, 1985; Zuckerman, 1979, for reviews).

- The social cognition research literature also provides much evidence suggesting that people positive information about the self is efficiently processed and easily recalled than negative information (e.g., Kuiper, Olinger, MacDonald, & Shaw, 1985). More specifically, happy people have higher opinion of themselves than unhappy people.

- Taylor and Brown (1988), after reviewing much of the research in mental health, concluded that normal people have an inherent motive to view themselves not only positively but also unrealistically so. There exists a pervasive tendency to see the self as better than others. People have illusions of control. That is, people think they control their environment, but in reality they do not. People are unrealistically optimistic about the future, even when confronted with evidence that suggests otherwise. In contrast, people who are depressed or have low self-esteem do not have those *illusions*. Depressives have more accurate self-knowledge than non-depressives. This pronouncement by Taylor and Brown has generated quite a bit of a stir in the mental health profession. For many decades the hallmark of mental health has been: getting the patient to face reality, confront it, and deal with it. *Accurate* self-knowledge has been *sine qua non* of mental health, i.e., that psychological adjustment dictates that the patient "gets in touch with reality." Hence, Taylor and Brown have managed to debunk the notion of accurate self-knowledge as being central determinant to mental health. Conversely, they argued that mental health requires a certain degree of positive illusions. For example, a study of cancer patients found that certain beliefs to be associated with successful adjustment to the cancer. These beliefs are that one's coping abilities were extraordinary and that one could personally prevent cancer recurrence (Taylor, Lichtman, & Wood, 1984; Wood, Taylor, & Lichtman, 1985). Positive illusions (positive view of the self, illusion of control, and unrealistic optimism) are necessary for happiness or contentment. Positive illusions are necessary to motivate people to care for others--an important criterion of mental health. This may be due to the fact that positive illusions facilitate social function. People help one another if and when they have a positive outlook on life and when they are in a good mood. Positive illusions also are necessary to engage in creative and productive work, again an important criterion for mental health. This may be due to the fact that positive illusions facilitate intellectual functioning and motivate high levels of performance and persistence in light of failure (cf. Becker, 1973; Greenberg, Pyszczynski, & Solomon, 1986).

13.5.2 The Tendency to Enhance Subjective Well Being but not to Exceed an Upper Threshold

Based on many studies examining life satisfaction in different countries, Cummins (1998) estimated a ceiling on the normal range of life satisfaction to be about 80% of the scale maximum. One interpretation of this finding is that there may be a tendency to increase positive affect but up to some *ceiling*. Diener, Sandvik, and Pavot (1991) have conducted a study that illustrates this tendency. The study demonstrated that intense and frequent positive experiences are related to subjective well being because they are easily evoked from memory when a person is asked to evaluate his life. However, they also demonstrated that frequent positive experiences are more related to long-term well being than intense ones. They explained this finding by arguing that frequent positive experiences tend to play a more important role in subjective well being than intense positive experiences because they are recalled more readily and accurately. Intense positive experiences, although they occur, may be experienced more rarely than occurrences inducing low-to-moderate positive affect. The authors theorised that people avoid experiences because they come at a cost. There are two costs: (a) intense negative affect and (b) lower positive affect of future positive experiences.

Intense positive experiences are usually followed by increased negative affect and decreased positive affect of other good experiences. This logic is based on Solomon's *opponent-process* theory (Solomon, 1980), which predicts that intense emotional peaks often come at the cost of negative affect. That is, those who experience intense positive feelings are likely to experience intense negative feelings too. Therefore, those who experience intense positive experiences typically do not report higher levels of subjective well being. This is due to the fact that the positive affect generated from intense positive experiences is offset by the negative affect generated from intense negative experiences (Diener, Colvin, Pavot, & Allman, 1991; Diener & Larsen, 1984; Diener, Larsen, Levine, & Emmons, 1985).[8]

Diener et al. explained that the experience of an intense positive event is likely to dampen positive affect of future related events. Intense positive affect is generated when an event is judged to be significantly above the adaptation level (satisfaction reference from past events). Thus, an intense positive experience raises the adaptation level (referent) by which future related positive events are judged. The higher the adaptation level the more likely that future positive events will be judged as less satisfying. The logic of this argument is based on Parducci's (1968) *range-frequency* theory, which will be described in some detail in a subsequent chapter.

Thus, there may be a homeostatic mechanism to control life satisfaction that it generally remains positive but not to exceed an upper threshold (Cummins, 1995, 1998; Headey & Wearing, 1988, 1992). The maintenance of positive affect is highly adaptive to the human species. Such a positive outlook on life, according to Cummins, is adaptive for food acquisition, predator avoidance, and mating.

Janoff-Bulman (1989) advanced the notion of "world illusions" that posits that people hold on to simplified views of the world for the purpose of generating and maintaining positive affect. World illusions take form in *benevolence* (people are inherently good and that the world is a place where good things usually happen), *meaningfulness* (there is good reason for everything that happens in life), *worthiness* (people are inherently praiseworthy because they are decent), *optimism* (the future will be better than the present), and *competence* (people tend to be self-resilient in taking care of themselves).

13.5.3 The Tendency to Prevent Subjective Well Being from Sliding below an Intolerable Threshold

Based on many studies examining life satisfaction in different countries, Cummins (1998) estimated a floor on the normal range of life satisfaction to be about 60% of the scale maximum. One interpretation of this finding is that there may be a tendency to prevent negative affect from sliding below an intolerable threshold. When people become too dissatisfied with life they slide into depression. Severe and chronic depression usually leads to suicide, the ultimate act of self-destruction. Argyle and Martin (1991) have

---

[8] Stoics believe that extreme emotional experiences should be avoided. Extreme positive feelings should be dampened by negative feelings. Ascetic Christians and Buddhists propagate the same maxim.

argued convincingly that happiness has three components: (a) frequency and degree of positive affect or joy, (b) satisfaction with life over a sustained period and (c) the absence of negative feelings such as depression and anxiety. It is the third component of Argyle and Martin's conceptualisation of subjective well being that is of particular interest here.

Much research has shown a strong relationship between satisfaction with life and depression (e.g., Mechanic, 1979; Reich & Zautra, 1981; Tanaka & Huba, 1984). People who are clinically depressed have a pervasive sense of dissatisfaction with life. This relationship is best illustrated by a study by Lewinsohn, Reddner, and Seeley (1991) in two large-scale longitudinal surveys of a general community sample. The study clearly indicated that life satisfaction and depression are negatively related. That life satisfaction is related to depression but it is not reducible to depression. When people become dissatisfied with their lives they become depressed. In other words, the data show that dissatisfaction with life precedes the onset of depression. And since there is an inherent need for survival and self-preservation, people are motivated to prevent themselves from sliding into depression. The bottom threshold of life dissatisfaction is the point of no return, and people try to avoid that point of no return by attempts at reducing dissatisfaction with life.

13.6 *Strategies People Use to Optimise Subjective Well being*

There is much research in the quality-of-life studies literature that suggests satisfaction in one area of life may influence satisfaction in another (e.g., Andrisani & Shapiro, 1978; Bromet, Dew, & Parkinson, 1990; Crohan, et al., 1989; Crouter, 1984; George & Brief, 1990; Kabanoff, 1980; Kavanagh & Halpern, 1977; Leiter & Durup, 1996; Levitin & Quinn, 1974; Loscocco, 1989; Orpen, 1978; Rice, Near, & Hunt, 1980; Schmitt & Bedian, 1982; Schmitt & Mellon, 1980; Staines, 1980). For example, satisfaction with one's job may influence satisfaction in other life domains such as family, leisure, social, health, financial, etc. Wilensky (1960), an organisational psychologist, was the first to describe strategies of how people enhance their subjective well being. He argued that when people feel lack of satisfaction in one life domain and they realise they have little control in changing that outcome, they engage in activities in other domains in an attempt to maximise overall life satisfaction (or to ensure that overall life satisfaction does not drop below an intolerable level). Thus, experiencing satisfaction in one life domain may "compensate" for the lack of satisfaction in another. He described how affect from one domain "spills over" unto other domains. He also described how people "segment" their affect in certain domains preventing affect from spilling over. Wilensky identified two basic inter-domain strategies that people use to enhance their subjective well being—spillover (and segmentation, which is the inverse of spillover) and compensation. I break down the concept of spillover into three sub-strategies: bottom-up spillover, top-down spillover, and horizontal spillover. The major part of the remainder of this book addresses strategies used within a given life domain. These are: re-evaluation based on personal history, re-evaluation based on self-concept, re-evaluation based on social comparison, goal selection, goal implementation and attainment, re-appraisal. Finally, I describe a strategy that combines both inter-domain and intra-domain dynamics. This is the balance strategy. I will briefly review the essence of each strategy here and defer the details to the subsequent chapters.

Bottom-up spillover refers to the influence of affect in subordinate domains (e.g., family life) on superordinate domains (e.g., overall life). That is affect travels up the hierarchy of life domains. An example of bottom-up spillover is a person who is happy with family life, his social life, his sex life, his marital life, his leisure life, but is dissatisfied with his work life. The affect contained in these life domains travels upward in the domain hierarchy to affect the most superordinate domain of overall life. This is done in a compensatory manner, in that the negative affect in the work life domain is offset by the positive affect invested in the other life domains.

Top-down spillover refers to the influence of affect of superordinate domains (e.g., overall life) on subordinate domains (e.g., family, work, leisure, social, and health). It is used as a strategy to enhance subjective well being given that the most superordinate life domain (i.e., overall life) contains more positive than negative affect. The positive affect is allowed to spillover down the domain hierarchy to increase the positive valence of the subordinate life domains, which in turn feeds back to overall life. For example, a person who feels good about her life in general but feels bad about her work life allows the good feelings about life at large to spill over into the work domain. Doing so reduces the negativity associated with work life.

Horizontal spillover refers to the influence of affect in a life domain on another life domain that is neither subordinate nor superordinate to it (e.g., influence of work satisfaction on family satisfaction). Horizontal spillover can be used as a strategy to enhance subjective well being by focusing on a positive life domain and allowing the positive affect associated with that domain to reduce the negative valence of another domain. For example, a person may feel fulfilled in the religious domain but feels dissatisfied with family. He allows his good feelings about religion to influence his feelings about family.

With respect to *compensation*, this strategy involves making life domains in which the person feels good more important and other domains in which she feels bad less important. For example, a person feels bad about her work life but feels very good about her religious life. To increase her subjective well being, she begins to view her religious life as the most important thing in her life. Doing so multiplies her good feelings invested in that domain; and these feelings are allowed to spill over to the most superordinate domain--overall life. By the same token making her religious life domain to be the most important decreases the salience of her work life, which in turn serves to decrease the negative spillover from that domain to overall life.

With respect to *re-evaluation based on personal history*, this strategy to enhance subjective well being refers to the manipulation of expectancies (based on one's personal history) used in judging one's well being in a given domain. For example, a person is dissatisfied with work life, perhaps because he thinks he does not make enough money to make ends meet. He may re-evaluate this domain by noting that he has made progress over the past several years. He was able to achieve significant raises and promotions over the past years, and should feel proud of his achievements.

With respect to *re-evaluation based on self-concept*, this strategy to enhance subjective well being refers to the manipulation of expectancies in making judgements about well being in a given domain. These expectancies may be based on one's self-concept such as the ideal self, the social self, the deserved self, the aspired self, the competent self, etc. For example, if a person is dissatisfied with his standard of living because he compares himself with his friends and associates who make considerably more money than he does. He may re-evaluate this domain by comparing his actual self with his deserved self. His deserved self is the image of himself attaining a standard of living that he thinks he deserves. Perhaps he thinks that he has not worked as hard as others have. Therefore, he does not deserve to attain the same level of standard of living. Such a comparison is likely to make his evaluation of his current standard of living positive, thus generating satisfaction in that domain.

With respect to *re-evaluation based on social comparison*, this strategy to enhance subjective well being refers to the manipulation of the standard of comparison (based on significant others) used in judging one's well being in a given domain. For example, a person is dissatisfied with his family life because of minor communication problems encountered with his children. He may compare his family life to those who are less fortunate, i.e., those who have children with significant problems such as drug abuse. Doing so may help him feel better about his family life, thus increasing subjective well being.

With respect to *goal selection*, this strategy to enhance subjective well being refers to the selection of personal goals that should be capable of generating a great deal of positive affect. For example, a person is dissatisfied with his leisure life. He visits his relatives on vacations and ends up arguing with his children and wife during the vacation. It usually turns out to be an "ordeal" not a vacation. He reassesses his situation by selecting a different leisure goal. He decides to take the family on a cruise for vacation, instead of visiting relatives. This goal is capable of generating a great deal of positive affect. A successful visit can only reduce dissatisfaction; however, an unsuccessful visit can heighten dissatisfaction.

Another strategy that will be discussed at some length is *goal implementation and attainment*. The focus of this strategy is direct action designed to complete a set of the tasks that would allow him to attain the goal. The catch here is to select those tasks in ways to increase the likelihood of goal attainment. Consider the same person who decided on a cruise for the family vacation. Suppose he does not have the budget to do the cruise. In this case, his leisure well being is likely to plummet. The advice is to ensure that the selected goal can be implemented with given resources.

Re-appraisal is yet another strategy to enhance subjective well being. One can re-appraise a negative event in ways to shed new meaning on that event, and therefore extract positive feelings from the re-appraisal. For example, a person looses his job because of organisational re-structuring. Instead of interpreting this event as negative causing him to feel bad about his work life, he realises that this situation presents a new opportunity for him to start a new chapter in his life. He looks forward to it with optimism and enthusiasm. This re-appraisal has served to enhance his subjective well being.

Balance is the last strategy we will discuss in this book. By balance we mean engaging in events to generate both positive and negative affect within a given life domain and compensating across life domains. Positive affect in a domain serves to enhance subjective well being in the here and now. Negative affect serves to motivate the individual to plan ahead to correct past mistakes and to take advantage of new opportunities. Negative affect is the basis of motivation to strive to attain future goals. People look forward to future joy. Thus, people tend to seek to "balance" positive and negative experiences in life.

PART II:

INTER-DOMAIN STRATEGIES

This part of the book focuses on *inter-domain strategies*. These are personal growth strategies that focus on manipulating psychological aspects dealing with the inter-relationships among life domains. The strategies are bottom-up spillover, top-down spillover, horizontal spillover, and compensation.

Chapter 4 covers *bottom-up spillover*. The strategy refers to the influence of affect in subordinate domains (e.g., family life) on superordinate domains (e.g., overall life). That is affect travels up the hierarchy of life domains. This is done in a compensatory manner in that the negative affect in one life domain is offset by the positive affect invested in other life domains. I developed a set of psychological principles capturing how bottom-up spillover can be used to enhance subjective well being by describing the psychological mechanics involved with the means-end chain and domain salience.

Top-down spillover (Chapter 5) refers to the influence of affect from superordinate domains (e.g., overall life) on subordinate domains (e.g., family, work, leisure, social, and health). It is used as a strategy to enhance subjective well being given that the most superordinate life domain (i.e., overall life) generally contains more positive than negative affect. The positive affect is allowed to spillover downward in the domain hierarchy to increase the positive valence of the subordinate life domains, which in turn feeds back to overall life. Several psychological principles were developed to reflect how certain factors affect top-down spillover. Examples of factors affecting top-down spillover include personality and affect intensity.

Horizontal spillover (Chapter 6) refers to the influence of affect in a life domain on another life domain that is neither subordinate nor superordinate to it (e.g., influence of work satisfaction on family satisfaction). Horizontal spillover focuses on a positive life domain and allows the positive affect associated with that domain to reduce the negative valence of another domain. Several psychological principles were formulated to reflect how horizontal spillover could be used to enhance subjective well being. The literature identified several factors affecting this kind of spillover and corresponding principles were deduced. These factors include domain overlap, personality type, skills and abilities, and cultural pressures.

With respect to *compensation* (Chapter 7), this strategy involves increasing the importance of life domains in which the person feels good and decreasing the importance of other domains in which she feels bad. Doing so multiplies the good feelings invested in that domain; and these feelings are allowed to spill over to the most superordinate domain--overall life. By the same token, increasing the salience of the positive life domain serves to decrease the salience of the negative life domain, which in turn serves to decrease the negative spillover from that domain to overall life. A compensation principle was formulated and explained to help readers use it as a strategy for personal growth. Several factors affecting compensation were revealed in the research literature. These include repeated failure, low versus high status, personal crises, public versus private conditions, fixed sum of resources, and needs. Additional compensation principles were formulated by considering these factors.

4

BOTTOM-UP SPILLOVER

Social psychological strategies to enhance subjective well being are captured by four inter-domain processes. To reiterate, these are:
1. Bottom-up spillover,
2. Top-down spillover,
3. Horizontal spillover, and
4. Compensation.

In this chapter, I will concentrate on helping the reader understand the process commonly known as bottom-up spillover and how it is used as a strategy to enhance subjective well being. After discussing the bottom-up spillover principle, I will describe the psychological mechanics of how bottom-up spillover occurs using the cognitive algebraic rule referred to as the compensatory decision rule.

14. WHAT IS BOTTOM-UP SPILLOVER?

To remind the reader what bottom-up spillover is, here is another definition. *Bottom-up spillover* is the spillover of affect from subordinate life domains to superordinate ones, specifically from life domains such as leisure, family, job, and health to overall life. That is, feelings within a given life space within the overall hierarchy of life experiences spill vertically from bottom to top.

The bottom-up spillover strategy is graphically shown in figures 5 and 6. The top portion of the figure (Figure 5) shows a person who is moderately satisfied with life (overall life satisfaction is shaded in grey—the darker the shade the greater the dissatisfaction and, conversely, the lighter the box the greater the satisfaction). The bottom portion of the figure (Figure 6) shows this moderate level of overall satisfaction has changed. Now the person is experiencing a high level of life satisfaction (the overall life satisfaction box is not shaded). Why? The increase in overall life satisfaction is due to the bottom-up spillover. This spillover is coming from essentially two life domains, namely the family and work domains. That is, positive affect travels from the life domains of family and work and spills over to the most superordinate domain of overall life. Doing so, it causes the person to enhance his subjective well being (change from moderate to high satisfaction with overall life). Note that the individual is not happy with his leisure life, but he did not allow his negative affect from leisure life to spillover to overall life. Doing so implies that people have control over bottom-up spillover. They can control the gates. One can allow positive affect to influence one's feelings about overall life, and, by the same token, prevent negative affect from spilling over.

A similar principle applies at lower levels of the domain hierarchy. Note that there are two major family events (family event 1 and family event 2). These are represented as boxes underneath the family life box. Both sets of family events have generated positive feelings (represented by the lighter shade in the two boxes). More technically, the representation of these positive feelings is in the form of cognitions (beliefs about their positive feelings related to the family events). These positive feelings may have been generated consciously by a cognitive evaluation of these events or subconsciously through the experience of positive emotions such as joy, affection, and pride. Ultimately, the source of positive and negative affect derive from satisfaction of human developmental needs (biological, safety, social, esteem, and self-actualisation needs). The positive affect associated with these family sub domains is allowed to spillover unto the family life domain. Thus, the person feels happy in his family life mostly because of his awareness of the feelings related to these two sets of family events.

Now let us look at the work domain. In the top portion of the figure (Figure 5) we see that the person starts out being moderately satisfied in his work domain. In the bottom portion of the figure (Figure 6) we see that his satisfaction in his work life has increased. How? He managed to increase his satisfaction in his work life because he was able to allow the positive affect associated with work event 2 to spillover unto his work life while preventing the negative affect associated with work event 1 to do the same. Thus he was able to contain the negative affect in one of the two work sub domains while allowing the other to spillover. Doing so is a bottom-up spillover strategy designed to enhance subjective well being.

The *spillover* of affect from a life domain (e.g., economic life domain capturing feelings of well being in relation to personal income, standard of living, and material possessions) and overall life (or happiness) can be conceptualised using the hierarchy model. The basic premise is that overall life satisfaction is functionally related to satisfaction with all domains and sub domains. Life satisfaction (satisfaction in the most superordinate domain) is influenced by one's feelings in salient and subordinate life domains; and thus the greater the satisfaction with the major life domains (such as personal health, work, family, and leisure), the greater the satisfaction with life in general.

Satisfaction with a given life domain is determined by satisfaction with one's concerns in that domain. For example, it can be postulated that satisfaction with the material life domain is determined by satisfaction with the monetary value of one's house, car, furniture, clothing, savings, jewellery, accessories, etc. A person's evaluation of these dimensions of the material domain (and/or the direct experience of positive and/or negative affect) can be viewed as satisfaction/dissatisfaction with life conditions or concerns within the material life domain. The hierarchy model of life satisfaction thus argues that satisfaction with overall life is determined by satisfaction with the major life domains. Satisfaction with a given life domain is determined by satisfaction with the life conditions/concerns within that domain.

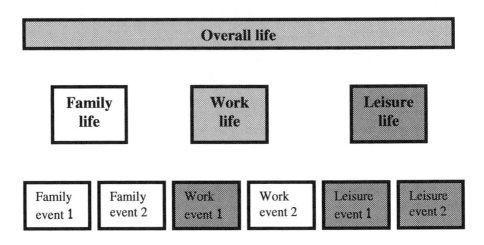

Figure 5. [Bottom-Up Spillover--Before]

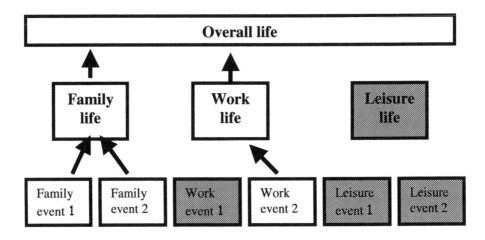

Figure 6. [Bottom-Up Spillover--After]

The concept of bottom-up spillover has been used by quality-of-life researchers (e.g., Campbell, Converse, & Rodgers, 1976; Diener, 1984; Diener et al., 1999; Efraty, Sirgy, & Siegel, 2000; Neal, Sirgy, & Uysal, 1999; Sirgy, Hansen, & Littlefield, 1994; Sirgy et al., 1991, 1998a, 1998b, 2000) to explain the psychological dynamics of subjective well being. The argument is that subjective well being can be explained and predicted from the various global feelings one has in relation to the different life domains (e.g., Campbell, Converse, & Rodgers, 1976). For example, one person may feel happy with life because he is mostly happy with what is important to him such as his health, job, family, friends, community, and material possessions.[9]

Many studies in the interdisciplinary field of quality of life have empirically demonstrated the vertical bottom-up spillover effect between satisfaction with specific life domains and overall life (Diener, 1984). Diener, in his classic literature review article (1984), concluded that subjective well being is mostly determined by subjective satisfaction from the various life domains. In commenting on Campbell's (1981) seminal study, he stated the following:

> . . . . the highest correlation was satisfaction with self (.55), suggesting that people must have self-esteem to be satisfied with their lives. Satisfaction with standard of living and with family life were also highly correlated with life satisfaction, whereas the correlation for satisfaction with work was moderate (.37), and satisfaction with health and community were somewhat lower (.29) (p. 552).

Here are additional study examples to help illustrate the concept of bottom-up spillover.

- In relation to health, much research has shown strong correlations between health satisfaction and subjective well being (e.g., George & Landerman, 1984; Larsen, 1978; Okun, Stock, Haring, & Witter, 1984).
- Much research in the work area has shown strong correlations between work satisfaction and subjective well being (see Rice, Near, & Hunt, 1980 for a review). For example, in a cross-cultural study comparing Japanese workers with workers from the U.S.A., Near (1986) has shown that job satisfaction explains 11 percent of the

---

[9] Tversky and Griffin (1991) have used the concept of "endowment effect" to refer to the positive affect resulting from a social judgement influence subjective well being--a concept comparable to spillover.

variance in life satisfaction among Japanese workers and 5 percent among American workers. She explained this finding by arguing that American workers are more likely to segment their work domain from other non-work domains. In contrast, the Japanese workers experience greater bottom-up spillover.

- Several studies have shown that satisfaction with the material life domain spills over to overall life (e.g., Day, 1987). For example, one study (Leelakulthanit, Day, & Walters, 1991) employed a consumer population in Thailand that demonstrated this effect. Specifically, they examined the relationship between satisfaction with one's own acquisition and possession of material goods and overall life satisfaction. The study results provided support for a positive relationship, especially for older and low-income people.
- Veenhoven (1991) has examined much of the evidence between income and subjective well being and concluded that satisfaction with income (or financial well being) correlates highly and positively with subjective well being.
- Tait, Padgett, and Baldwin (1989) conducted a meta analysis of 34 studies and found an average correlation of .44 between job satisfaction and subjective well being.
- Myers (1993, 1999) has amassed much evidence to show the strong contribution of close social relationships to subjective well being. The effect of close relationships on subjective well being is revealed through satisfaction with friendships and marital satisfaction.

The Bottom-Up Spillover Principle: Subjective well being can be increased by allowing positive life domains to spill over positive affect unto the most superordinate domain (overall life). The positive affect accumulates in life domains as a direct function of satisfaction of human development needs.

The *bottom-up spillover* principle implies that one has control over how one feels about life at large. This means that you can influence your own subjective well being by controlling which life domains you should draw from, and which ones you should shut off. The basic premise is to draw from life domains containing positive feelings, not those containing negative feelings. For example, a person seems pretty happy with his work, leisure life, and social life. However, he does not feel good about his family life. To enhance his subjective well being, he draws positive feelings from his work, leisure, and social life domains. At the same time, he makes an effort to block or shut off the negative feelings he has about his family from affecting his feelings about life overall. Yes, it can be done, and in the sections below, I will describe some tactical advice that can help you implement the bottom-up spillover strategy.

15. FACTORS AFFECTING BOTTOM-UP SPILLOVER

There are two factors that will be discussed in this section considered to play an important role in facilitating bottom-up spillover. One factor deals with making connections in a mean-ends chain and the other is the manipulation of domain salience and affect.

15.1 Means-Ends Chain

The means-ends chain is a concept popular in consumer psychology (e.g., Guttman, 1982; Reynolds & Guttman, 1988). It is designed to help marketers understand why some consumers feel that buying and owning their favourite car is very important in their life, and how their happiness revolves around that car. In contrast, subjective well being may have very little to do with the consumption of most consumer goods for most consumers. Figure 7 shows the means-end value chain. The means-end chain model posits that a product can be characterised in consumers' minds in terms of a chain of attributes, beginning from concrete attributes, followed by abstract attributes, functional consequences, social/psychological consequences, instrumental values, and ending with terminal values (see Figure 7). The main premise here is that, for some products, the chain extends to values that are central to one's life. Life satisfaction can be easily construed as a value that is commonly shared by people and is central to life. Marketers use the means-end chain model to cognitively map the product attributes and trace the cognitive connections leading to positive and negative values. Thus, the model is used as a tool for marketers to understand how a product affects consumers' instrumental and terminal values (and therefore consumers' quality of life). A product can be designed (or re-designed) to translate into a cognitive map (in the minds of consumers) that leads to important instrumental and terminal values with minimal conflict among these values. For example, suppose an automobile manufacturer decides to cater to an elderly population and enhance the quality of life of the elderly by providing them with an automobile that can meet their instrumental and terminal values. Suppose that safety and economy (instrumental values) are strongly associated in the minds of the elderly to happiness (terminal value). The question becomes "can a car be designed in such a way that satisfies the need of the elderly for both safety and economy?" Automotive engineers thus use this information to guide their design decisions.

The means-end chain can help us understand how evaluations of concrete events occurring in the context of a life domain can affect evaluations of life overall. Connecting the cognitive evaluations of life events with the evaluations of life domains, and the evaluations of life domains with evaluations of overall life can enhance subjective well being. Thus, controlling the "gates" that allow affect to spillover form the concrete to the very abstract is a matter of making meaningful connections between the concrete (a specific life event) and the abstract (life overall).

For example, suppose a college student does well on, let's say, an upper-division class in his major. She feels good about his accomplishments in that class because she evaluates his performance positively. These positive feelings can make a difference in enhancing that student's overall life satisfaction. To do this the student thinks about how the high grade in that class will pave the way to securing the kind of job she aspires to have, and how she will feel quite rewarded in life by doing that kind of work over the entire span of her career.

The Means-End Chain Principle of Bottom-up Spillover: Establishing meaningful connections between life events, life domains, and overall life can facilitate bottom-up spillover. Subjective well being can be enhanced by making meaningful connections with positive life events--events that can be evaluated positively. A life event is positive when it generates positive affect as a result of satisfaction of one or more human developmental needs. Conversely, an event is negative when it generates negative affect as a result of failing to satisfy one or more needs.

The *means-end chain* principle encourages us to become vigilant in making meaningful connections between the meaning of a positive event in a particular life domain and how that event contributes to overall well being. Establishing meaningful connections between the very concrete and the very abstract in the context of one's hierarchy of life domains facilitates bottom-up spillover. Of course, we would want to establish meaningful connections among mental constructs in such a way as to facilitate bottom-up spillover of positive affect, not negative affect. Hence, the trick is to make meaningful connections among mental constructs that are positive in valence. Doing so is likely to facilitate spillover of positive affect, not negative affect.

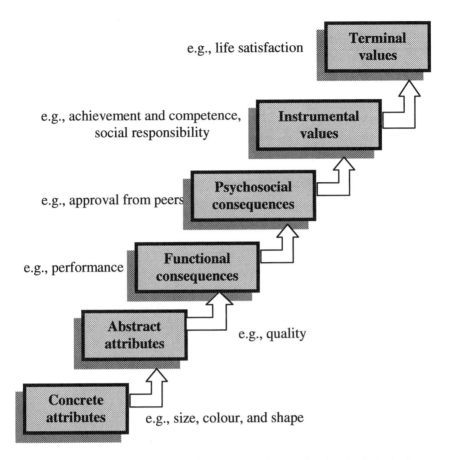

Figure 7. [The Means-End Chain Model Popular in the Marketing Literature]

15.2 Manipulating Domain Salience and Affect

In order to understand how bottom-up spillover works, we need to make reference to the concept of domain salience. This is because bottom-up spillover occurs as a direct function of domain salience. Specifically, domains that are highly salient are those that impact other domains by inducing spillover, thus influencing the affect in other domains. To reiterate, a particular life domain (e.g., material, health, job, community, family, or leisure) may vary in salience in relation to other life domains. For some people, a particular life domain may be highly salient, while for others the same domain may be low in salience. The higher the salience of a domain, the more emotionally involved the person is in that domain. Emotional reactions to outcomes and events in that domain are likely to be experienced much more intensely than similar outcomes and events in other less-salient domains. Thus, affect in salient life domains is more likely to spill over, contributing more to subjective well being than affect in less salient domains.

Now let us go through the compositional logic of this argument. Subjective well being is likely to be most affected by the spillover of affect in one particular domain than by affect from other life domains, *given that the domain in question is highly salient*. For example, materialistic people (those who are emotionally involved in the world of shopping and material goods) are likely to experience a high level of subjective well being if they accumulate sufficient positive affective experiences in the material life domain. Conversely, materialistic people are likely to feel unhappy if that they accumulate negative experiences in their material domain.

Here is suggestive evidence of this argument:

- Oishi, Diener, Suh, and Lucas (1999) found students with high achievement values felt "better" on days when they did well in school, and students with strong social values felt "better" on days when they had a more satisfying interpersonal life. In other words, students with achievement values are those who are emotionally involved with education and work. These students felt quite satisfied when they did well in school because their achievement values magnified these feelings of satisfaction. Students with interpersonal values also felt highly satisfied on days when they interacted successfully with others. The interpersonal values served to magnify those feelings considerably.

- LaBarbera and Gurhan (1997) found that income's positive relationship with subjective well being increases as people become more materialistic. Obviously, materialistic people place more importance on income than non-materialistic people.

- Oishi et al. also found that satisfaction with travel was a more important predictor of subjective well being in the more-developed countries than the less-developed ones. This is because in the more-developed countries people place more importance on leisure than those in the less-developed countries. This emphasis on leisure serves to magnify satisfaction with leisure spilling over unto overall life.

- One study has found that married women are happier than married men and unmarried people in general (Williams, 1988). This is because women rate the quality of marriage as more important than men do.

- Steiner and Truxillo (1989) conducted a study that showed that job satisfaction and life satisfaction are more strongly correlated among employees with higher work involvement than those who are not emotionally invested in their work.
- Diener and Diener (1995) found that financial satisfaction is a stronger predictor of life satisfaction in poor nations than in wealthy ones.   Conversely, self-esteem is a stronger predictor of life satisfaction in the developed than the developing countries. Again, the explanation here is that income and financial security is more important to people in the developing than in the developed countries. By the same token, the focus on the self is more important to people in the developed than developing countries.

Now given that we understand how spillover is guided by domain salience, we are now ready to ask the most important question: How can we model and predict subjective well being by accounting for the magnitude of affect (satisfaction/dissatisfaction) in each life domain and the salience of these domains? Consider the following situation belonging to a person, let us call him Patrick. Patrick is evaluating his life. He generates the following self-evaluations (we will refer to these self-evaluations in figures denoting intensity of valence on a scale varying from very positive self-evaluations [+5} to very negative self-evaluations [-5]:

+3 reflecting his evaluation of his standard of living,
+2 reflecting his family life,
+1 for his religious life,
-2 for his social life,
-3 for his sex life,
-1 for his leisure life, and
+2 for his work life.

The question is how will these feelings of satisfaction in these different life domains spillover in the most superordinate life domain, namely overall life? The answer lies in the moderating effect of domain salience. One can model this process and outcome using a weighted sum calculus--multiplying the evaluations of the different life domains by the perceived importance of the different domains and summing the resultant scores (see Table 5). Suppose the event that precipitated Patrick's evaluation of his life was getting fired from his job. His previous evaluation of his work life domain plummets from +2 to -2. The salience of his work life domain is likely to be extremely high at that moment. On a total percentage scale, one can assign an importance weight of 90% reflecting the current salience of the work domain. The exact breakdown of perceived importance scores may be as follows: 3% importance for his standard of living, 3% importance for his family life, 1% importance for his religious life, 1% importance for his social life, 1% importance for his sex life, 1% importance for his leisure life, and 90% importance for his work life. Hence, if we take a sum of all the life domain evaluations, we compute a total score of -1.75, reflecting an overall dissatisfaction with life (scale varying from +5 to -5). In this formulation of the sum of satisfaction ratings (weighted by perceived importance) the reader can see how the effect of spillover can be captured.

The theoretical logic of this process is explained by much work in social psychology in multiattribute attitude formulations (e.g., Fishbein & Ajzen, 1975). For example, using the language of multiattribute attitude, a person's attitude toward life is a direct function of the person's evaluations of the various life domains (moderated by the belief strength associated with each life domain). That is, evaluation of each life domain is viewed as satisfaction in that domain, and overall life satisfaction is conceptualised to be determined by satisfaction with each life domain--job, family, personal health, leisure, material possessions, and so forth (e.g., Frisch, 1998, 1999, 2000, 2001, in press).

We can show this principle mathematically as:

$$SWB = \sum_{i=1}^{n} A_i S_i$$

where

SWB = Subjective well being
A_i = Positive/negative affect experienced in domain (i), i = 1, 2, . . . n (scale: +5 (very positive) to -5 (very negative)
S_i = Salience of domain (i), i = 1, 2, . . . n (scale: percent)
n = Total number of life domains considered by the individual

Table 5. [The Effect of Spillover of Satisfaction from Life Domains on Satisfaction with Life Overall]

Life domain	Satisfaction rating (SR)	Perceived importance (PI)	SR x PI
Standard of living	+2	3%	.06
Family life	+1	3%	.03
Religious life	-2	1%	-.02
Social life	-3	1%	-.03
Sex life	-1	1%	-.01
Leisure life	+2	1%	.02
Work life	-2	90%	-1.80
Total		100%	**-1.75**

NOTE: Scale of satisfaction ratings and total scores: from +5 (very positive evaluation) to -5 (very negative evaluation)

The Multi-domain Satisfaction Principle of Bottom-up Spillover: *Subjective well being can be enhanced by increasing the salience of positive life domains, decreasing the salience of negative domains, increasing positive affect in positive domains, and/or decreasing negative affect in negative domains. A life domain is positive when it contains significantly more positive than negative affect generated from satisfaction of human developmental needs. Conversely, a life domain is negative when it contains significantly more negative than positive affect.*

The *multi-domin satisfaction* principle outlines at least three sets of strategies to enhance subjective well being. The first set deals with manipulation of domain salience—increasing salience of positive life domains and decreasing salience of negative ones. The second set involves the manipulation of affect—increase positive affect in positive life domains and decrease negative affect in negative life domains. I will not delve in this chapter into describing the very specific tactics related to these two sets of bottom-up spillover strategies. This is because these tactics will be fully explored in the context of other chapters. For example, the chapters on re-evaluation (there are three chapters devoted to re-evaluation based on different standards of comparisons) focus on how people can increase domain-specific positive affect (and decrease negative affect) by manipulating the standard of comparison. There is one chapter dealing with re-appraisal. The focus of that chapter is to increase positive affect and decrease negative affect through re-interpretation of life events. There is a chapter on compensation that deals with domain salience and how it can be manipulated to increase positive affect and decrease negative affect. We have several chapters on goal-oriented action. These chapters focus on how people can do a better job selecting goals and engaging those goals to produce positive affect (and decrease negative affect). So the reader will learn how to further implement the bottom-up spillover strategy by learning about those other subjective well being strategies.

The third set of strategies implied by the multi-domain satisfaction principle is what Frisch calls "boost satisfaction in other areas not considered before" (Frisch, in press, Chapter 4). Frisch argued that since a person's subjective well being is the sum of their satisfaction in particular valued life domains, people could enhance their subjective well being by experiencing positive affect in new life domains. This can be done by exploring new domains and experiencing pleasure in those new areas.

15.3 The Positivity Bias in Life Domain Evaluations

Cummins et al. (2002) have argued and presented evidence suggesting that there is a posivity bias in life domain evaluations. People are motivated to evaluate their life overall in positive terms. They are motivated to enhance or at least maintain a positive view of themselves. This positivity bias has been well documented in the social cognition literature. One example of a program of research supporting this point of view is the work by Tesser et al (1989) on self-evaluation maintenance. The self recognises good performance in many areas, but aspires to improve in only few areas. Therefore, self-evaluations of one's performance are usually positive. Negative self-evaluations tend to be limited to non-valued areas of one's life, thus becoming less threatening to the need for self-esteem.

This positivity bias varies as a direct function of two factors: (1) the level of abstractness of the life domain, and (2) the level of the domain proximity to the self. With respect to the level of *abstractness*, consider the following three life domains--overall life, home life, and sex life. These three life domains do indeed vary in terms of the level of abstractness of the experiences housed within those domains. Overall life is most abstract because it is a life domain most superordinate in the domain hierarchy. Overall life contains affective expereinces related to many other subordinate life domains (e.g., home life, work life, leisure life, and community life). Note that home life is subordinate to overall life. One can also argue that sex life may be a sub-domain under home life. That is, in the context of a family, experiences related to home life may involve family life, social life, neighborhood life, and sex life. Because sex life is subordinate to home life, which in turn is subordinate to overall life, it is considered to be most concrete. Overall life is considered most abstract, whereas home life is somewhere in between.

Cummins and his colleagues theorise that the greater the abstractness of a life domain the greater the motivation to maintain a positive view of the self. This tendency leads people to rate their overall life most positive, but the positivity bias diminishes as the person rates life domains that are increasingly more concrete. That is, people are more likely to rate their sex life more accurately as a direct function of their actual experiences in that area than if they were to rate their home life and overall life. Again, the underlying motive is the need for self-esteem. It is easier to satisfy the need for self-esteem in rating abstract life domains because these domains are "less real". The more concrete the life domains the more they become subject to reality checks.

> *The Abstractness of Life Domain Principle of Bottom-up Spillover:*
> *Subjective well being can be enhanced by evaluating abstract life domains, if these evaluations are anticipated to be positive. If the evaluations are anticipated to be negative, then the damage to subjective well being can be minimized by diverting the evaluation to concrete domains.*

The advice from the *abstractness principle* is to focus on evaluating abstract rather than concrete life domains. However, does this mean that people should not evaluate their concrete life domains? No! They should do so if and when the affective experiences housed within the concrete domains are positive. Positive affect is sure not threat to subjective well being. It is the negative affect that should be avoided.

With respect to the *proximity-to-the-self* factor, Cummins and his colleagues have argued that life domains also can vary in relation to their proximity to the self. Some life domains are close to the self (e.g., overall life, health life, sex life, work life, and leisure life), whereas other domains are distal from the self (e.g., community life, life in the greater community or region, life in the state or province, life in the country, and so forth). The positivity bias applies more to evaluations of life domains proximal to the self and less to domains distal from the self. In other words, people are motivated to evaluate their overall life positively but "call it as they see it" in relation to their evaluations of their community life, life in their state or province, life in their country, and so forth. The underlying motive is self-enhancement (i.e., the need for self-esteem). Negative evaluations of one's life in the community (distal life domain) are less threatening to the self than negative evaluations of one's overall life (proximal life domain).

> *The Self-proximity Principle of Bottom-up Spillover: Subjective well being can be enhanced by evaluating life domains proximal to the self, if these evaluations are antiicipated to be positive. If the evaluations are anticipated to be negative, then the damage to subjective well being can be minimized by evaluating domains distal to the self.*

The advice from the *self-proximity principle* is to focus on evaluating life domains that are most proximal to the self, if and when these evaluations are anticipated to be positive. These evaluations are likely to be rich in the intensity of the positive affect, and therefore they can play an important role in enhancing subjective well being. The caveat, of course, is to watch out if these evaluations in those self-proximal domains are negative. If so, the advice is to refrain from evaluating those domains. Instead choose the least threatening strategy. Focus on those life domains most distal to the self. The negative evaluations associated with these domains are not likely to do too much damage to subjective well being.

TOP-DOWN SPILLOVER

This chapter describes top-down spillover as a strategy people use to optimise subjective well being. The strategy is described in some detail. Empirical evidence is presented to demonstrate its use. I will provide a little bit of advice based on the principle of top-down spillover. Furthermore, a discussion will ensue regarding how personality traits and other factors facilitate the top-down spillover process.

16. WHAT IS TOP-DOWN SPILLOVER?

Top-down spillover is the influence of affect from overall life on affect embedded in various life domains. That is, affect flows from a superordinate domain to subordinate domains.

The process of top-down spillover is shown in figures 8 and 9. Let us go through the process and use an example to further illustrate the process. The top part of the figure shows the domain hierarchy before the top-down process, and the bottom part shows the outcome of top-down spillover. The top part (Figure 8) shows a graphical illustration of a person (let us call her Wanita) who feels satisfied with her family life (represented by white fill-in). The events and concerns within the family domain are positive too (represented by white fill-in). For example, events related to her relationship with her husband have been quite positive. Also, she has two children, ages 7 and 12. Both children are doing great in every way. They are doing well in school; they are healthy and well behaved; and most importantly, Wanita feels close to her kids.

With respect to her work life, the figure shows a grey fill-in, which signals a state of moderate dissatisfaction. Note that there are two sets of work events subsumed under the work domain, one negative (dark in shade) and the other is positive (light in shade). Perhaps Wanita is happy with the people at work. She has a good relationship with her boss and all her other colleagues. However, she feels dissatisfied with her pay and the benefit package she receives from work. Her last raise was several years ago, and it was not much to speak of. The reason given was "the firm is in a mature market and is barely breaking even. The business is not making a profit." She realises that she can increase her income significantly if she were to quit and join another company that is in a growth market.

With respect to her leisure life, note that the box is larger than the boxes pertaining to her work life and family life. The size of the box represents how important that life domain is to the person in question. In this case, it represents the fact that Wanita's leisure life is considered to be very important to her, more important than her family and work life. Note that the leisure life box is shaded with a darker shade representing negative affect. This means that Wanita feels quite dissatisfied with her leisure life. The leisure events subsumed in the leisure life domain are also shown with a dark fill-in, representing negative affect. Wanita has two passions, one is aerobic exercise and the other is foreign travel. She injured her knee a year ago, and this injury put her out of commission. She no longer can enjoy her aerobic passion. Money is tight, family expenses are high with two growing kids, and the fact that she has not received a decent raise for quite sometime now. Therefore, she no longer indulges herself (with her husband) going overseas on their summer vacations. Her husband's income has not increased significantly either. Hence, her two passions in life have been in a "state of oblivion". Furthermore, note that she feels satisfied with life overall (represented by the white fill-in in the box pertaining to overall life). She is a happy person; she has a positive outlook on life, and always sees the good in people and things. Perhaps this happiness was brought about by having had wonderful parents who gave her unconditional love and taught her how to appreciate life in its fullest.

Now let us look at the bottom part of the figure describing and illustrating the process of top-down spillover. Wanita allows her satisfaction with life overall to spill down to influence her dissatisfaction in the leisure domain and to a lesser extent her work domain. She may do this by being optimistic, e.g., "Things are likely to turn around at work, and eventually I will get a significant pay increase." With respect to the leisure domain, she may rationalise also by convincing herself that the lack of travel is only a temporary setback. That when things get better at work the family will be able to afford to do some summer travel in Europe. In the mean time, travel has to be restricted domestically, and this is not bad. With respect to aerobics, she may think that this is also a temporary setback, and she actually appreciates the time off from aerobics to allow her knee to heal. The time off from aerobics allowed her to spend more time with the kids, which brought them even closer than they were before.

Note that this top-down spillover is shown in Figure 9 to flow back up to register its final influence on satisfaction with life. That is, although the top-down spillover effect does not speak to how top-down spillover affects satisfaction with life, one can easily extrapolate its strategic use to enhance subjective well being. Specifically, the top-down spillover principle posits that positive affect is induced from the most superordinate domain (life overall) to influence affect in the various sub domains, which in turn influences satisfaction in the most superordinate domain.

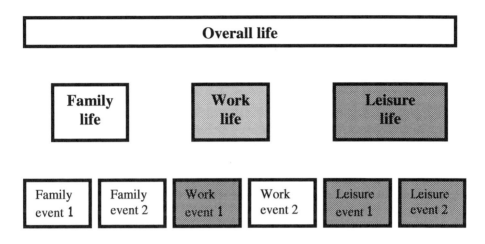

Figure 8. [Top-down Spillover--Before]

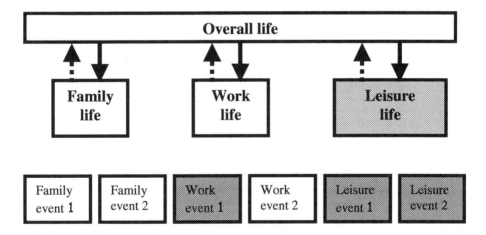

Figure 9. [Top-down Spillover--After]

Lykken (1999) maintains that people are endowed (from their genetic/biological makeup and/or from early childhood socialization) with a certain amount of happiness they carry around from one situation to another. His metric for happiness is "haps". Some people are endowed with, let us say, 20 haps, some 35 haps, and some, perhaps 5 haps. Those who are characterized as having more "haps" are called "happy people", and those with less haps as "unhappy". As with my theory, Lykken proposes that people experience events and these events generate positive and negative affect. Life events serve to add a few haps to the person's repertoire of haps (the person's set point of happiness), thus enhancing subjective well being in a given situation at that time. However, according to Lykken, these additional increases in subjective well being are not permanent additions to the person's overall happiness repertoire (the person's set point of happiness). These increases in subjective well being reflect only a temporary "boost". The person, in the absence of experiencing other positive or negative events, returns to his endowed set point. These positive events are emotional uplifts. Conversely, there are hassles. These are negative events that temporarily reduce the person's overall repertoire of happiness.

The point here is that people have a set point of happiness, an overall bank of positive and negative affect representing the person's level of subjective well being. One can add or take away from this bank, but these additions and subtractions are temporary and reflect how the person feels overall in a given instance or in a given situation. Suppose a teenager, wc will call Mark, has a happiness endowment of, let's say, +20 haps. He goes to school and sees his girlfriend flirting with a guy. He feels pretty bad. These negative feelings amount to, let's say, -5 haps. Therefore, at the time he experienced the negative affect (seeing his girlfriend flirting) his subjective well being amounted to +15 haps, i.e., +20 haps from his endowment and -5 haps from the negative affect generated from that situation. After a couple of days, assuming no incidents that made him feel particularly good or bad occurred, he returns to his set point, which is +20. In other words, his level of subjective well being was measured at +20, two days after the flirting incident. This set point of happiness, this natural endowment or repertoire of happiness, is quite similar to the *top-down spillover* effect.

Much research in subjective well being has suggested that happy people (compared to unhappy people) tend to perceive their selves more positively, and this positive self-regard biases their perception about outcomes in specific domains. This bias may be partly responsible for the experience of satisfaction across a variety of life domains. This influence of overall happiness on affect experienced in specific life domains is what we call here *top-down spillover.* For example, a longitudinal study by Judge and Wantanbe (1993) has shown that the pattern of influence between job and life satisfaction is mutual. That is, job satisfaction influences life satisfaction (bottom-up spillover), and that life satisfaction reciprocally influences job satisfaction (top-down spillover) (cf. Judge & Hulin, 1993; Judge & Locke, 1993).

The Principle of Top-Down Spillover: Subjective well being can be increased by allowing spillover of positive affect from overall life to important life domains. This should increase positive affect (or decrease negative affect) in these life domains. Positive affect is generated as a direct function of satisfaction of human developmental needs.

The principle of *top-down spillover* reminds us of how important child rearing and early socialisation is to subjective well being. If parents would do their best to raise a child who is positive and has a high level of subjective well being, this child will have an enormous advantage. The high level of subjective well being should empower the child in every way. High levels of subjective well being will be used throughout life to further influence affect in the various life domains.

I like to think of the top-down spillover using the analogy of the "rich get richer and the poor poorer." This is an unfortunate reality for the poor, but this reality instructs us that the rich have a head start on making money. It is easier to make money when you have money than if you are starting out from scratch. The same applies to subjective well being. If you start out with high levels of subjective well being, you are likely to get more of it. If you start out low, then the tide is against you. You have to swim against the tide, and possibly if you get tired, you drown.

That is not to say that those who are dispositionally unhappy people cannot do much to improve the quality of their lives. This entire book is replete with personal strategies. The obvious recommendation is to learn to use these strategies.

17. FACTORS AFFECTING TOP-DOWN SPILLOVER

The literature has identified two factors I believe influence the top-down spillover process. These are personality and extreme levels of subjective well being.

17.1 Personality

There is much research that suggests that *extraversion* is positively correlated with subjective well being (see Diener 1984 and Diener et al. 1999 for literature reviews). For example, Costa, McRae, and Norris (1981) found that extraversion predicted happiness 17 years later. This is typical of the research findings reviewed by Diener (1984). There is a strong relationship between extraversion and subjective well being. To illustrate this research, consider the study conducted by Headey and Wearing (1991). These quality-of-life researchers found that extraversion was positively related with life satisfaction and positive affect (cf. Diener et al., 1992; Kette, 1991). Costa and McCrae (1980) have argued that *neuroticism* is linked with negative affect, whereas extraversion is linked with positive affect. Watson and Clark (1984) made the point that neurotics and extraverts have a temperamental disposition to experience negative and positive affect, respectively.

Other personality traits have been linked with subjective well being. These include *self-esteem* (e.g., Dunning, Leuenberger, & Sherman, 1995), *optimism* (e.g., Scheier & Carver, 1985), *expectancy of control* (e.g., Grob, Stetsenko, Sabatier, Botcheva, & Macek, in press), *pollyannaism* (e.g., Matlin & Gawron, 1979), and *genetic predisposition to be happy* (e.g., Lykken & Tellegen, 1996; Tellegen, et al., 1988).

The Personality Principle of Top-down Spillover: Top-down spillover of positive affect from overall life to various life domains is likely to occur more readily for people who are extraverts, optimistic, have high self-esteem, have high expectancies of control, have the Pollyanna syndrome, or have a genetic predisposition to be happy. Conversely, top-down spillover of negative affect from overall life to various life domains is likely to occur more readily for people who are introverts, pessimistic, have low self-esteem, have low expectancies of control, do not have the Pollyanna syndrome, or do not have a genetic predisposition to be happy.

The *personality principle* tells us that if you are the kind of person who is either an extravert, an optimist, has high self-esteem, has high expectancies of control, has the Pollyanna syndrome, or has a genetic predisposition to be happy, then you can take advantage of this by allowing positive affect to spillover in the various life domains. Doing so will enrich the life domains with positive affect. However, if you are an introvert, a pessimist, have low self-esteem, have low expectancies of control, do not have the Pollyanna syndrome, or do not have a genetic predisposition to be happy, then beware. Again, BEWARE! This is because you may have a tendency to create havoc in your life by allowing top-down spillover of negative affect. This tendency will infect your life domains with negative affect, and you will feel bad about your life most of the time.

Preventing top-down spillover of negative affect is very difficult but possible. It can be done through through the application of many of the personal strategies discussed in this book and/or psychotherapy. The focus of psychotherapy is to teach the client to use cognitive, affective, and behaviour strategies to block the flow of top-down negative affect. Since I am not a clinical psychologist (but a mere social/industrial psychologist) I am not in a position to give expert advice on psychotherapeutic techniques to use. I would assume different psychotherapeutic approaches could have their own "bag of tricks." However, if you would like to read an excellent book on the use of quality-of-life therapy to enhance subjective well being, read Frisch (in press). His book gets into many of the psychotherpeutic techniques, and Michael Frisch is a Professor of Clinical Psychology and a practicing psychotherapist.

17.1.1 The Very Happy and the Depressed

People who are extremely high or extremely low on subjective well being are more likely to experience a top-down spillover than those who are less extreme. This is because these people have so much positive or negative affect vested in the most superordinate domain, and such intense feelings are likely to be contagious.

Evidence of this hypothesis is supported by research in depression. For example, Sweeney, Schaffer, and Golin (1982) have shown that clinical depression leads to failure to feel pleasure when engaged in normally pleasant events. The converse is argued for very happy people. Additional evidence comes from a study conducted by Diener, Oishi, Lucas, and Suh (2000). They examined the relation between the best life domain and life satisfaction, and between the worst domain and life satisfaction. Two types of measures were used--global life satisfaction and domain satisfaction ratings. The study found that happy people were more likely to weight good domains in judging their life satisfaction and weight bad domains relatively less. In contrast, unhappy people were more likely to give greater weight to their worst domain.

The Very Happy and the Depressed Principle of Top-down Spillover:
Top-down spillover of positive affect from overall life to various life
domains is likely to occur more readily for people who are very happy.
Conversely, top-down spillover of negative affect from overall life to

various life domains is likely to occur more readily for people who are very depressed.

What advice can we deduce from the *very-happy-and-depressed* principle? The same advice discussed under personality. That is, those who are already happy, take advantage of this "overflow" of happiness. Use it as a shield to help in situations in which truly negative events occur. This shield acts like a "cushion". It softens the painful blows of life. For those who are depressed, the advice is, get professional help. This is because the depression is working against attempts to enjoy life and experience happiness. Remember top-down spillover of negative affect! This is the danger. Realise the danger and get help.

6

HORIZONTAL SPILLOVER

I describe in this chapter how some people attempt to *enhance subjective well being* by implementing a strategy referred to as horizontal spillover. Once this strategy is described in some detail, we will show how this strategy can be implemented, under what conditions, and how understanding the dynamics of this strategy can help us enhance our own quality of life.

18. WHAT IS HORIZONTAL SPILLOVER?

Horizontal spillover refers to the effect of satisfaction or dissatisfaction of one domain on a neighbouring domain. For example, work satisfaction or dissatisfaction spills over in the family domain thus affecting satisfaction or dissatisfaction with family life.

There is much evidence in the quality-of-life literature to suggest that affect in one life domain does indeed influence affect in another domain that is not superordinate or subordinate to it but is on the same plane in the overall hierarchy of life domains and concerns. For example, we may address the spillover between the material domain and the family domain, between the family domain and the job domain, and so on. Tthe family, job, and material domains are considered to be subordinate to the most superordinate domain of all, namely life overall. Within the family, material, and job domains, we may have sub-subdomains referred to as *life events*.

Here is an example of horizontal spillover as offered by Wilensky (1960) in his classic work on spillover, compensation, and segmentation:

> . . .the Detroit auto-worker, for eight hours gripped bodily to the main line, doing repetitive, low-skilled, machine-paced work, which is wholly ungratifying, . . . goes quietly home, collapses on the couch, eats and drinks alone, belongs to nothing, reads nothing, knows nothing, votes for no one, hangs around the home and the street, watches the "late-late" show, lets TV programmes shade into one another, too tired to lift himself off the couch for the act of selection, too bored to switch the dials. In short, he develops a spillover leisure routine in which alienation from work becomes alienation from life; the mental stultification produced by his labour permeates his leisure.

Figures 10 and 11 show a visual illustration of hoe horizontal spillover works. The figure's top part (Figure 10) shows the domain hierarchy without any spillover in any direction (top-bottom, horizontal, and bottom-up). The bottom figure (Figure 11) shows how horizontal spillover occurs. Note the spillover is from the family life domain to the work domain. No spillover is evident from the leisure domain to the work domain.

Normatively speaking, one can argue that spillover can be induced from positive life domains to less positive ones to increase overall life satisfaction or decrease life dissatisfaction. Spillover of negative affect is dysfunctional or maladaptive. Positive spillover is adaptive when we consider the ultimate goal is to enhance the positive valence of important life domains. This is because increasing the positive affect of important life domains enhances subjective well being by allowing bottom-up spillover from the affected domains to overall life.

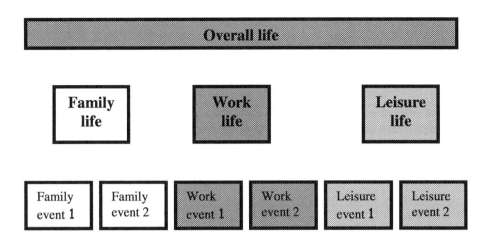

Figure 10. [Horizontal Spillover--Before]

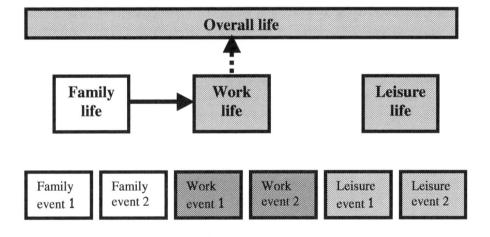

Figure 11. [Horizontal Spillover--After]

Consider this story. John is a middle-age stockbroker. His wife thinks he is going through a mid-life crisis. He is not happy with his career and is complaining about the fact that he invested so much of his life in a career for which he has no passion. The teaching profession fascinated him throughout his childhood. He admired his teachers and wanted to grow up to become a teacher.

Back in college he befriended a number of college students from a fraternity house who were all business majors. All they talked about was business and the stock market. He also met his future wife in college. Her name was Samantha, and she was a marketing major. He always thought that she was the ultimate consumer. She had lavish tastes in clothes, dinning in fine cuisine, and travelling to exotic places. Samantha was mesmerised by the prospect of mingling with the rich and famous. She wanted to marry a successful businessman who would be able to provide her with an extravagant lifestyle. John fell in love with her and sought her love and respect. She had a passion for life, and he sipped and drank from her cup of life. Thus, his interest in business and finance peeked, and he decided to major in finance. He married her, and he became increasingly motivated to fulfill *her* dream of joining the economic elite and mingling with people of high society.

Right out of college, he worked in a bank as a loan officer for a few years and then switched to a large brokerage house in New York. Samantha became a housewife and a homemaker. They tried to have kids, but they had no luck in that department. She thought about adopting but decided against it. This is mostly because Samantha could not see herself raising a child that was not "hers". Nevertheless, she was very content with her homemaker role. She wanted to live in style. John went along with her life vision. He remembers the day he came home and told Samantha about the prospect of taking on this high-salary position in a large brokerage house in New York. Samantha was absolutely delighted. She thought that moving to New York was a great move. She did not mind the move at all. Leaving friends and family behind was a small price to pay. He felt wonderful the first year when the family moved to New York. He worked hard realising Samantha's dream, and he felt quite happy knowing he had his wife's love, respect, and approval.

But then things got rough. The pressure of making money was onerous. His colleagues at work were like sharks. He felt that they were constantly stabbing one another in the back. The culture at the office was "everyone is looking outfor number one". The goal was to sell as as possible because of the high commissions they were making on new and large accounts. Life at work had become very stressful. His job demanded more time, and he spent less time with his family. Most importantly, his social life dwindled to a halt. He felt he had no friends and no social life to speak of. The few social get-togethers were job related.

John is now middle aged and is questioning whether he chose the right career. Did he embark on the wrong path in life? He wanted to become a teacher. That was his passion. Now he finds himself alienated from his job, family, colleagues, neighbours, and community. Life now seems meaningless. His marriage to Samantha has reached a boiling point. Arguments lately have been quite heated. He blames Samantha for "selling his soul to the devil". He feels angry and embittered. He has been thinking of divorce.

Recently, he ran into an associate from work, Tom. Tom was a college administrator of an executive MBA program. They started a conversation that made John excited about the prospect of becoming an adjunct faculty in that program, teaching people a course or two on finance. After a couple of days, he called Tom and explored with him the possibility of teaching a night course in the executive MBA program. Lo and behold, Tom responded positively. It just happened that he was looking for a person who had the experience and background that John has in financial management. Thus, John became an adjunct faculty teaching a night class in financial management. He now feels much better about life. He has a more positive outlook on things. The stress at work is much more tolerable. Even his relationship with his wife seems to be getting better. His childhood passion of finally becoming a teacher is slowly but surely becoming realised. Although he did not quit his job at the brokerage house, night teaching seems to have made quite a bit of difference in improving John's subjective well being.

What has happened to John is what quality-of-life researchers call *horizontal spillover*. We can think of his nighttime teaching as essentially a "hobby". It is leisure in one sense. The positive affect he is experiencing from his leisure life is spilling over to his work life making his job less stressful. His satisfaction with teaching is also spilling over to his family life making his relationship with his wife more bearable. At least now, he is not thinking of divorce, and he and his wife are not arguing.

Now let us examine the evidence in the literature concerning the horizontal spillover effect.

- Diener and Larsen (1984) were able to demonstrate the effect of horizontal spillover across a variety of life domains. For example, they found that average levels of pleasant affect in work situations correlated highly and positively with average moods in recreation situations, and average levels of negative affect in work situations correlated highly and positively with average mood levels in recreation situations.

- Shepard (1974) has shown that work satisfaction/dissatisfaction can spill over to the leisure domain affecting involvement and satisfaction in that domain.
- Lacy, Hougland, and Shepard (1982) have demonstrated a moderately positive relationship between job satisfaction and satisfaction in non-work domains such as family, friends, marriage, hobbies, and place of residence.
- Kremer and Harpaz (1982) were able to demonstrate support for horizontal spillover between work and leisure in retired people. Leisure patterns of activities had semblance to their previous work patterns.
- Wilson (1980) reviewed studies dealing with the spillover between work and leisure and concluded that satisfaction from work tends to spillover to the leisure domain, affecting satisfaction in that domain (cf. Furnham, 1991).
- Crouter (1984) was able to demonstrate a spillover effect from the family domain to the work domain, particularly for mothers of young children.
- Shamir (1986) showed that the unemployed reduce their activities in many other life domains, i.e., that the effect of dissatisfaction arising from unemployment spills over to other life domains.
- Similarly, positive relationships between work and nonwork were demonstrated by Frone, Yardley, and Markel (1997), Karasek (1976), Lipset, Trow, and Coleman (1956), Safilios-Rothschild (1970), Seppanen (1958; cited in Allardt, 1976), and Staines and Pagnucco (1977).

Hopefully by now the reader has a good appreciation of horizontal spillover and how it can be used to enhance subjective well being. We can formulate a principle that captures how people can use this strategy to enhance their own subjective well being as follows:

The Horizontal-Spillover Principle: *Subjective well being can be enhanced by inducing positive affect in a particular life domain to horizontally spill over to neighbouring important domains. Doing so increases the positive valence of the neighbouring domains (or decreases negative valence). This, in turn, should enhance subjective well being through a bottom-up spillover of positive affect from the neighbouring domain to overall life.*

Based on the *horizontal-spillover principle*, the obvious recommendation is to do your best to increase positive affect in one area of life likely to affect other areas. Increasing satisfaction in that area will play an important role not only in enhancing overall life satisfaction directly (through bottom-up spillover), but also indirectly through the satisfaction spillover from the other areas (horizontal spillover). The obvious way of doing this is to engage in life events in that domain likely to generate positive affect. This positive affect should in turn spillover to the life domain and further up the domain hierarchy to life overall.

Decreasing dissatisfaction should also work the same way. By diminishing the negative feelings in the domain that is spilling over in neighbouring domains, one can decrease overall life dissatisfaction directly and indirectly. This can be done in one of two ways. First, one can engage in life events that should guarantee positive emotional outcomes. Experiencing positive life events within an overall negative domain should help make the domain less negative, and diminishing the overall negativity of that domain should affect overall life less adversely. Second, one can make thepsychological wall of the negative domain less permeable (or more impermeable). In other words, contain the negative affect of that domain so that once could decrease spillage to the neighbouring domains and to life overall.

How can people contain the negative affect in a domain to prevent spillage? Consider the following example. Susan is unhappy at work. She believes that her boss is discriminating against her because she is a woman, and her chance for a good promotion was lost to a male colleague. She believes that she deserves that promotion because she is more qualified than her male colleague. She comes home and her bad feelings about work affect her home life. She takes it out on her husband and children. This is horizontal spillover from work life to family life. The resultant outcome is her subjective well being plummets. How can she prevent this situation by containing her feelings of work, i.e., making the "walls" containing the negative affect *impermeable*? Many people do, but some do it better than others. Here are some things that Susan could do. She could convince herself that she will not talk about work with her husband or with her children. She should not bring work at home either. She should allow nothing about work to come into the house, perhaps her briefcase too. She should discourage her officemates from calling her at home to discuss any work-related matter. She should make it a point not to socialize with people at work outside of the office. At home and in other settings, she should engage herself fully and become more emotionally involved in other areas of her life--at least until the negative feelings in her work life decrease in intensity and magnitude. This is not so difficult to do as some might think. Right?

19. FACTORS AFFECTING HORIZONTAL SPILLOVER

In this section several mechanisms are described that helps the reader further understand the conditions under which horizontal spillover is likely to take place. These conditions include overlap, high involvement, skills and abilities, and cultural norms and pressures.

19.1 Overlap

Staines (1980) has argued that horizontal spillover may occur under conditions in which the individual is highly involved in the two life domains (e.g., work and family). High involvement in the two domains (in which affect in both domains spillover on each other) may occur when there is significant overlap between the two life domains in terms of time, place, people, and activities.

For example, suppose we have a family in which the husband and wife are professors at the same university, the same department, and collaborating together on joint research projects. In this case, their family life overlaps significantly with their work life. They share the same activities, they have the same colleagues, and they work at the same place, and so on. This overlap between the two life domains facilitates spillover of affect (positive or negative) from one domain to the next.

Now suppose the husband professor was denied promotion at the university. He is likely to feel quite dissatisfied in his work life because of this significant negative event. Will this dissatisfaction spillover to his family life? Perhaps! This may be due to the association of his wife and family life with aspects of his work life.

The same principle applies to positive affect. If he gets his promotion, he is likely to feel quite happy with his work life, which in turn is likely to spillover to his family life.

The Overlap Principle of Horizontal Spillover: Horizontal spillover is likely to occur when the individual is highly involved in the two life domains and these domains overlap in time, place, people, and/or activities.

What can one learn from the *overlap principle* that can enhance subjective well being? Pay much attention to those areas in your life that overlap considerably. Make sure you are satisfied in these areas of your life. If you are satisfied with the overlapping areas, then use this overlap to your advantage. Reinforce the overlap by engaging in life events in the overlapping domains to guarantee the experience of more positive affect and less negative affect. This overlap serves to magnify the positive affect and faciltate spillage to overall life.

Conversely, if there is more dissatisfaction than satisfaction in the two overlapping domains, then one strategy to pursue is to decrease the overlap. Doing so serves to lessen the affect attenuantion resulting from the overlap. Not doing so may cost much in overall life satisfaction.

19.2 High Involvement

Staines (1980) also has argued that horizontal spillover can be facilitated when the person has a personality that induces a high level of involvement in the two domains in question. Example of a personality trait that induces high level of empotional involvement in one or more life domains is *Type A personality*. Type A personality is described as the kind of person who is always on the go. This person juggles too many things at once. He thrives on a life full of stress. This personality type is related to higher incidence of coronary heart disease (e.g., Rosenman, Friedman, Straus, Wurm, Jenkins, Messinger, Kositchek, Hahn, & Werthessen, 1966). People with such personalities are more likely to experience spillover among many of their life domains—work, leisure, family, health, social, etc.

Of course, Type A personality is about stress. There are other personality traits that induces high level of emotional involvement but reflect positive emotions. A good example is the *autotelic personality*. This is a personality trait that was coined by Mihaly Csikszentmihalyi (1997), the renowed psychologist who spoke so much about flow and zest for life. The autotelic personality is the kind of person who is usually totally absorbed with many things he or she does. Csikszentmihalyi maintains that this kind of person experiences *flow* more so than others. Autotelic people derive intrinsic satisfaction from the things they do. They are not motivated by extrinsic sources of satisfaction. For example, a worker is very involved with his job and excels at it. He is involved with the job not because the job pays well but because he finds the job challenging. He finds pleasure from mastering the job-related tasks. He is highly involved in his work life. He approaches his leisure life with the same level of intensity. He likes to master every game he plays and every sport he engages. He finds pleasure learning the rules of the game and beating his challengers. Because of his high level of involvement in both leisure and work, this person is likely to experience horizontal spillover between the work and leisure domains. Any affect (positive or negative) from either work or leisure life is likely to spill over in the other.

The point here is that horizontal spillover is facilitated between two life domains if the person is emotionally engaged in these domains. A high level of involvement in the two domains precipitates spillover.

> *The High Involvement Principle of Horizontal Spillover: Horizontal spillover between two life domains is more likely to occur if the individual is emotionally involved in both domains than if he or she is not emotionally involved.*

Based on the *high involvement principle of horizontal spillover*, the advice one can take here is to assess your personality and the extent to which your personality makes you experience life events in certain areas of your life with high intensity. For example, are you a Type A person? If so, then make sure to do your best to feel satisfied in those life domains you feel are most important. If you do not, because of your high level of emotional involvement in life, you are likely to feel overwhelmed with stress, which in turn will spillover to feelings of unhappiness. In contrast, if you are an autotelic person, then the high intensity is in your favor. Capture the intensity you experience in one area of life and allow it to spillover to other areas of life. You can do so by applying the same type of intensity in engaging life events in the other areas of your life.

19.3 Skills and Abilities

Another moderator identified by Staines (1980) is skills and abilities. Staines surmised that horizontal spillover is likely to increase when the skills and abilities in one life domain transfer over to another (cf. Meissner, 1971). For example, negotiations and bargaining skills learned at work are applied to the consumer domain. Thus, the person becomes a better bargain hunter in buying consumer goods as a direct result of learning those skills from work. Social skills learned in family life can transfer over to the work domain, enhancing the person's management skills. And so on.

Note that the previous discussion of overlap focused on overlapping situations and roles. Here we have a semblence of "overlap" too but the nature of overlap is related to skills and abilities.

The Skills Principle of Horizontal Spillover: Horizontal spillover is likely to occur if the individual uses skills learned in one life domain in the context of another domain.

The *skills principle* of horizontal spillover advises us to take advantage of skills we have in one domain and to actively transfer those skills in other domains. Of course, this principle applies only if and when those skills are at least partly responsible for goal attainment and resultant satisfaction.

19.4 Cultural Pressures

Cultural pressures is a concept that signals the extent to which society socialises people to either segregate life domains or conjoin them. Dubin (1956, 1973, and 1976) argued that many people segregate the various domains in their lives. That the present structure of society encourages the segregation of work from other major institutions. That is, they segment their feelings in one domain from their feelings in another. In a cross-cultural study comparing Japanese workers with workers from the U.S.A., Near (1986) has shown that American workers are more likely to segment their work domain from other non-work domains. In contrast, the Japanese workers do not segment their attitude toward work from their attitude about other aspects of their lives.

Staines (1980) hypothesised that horizontal spillover can be predicted under conditions in which cultural pressures in one life domain induces the person to become highly involved in another domain. For example, corporate executives who are highly involved in their work life may become equally involved in social activities. Their job requires them to socialise with colleagues outside of work to foster a sense of collegiality. Many corporate executives pride themselves on negotiating their finest deals in social settings, e.g., on the golf course (Levison, Price, Munden, Mandl, & Solley, 1962).

The Cultural Pressures Principle of Horizontal Spillover: Horizontal spillover between two life domains is likely to occur if the individual feels cultural pressure arising from one of the domains (a high involvement domain) to be involved in the other domain.

What advice does the cultural-pressures principle offer? If cultural pressures dictate high involvement in two life domains, then the individual should realise that feelings from one of these domains are likely to spillover on the other domain. So try your best to experience satisfaction in at least one of those neighbouring domains. Those positive feelings are likely to spillover to the neighbouring domain, and in turn both domains will contribute positively to your subjective well being.

COMPENSATION

I will describe in this chapter how people use compensation as a strategy to optimise their subjective well being. When people feel dissatisfaction in one life domain they deflate the importance of that domain and inflate the importance of other life domains in which they have experienced satisfaction. I will describe the compensation principle in some detail. Furthermore, I will describe at least possible mechanisms or conditions in which compensation is proven evident. These are related to a fixed sum of resources and personal needs.

20. WHAT IS COMPENSATION?

People are motivated to optimise their subjective well being. To do so, they manipulate the salience of life domains. When they feel dissatisfaction in one life domain they deflate the importance of that domain and inflate the importance of other life domains in which they have experienced satisfaction. Doing so prevents the overall loss of satisfaction, thus reducing the possibility of sliding into depression. Therefore, experiencing satisfaction in one life domain "compensates" for the lack of satisfaction in another (Wilensky 1960).

In certain philosophical and religious traditions, advice about well being is offered that appears to be designed to reduce the intensity of one's emotions, especially emotions such as anger, shame, sadness, and guilt. For example, mental detachment from the world is recommended in some religious traditions (e.g., Hindu) in order to dampen one's unpleasant emotions. Philosophical traditions such as stoicism also recommend thinking in a certain manner in order to protect oneself against adversity. This mental detachment or guarding oneself against adversity can be understood and appreciated as compensation.

Figures 12 and 13 illustrate graphically the process of compensation. The top part of the figure shows a person very dissatisfied with his leisure life (denoted by the dark shading in the leisure life box), somewhat dissatisfied with his work life (denoted by the grey colour in the work life box), and satisfied with his family life (denoted by white in the family life box). Also, note that the size of the leisure box is larger than the size of either work or family. The size denotes the level of importance of that domain in relation to others. In this case, the leisure domain is considered to be more important than either the work or family domain.

The bottom portion of the figure shows the process and outcome of compensation. In the case shown in the figure, the person compensated by changing their valuation of the leisure domain to least important and his family domain as most important. He shifted salience from a domain in which there is much negative affect to a domain that has much positive affect. Doing so minimises the negative affect spillover from the leisure domain on overall life, thus decreasing life dissatisfaction. Similarly, increasing salience of the family domain serves to increase positive affect of overall life through a bottom-up spillover. This person feels much better about his life because he obtains fulfillment from his family, a need not considered strong in the past, now considered very strong because of the shift of life priorities.

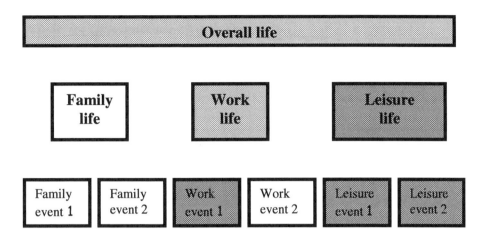

Figure 12. [Compensation--Before]

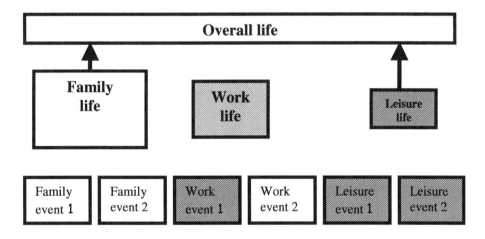

Figure 13. [Compensation--After]

Suggestive evidence of the compensation effect can be described as follows:

- Miller and Weiss (1982) have effectively argued that people sometimes compensate for work deficiencies through leisure activities. For example, they found evidence that people in low-status jobs tend to compensate by *stressing the importance* of prize winning in leisure activities related to organised league bowling (cf. Shepard, 1974). They did this more so than people with high-status jobs to compensate for their lack of satisfaction at work (cf. Furnham, 1991; Staines, 1980).

- Best, Cummins, and Lo (2000) have conducted a study on the quality of rural and metropolitan life and found that both groups report equivalent levels of life satisfaction. However, metropolitan residents reported more satisfaction with family and close friends, while farmers reported more satisfaction with the community and productivity. The authors explained this finding by suggesting that life satisfaction is maintained through *domain compensation*. That is, decreases in satisfaction in one domain are compensated by increases in satisfaction in another.

- Another type of evidence supporting the compensation effect is the significant correlation between domain satisfaction and domain importance. Domains in which people express high levels of satisfaction are likely to be treated as more salient than domains with low satisfaction (or dissatisfaction). Thus, people jack up the salience of domains they feel satisfied in and jack down the salience of domains they feel dissatisfied in. Scott and Stumpf (1984) conducted a study of this sort. They collected data on subjective well being, domain satisfaction, and domain importance using a population of immigrants to Australia. The data clearly revealed a pattern of correlations in which most domain satisfaction scores were significantly correlated with their corresponding domain importance scores—friendship, material possessions, family recreation, and nation.

- Other evidence of the compensation effect comes from evidence showing a negative correlation between involvement in one life domain and involvement in another. For example, in organizational psychology, many studies produced negative correlations between work and non-work involvement. These include comes from Cotgrove (1965), Clark and Gecas (1977), Clark, Nye, and Gecas (1978), Fogarty, Rapoport, and Rapoport (1971), Goldstein and Eichhorn (1961), Haavio-Mannila (1971), Haller and Rosenmayr (1971), Rapoport, Rapoport, and Thiessen (1974), Shea, Spitz, and Zeller (1970), Walker and Gauger (1973), and Walker and Woods (1976).

- Research in social psychology has shown that the things that people are not proficient at are perceived as less important than the things that they are proficient at (e.g., Campbell, 1986; Harackiewicz, Sansone, & Manderlink, 1985; Lewicki, 1984; Rosenberg, 1979).

The Compensation Principle: *Increasing the salience of a domain having more positive than negative affect can enhance subjective well being. Conversely, decreasing the salience of a domain having more negative than positive affect can enhance subjective well being.*

Based on the *compensation principle* the advice is to compensate when you are failing in one area of your life. Do so by finding another area of your life in which you think you may find peace and joy. Once you make that decision, treat the area of your failed life less important. Conversely, treat the area you chose to invest more time and energy more important.

Frisch (in press) has developed a model of quality-of-life therapy that advocates the use of five strategies therapists can use to help enhance the quality of life of their clients. One of these five strategies deals with *changing priorities* in life (Chapter 4). The idea here is to help clients rearrange their priorities by assigning lower importance to areas they are not doing well in and higher importance to positive domains. Frisch used the example of a patient who decides to work on friendships even though the main reason why he was feeling unhappy was that he did not have a love life. Instead of focusing on his love life, he decided to channel his energy into friendship because he knew he is capable of making friends easily. Making friends is a guaranteed success and is likely to enhance his quality of life. Finding a romantic partner is risky and is likely to cause more displeasure than pleasure. Therefore, good friendships can compensate for a poor love life.

21. FACTORS AFFECTING COMPENSATION

In this section, I will explore with the reader several factors influencing the use of compensation. In other words, there are certain conditions that make the compensation effect more likely. Examples include repeated failures, low versus high status, personal crises, public conditions, fixed sum of resources, and needs.

21.1 Repeated Failure

There is much evidence that suggests that compensation occurs when a person fails repeatedly in a given domain. To cope with this failure, he de-emphasises the goals in the failure domain and refocuses on other goals in other domains. Pyszczynski (1982) has effectively argued (and empirically demonstrated) that when a person fears failure, he may convince himself that the goal is less important (or less desirable) than he originally thought. The same point has been made by research in cognitive evaluation theory (Dea & Ryan, 1984).

Research in accounts theory lends support to the compensation effect under significant or repeated failure conditions. For example, Tedeschi and Riess (1981a, 1981b) have argued that when people engage in action producing negative consequences, these people try to *justify* their action by arguing that the consequences are not as negative as some may claim. And conversely, when people engage in action producing positive consequences, they try to *enhance* these actions by magnifying the positivity of the consequences. Account researchers refer to these strategies as justification and enhancement strategies that protect and enhance the person's self-esteem.

The Repeated Failure Principle of Compensation: Compensation between two life domains is likely to occur when failure is experienced repeatedly in one domain. The repeated failure causes the individual to decrease the importance of the failure domain and compensate by increasing the salience of a success domain. Doing so enhances subjective well being.

Based on the *repeated failure* principle, the advice you can take away is to compensate in life domains in which you suffer repeated setbacks. Do not let these setbacks get you down. Instead shift your focus to another domain in which you have a history of success. Play up the importance of the success domain, and play down the significance of the failure domain. For example, if you are not doing well at work (you have not received decent raises and promotion over the past years and you feel like you are stagnating at work), then perhaps you cannot rely on your work to play a significant role in finding joy and happiness in life. Face up to that fact and shift your mental energy. Convince yourself that life is not about work. You work to simply earn a living, and this is the best you can expect out of work. Concentrate on another life domain that has given you joy and satisfaction in the past. Perhaps you have volunteered at church to be a guidance counsellor for the teenagers. You have felt great because many of the teens you have counselled have come back and thanked you for your guidance in their hour of need. Perhaps this is where you need to channel your energies. Perhaps church is very important in your life, and your involvement in church activities should be at least maintained, if not increased. Compensating, thus, can enhance your quality of life.

21.2 Low versus High Status

From research in sociology, a good deal has been written on variations in self-esteem in blacks. The research indicates that blacks have slightly higher self-esteem than whites (Jacques & Chason, 1977; Rosenberg & Simmons, 1972; Taylor & Walsh, 1979; Yancey, Rigsby, & McCarthy, 1972). This counterintuitive finding has generated theoretical speculation. Rosenberg and Simmons proposed a *value selectivity* explanation. This explanation asserts that a minority individual devalues the domain in which he has low status and places greater value on the domain that allows him to have high status (see Gecas, 1982, Porter & Washington, 1979, for a review of this literature). Doing so allows blacks to generate greater positive self-evaluations than whites.

For example, a black woman may perceive that leaders within her community advocating togetherness, solidarity, and justice are people who demand respect and have social status. She decides to strive to become a community leader. Doing so allows her to evaluate herself more positively than before. This personal striving results in greater self-esteem and an enhance sense of subjective well being.

The Low-versus-High-Status Principle of Compensation: Compensation between two life domains is likely to occur when the person recognises that he has high status in one domain but low in another. Recognition of low status in one domain causes the individual to decrease the importance of that domain and compensate by increasing the salience of the high-status domain.

The *status* principle prompts us to take stock of our life. Which domains we feel good about because we are treated with status and respect by others, and which domains we are not? We should play down the importance of those areas of our lives in which we feel we are not treated with respect. We should do the converse in those areas in which people treat us with respect and think highly of us.

Consider Tim's story as an example. Tim is an investment broker. He is a telemarketer—he gets on the phone, contacts prospective investors and tries to sell them stock over the phone. Many of the people he contacts treat him like dirt. Hardly anyone thinks highly of telemarketers trying to sell stocks on the phone. He knows he does not get much respect from his customers or prospective customers, and even from his own colleagues at the brokerage firm. Nevertheless, Tim manages to make quite a bit of money. Tim is married and has two young children. His wife is a homemaker. She thinks highly of Tim. He is a good family man and "he brings home the bacon," plenty of "bacon". His two children think Dad is great, Dad is superman, and Dad is their ultimate hero. To enhance the quality of his life, Tim realises that his brokerage job is just a job. It is not a career. His passion is his family. What is most important is family. He channels whatever time he has away from work into family life. Doing so enhances his quality of life.

21.3 Personal Crisis

From personality-clinical psychology, a number of researchers have addressed issues related to adaptive change given personal crises. For example, Bulman and Wortman (1977) and Taylor (1983) have argued that people may cope with personal crises by decreasing the importance or desirability of the goals and expectations that were dominant before the crises. This is a cognitive strategy that may reduce the negative affect associated with the crisis.

> *The Personal Crisis Principle of Compensation: Compensation between two life domains is likely to occur when the person experiences a crisis in one domain. To deal with the crisis, the person decreases the importance of that domain and compensates by increasing the salience of another domain.*

The *personal crisis* principle advises us to compensate when we are faced with a personal crisis in our lives. Suppose a family has a devastating car accident in which the children perish and no one survives except the mother. She grieves for her family, but eventually she re-marries and has two kids. But this time she does not become a homemaker. She channels her life passion in her work, not her family. She did this to compensate as a strategy to ensure that her future subjective well being can be maintained. She cannot afford to invest much of her life and passion in her family again. It is too risky. All of it can "go down the tubes in a flash." She is not making that mistake again. This strategy helps her deal with her personal crisis in the best way she can, and it works for her. She is able to cling to life and derive more satisfaction from work than her family.

21.4 Public Versus Private Conditions

Research in compensatory self-inflation theory suggests that people may compensate for their failure experiences in one domain by decreasing the relative salience of that domain and increasing the salience of success domains; and this tendency is more evident in public than private conditions (Baumeister & Jones, 1978; Frey, 1978; Greenberg & Pyszczynski, 1985). That is, people try to look good in the eyes of others. When they fail in an important event, they explain that failure to those who have witnessed the event by deflating the importance of that event. On the other hand, if they succeed they carry on by highlighting the importance of that event to others. This "compensatory self-inflation" is less evident when these life events are experienced privately, i.e., the events are not witnessed by others.

The Public Condition Principle of Compensation: Compensation between two life domains is more likely to occur when the person experiences failure in one domain in a public way (significant others have knowledge of the failure). To deal with public humiliation, the person decreases the importance of that domain and compensates by increasing the salience of another domain.

The *public condition* principle prompts us to use compensation as an effective means to deal with public humiliation when we experience failure and everyone (our significant others) knows about it. An eight-year old child invests much of her energy into playing the piano and doing gymnastics as extra-curricular activities. She has a recital, which was well attended by her parents, classmates, friends, and other family members including her two brothers, several cousins, two aunts and uncles, and her grandmother. She blew it at the recital. Although her parents, aunts, uncles, and grandmother were polite in saying she did well, her two brothers told her flat out that she did horrible. Her cousins did not say much. Deep down she knows she blew it, and she has to face up to it. What is she to do? She decides to stop playing the piano. She derogates piano playing and the people who play piano. She calls them stupid. Gymnastics now is for the heroines and heroes. She loves gymnastics. This was her way to deal with the loss of self-esteem when she felt public humiliation after that recital. She *compensated* by denigrating piano playing and emphasising gymnastics. Doing so allowed her to maintain her self-esteem and restore subjective well being.

21.5 Fixed Sum of Resources

One moderator that may make people compensate between life domains is resources. People have a limited amount of resources such as time and energy. If they fail in one domain (e.g., work), they may decide to allocate their energies elsewhere (e.g., family). These resources once spent can further accentuate the compensation effect. That is, the compensation effect becomes more evident in situations in which compensation entails expenditure of personal resources. Since personal resources (e.g., time, energy, and money) are usually limited, people allocate these resources in domains they are likely to derive satisfaction from (cf. Clark, Nye, & Gecas, 1978).

For example, consider two college students who declared their major in cinematography, one rich and one poor. The rich student has more financial resources than the poor person, by definition. This is the first semester in the junior year. They took a class in filmmaking. All students were required to finance their filmmaking efforts in that class. The rich student asked her parents for funding, which was provided to her with no if's and but's. The poor student had to work extra hours to raise the money for the filmmaking project. Both students ended up with a failing grade in the class. The poor student decides to change her major. In contrast, the rich student decided to stick it out. What happened, psychologically speaking? We can explain this situation through the *fixed sum of resources principle of compensation*. The poor student drops out because her resources are quite limited. Indeed she has exhausted her limited resources in this class and ended up failing the class. She cannot afford to continue with a major requiring her to expend additional resources she does not have. Consequently, she becomes highly motivated to resolve this situation with the minimum amount of emotional damage. She compensates by playing down the value of careers in cinematography. The rich student is less motivated to compensate because she has more resources. She can afford to try out other classes in cinematography. Therefore, she hangs on to her major in cinematography-- at least temporarily.

The Fixed-Sum-of-Resources Principle of Compensation: Compensation between two life domains is likely to occur when satisfaction derived from these domains require significant resources and given that these resources cannot be provided.

Based on the *principle of fixed sum of resources*, one recommendation to enhance subjective well being is to realise that spending more resources (time, energy, and/or money) in one domain usually comes at the expense at another. Do not try to extend yourself in one area of your life without knowing full well that something has to give in another area. This is particularly important when both areas of your life require significant resources.

21.6 Needs

Compensation can take place more easily if the new more-salient domain can satisfy the same needs of the domain made less salient (cf., Meissner, 1971). For example, suppose that a person, call her Linda, has trouble with her marriage. For the last several years her relationship with her husband has been at an all-time low. Her husband, Tom, used to be her close friend and confidant. She misses the friendship, the companionship, and the laughter. She believes that her marriage cannot be salvaged. This is because Linda strongly suspects that he has a mistress. Sooner or later he will come to her asking for a divorce. Linda decided to get more involved with her church. She became involved in the church choir and consolidated her friendship with two choir members, Janice and Maggie. Now she socialises regularly with Janice and Maggie outside of church. She feels she has made good friends. She now enjoys her time with them and her sense of humour has returned because of Janice and Maggie. She is still married to Tom, but they hardly interact any more. They have finally discussed divorce, and he is planning to move out of the house soon. She does not feel bad about the divorce because that part of her life is no longer important. Her life at church, the church choir, and her friends compensated quite well for the dissatisfaction she experienced with her marriage to Tom. Note that Linda managed to compensate well because the same needs she was not able to satisfy in her marital life were effectively compensated in her church life.

The Needs Principle of Compensation: *Compensation can be facilitated if the new salient domain can satisfy the same needs of the domain made less salient.*

Based on the *needs principle*, we can recommend that you compensate but make sure that the new areas of your life in which you choose to invest more time and energy can satisfy the same needs in the area of your life that you want to make less important. So do some thinking about which areas of your life you would like to invest yourself in to compensate for the one area in which you are failing. Select wisely based on your understanding of the needs you seek to satisfy in the area in which you failed. Test out your new passion. Does your new passion serve you well by satisfying the needs you longed to satisfy in the failed area?

PART III:

INTRA-DOMAIN STRATEGIES

Part III of the book focuses on intra-domain strategies. These are personal growth strategies that focus on manipulating the psychological aspects within a life domain. I describe six major intra-domain strategies: re-evaluation based on personal history, re-evaluation based on the self-concept, re-evaluation based on social comparisons, goal selection, goal implementation and attainment, and re-appraisal.

Chapter 8 describes *re-evaluation based on personal history*. This strategy to enhance subjective well being refers to the manipulation of expectancies that are based on one's personal history. These type of expectancies are commonly used in judging one's well being in a given domain. For example, if a person is dissatisfied in a particular life domain, he or she may re-evaluate this domain by noting progress toward goal attainment based on his or her history of activities. After fleshing out the underlying psychological principle of re-evaluation based on personal history, I examine the factors affecting this principle and derive additional principles. These additional principles are based on adaptation level, range-frequency, adaptation over time, and sensitisation.

With respect to *re-evaluation based on self-concept* (Chapter 9), this strategy to enhance subjective well being refers to the use of the self-concept in making judgements about well being in a given domain. The self-concept involves expectancies such as the ideal self, the social self, the deserved self, the aspired self, the competent self, etc. Thus, a person dissatisfied in a particular life domain may re-evaluate this domain by comparing his actual self with another type of self-concept that would ensure positive evaluation. I develop a psychological principle to help guide the reader in using this behavioural phenomenon and provide advice on how to use this principle. Then I examine the many factors affecting the use of this principle and develop additional principles to qualify the main concept. These additional principles are based on my understanding of how people evaluate themselves using their ideal self, social self, deserved self, minimum-needs self, predicted self, competent self, aspired self, and self-concept integration.

With respect to *re-evaluation based on social comparison* (Chapter 10), this strategy to enhance subjective well being refers to the manipulation of the standard of comparison (based on significant others) used in judging one's well being in a given domain. People can enhance their subjective well being by comparing themselves to others in ways to generate positive affect and reduce negative affect in a given life domain. Based on this understanding I describe the general principle behind re-evaluation based on social comparison. I further develop additional principles based on the psychological dynamics of self-enhancement, self-improvement, self-identification, and the use of fictitious occurrences.

With respect to *goal selection* (Chapter 11), this strategy refers to the selection of personal goals capable of generating a great deal of positive affect within a life domain. In other words, people can induce maximum positive affect within a life domain by selecting goals that can generate much positive affect. I develop a list of principles based on the following factors affecting goal selection: goal meaningfulness, intrinsic versus extrinsic goals, high- versus low-level goals, goals related to growth needs, approach of desired states versus avoidance of undesired states, goals related to intensity versus frequency of positive affect, goals related to cultural norms, goals related to deprived needs, achievement versus non-achievement goals, autonomy in goal setting, and flow. Then I identify many factors affecting the selection of goals that are likely to be attained and develop corresponding principles. These factors include setting goals to adapt to changes, feedforward, goal-motive congruence, goal-cultural value congruence, goal-resources congruence, goal realism, and goal conflict.

Another strategy that will be discussed at some length is *goal implementation and attainment* (Chapter 12). The focus of this strategy is direct action designed to complete a task that would ensure goal attainment. Many factors were uncovered in the research literature and corresponding principles were formulated. Factors affecting goal implementation include goal commitment and feedback. Factors affecting goal attainment include recognition of goal attainment, goal concreteness, and progress toward goal attainment.

Chapter 13 or *re-appraisal* refers to the strategy of re-interpreting significant negative events to generate positive affect and to diffuse negative affect. Doing so serves to decrease dissatisfaction with that domain housing the experience of these events. Conversely, re-interpreting significant positive events can enhance the positive valence of the events, thereby increasing satisfaction in the domain housing these events. The research literature shows that this type of re-appraisal can be facilitated by active teaching, spirituality, social support, and the passage of time.

RE-EVALUATION BASED ON PERSONAL HISTORY

One could evaluate oneself in ways to increase positive affect (or decrease negative affect) in a particular life domain. This is a strategy that serves to enhance subjective well being. This strategy focuses on changing affect in a particular life domain by manipulating the expectancies or standard of comparison in evaluating one's current state of affairs in that domain. In this chapter I will show the reader how subjective well being can be influenced positively through a variety of principles related to self-evaluation using personal history as a standard of comparison. These principles include adaptation-level, range-frequency, adaptation over time, and sensitisation.

22. WHAT IS RE-EVALUATION BASED ON PERSONAL HISTORY?

Re-evaluation based on personal history is a strategy to enhance subjective well being. It is illustrated in figures 14 and 15. The top part of the figure shows a person (I call Jay) who is satisfied with his family life, somewhat dissatisfied with his work life, and very dissatisfied with his leisure life. The bottom part shows the effect of using the re-evaluation strategy. Here, Jay focused on the leisure domain and managed to change how he feels about his leisure life. He did so by manipulating standards of comparisons within that domain and re-evaluating that domain with new standards. For example, suppose that the reason for feeling very dissatisfied in leisure was due to the type of leisure events he experienced the last few months. Upon his wife's insistence, he spent his summer vacation with his family at his in-laws. His relationship with his in-laws has been strained for a long time. His wife thought that spending time with her parents would make things better. Therefore, he felt that his last vacation was a waste; that he did not really have a vacation *per se*. He now re-evaluates his leisure life by comparing what happened during the last visit with all the previous visits they had over the years. He realises that the most recent vacation was actually a pleasant one compared to past visits. This time, Jay managed to get along with his in-laws, and the time that he spent with his family was not bad after all (again compared to all the previous visits from past years). Jay's in-laws did their best to be pleasant and hospitable. Everybody was on his or her best behaviour. This type of evaluation made him feel better about his vacation and thus his leisure life. He no longer feels bad about missing out, but actually feels good about having spent vacation time with his immediate and extended family. Note that the strategy here was merely an attempt to re-evaluate events in his leisure domain by using expectations based on personal history, expectancies that induced a positive self-evaluation.

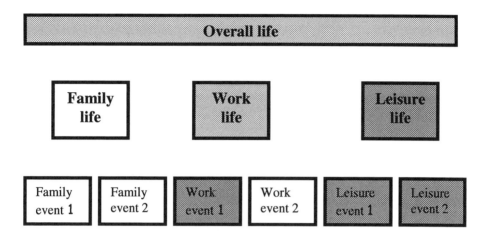

Figure 14. [Re-evaluation based on Personal History--Before]

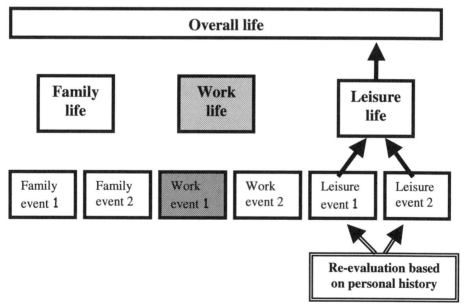

Figure 15. [Re-evaluation based on Personal History--After]

The Personal History Principle of Re-evaluation: Satisfaction results when a life event or outcome is evaluated to equal or exceed one's expectations of that outcome based on what the person has grown accustomed to in the past. The better the outcome compared to what the person is accustomed to the higher the satisfaction. Dissatisfaction results when the outcome is evaluated to fall short from what the person has been accustomed to in the past. The greater the discrepancy from what the person has been accustomed to the greater the dissatisfaction.

The advice delivered by the *personal history* principle is simple. If you believe that you have made incremental progress here and there in one or more of your life domains, then you should evaluate your achievements in light of your past. Doing so will most likely generate positive self-evaluations and you will feel satisfied with your accomplishments. This is because you see current achievements as delivering something better than the past.

23. FACTORS AFFECTING RE-EVALUATION BASED ON PERSONAL HISTORY

In this section I will make an attempt to describe a variety of factors affecting how this type of re-evaluation works in different situations and over time.

23.1 Adaptation Level

Helson (1947, 1948, and 1964) described the effect of past stimuli on the subjective experience of a current stimulus. He introduced the concept of *adaptation level* (AL). He described AL as the level of a stimulus that elicits no response (the level that is hedonically neutral). Helson theorised that AL is determined by an average of past stimulus levels. For example, a person develops an expectation of what pizza tastes like based on past experiences with eating pizza. Every time he eats a pizza, his expectation level of what pizza tastes like changes as a direct function of the new experience averaged with all other past experiences. Of course, more recent experiences with eating pizza play a more significant role on the person's expectation of what pizza tastes like than less recent experiences. Therefore, the cognitive calculus may be a weighted average rather than a simple average.

Using a more macro example, consider the following person who is evaluating his standard of living. This person has been accustomed to a high standard of living, because his parents and relatives were quite affluent. In other words, his past experiences dictate that his AL with respect to the standard of living is high. But then, let us say that in the recent past he had several financial setbacks causing him to live modestly. Thus, we would expect that his AL in relation to the standard of living could decrease as a direct function of the recent financial setbacks.

Furthermore, Helson theorised that an individual's hedonic state at any given time is a direct function of the difference between the current stimulus level and the person's adaptation level. If the hedonic level of the current stimulus exceeds that of the AL, the person experiences satisfaction. Conversely, if the hedonic level of the current stimulus falls below the AL, the person experiences dissatisfaction. Furthermore, the degree of satisfaction or dissatisfaction can be predicted from the degree of discrepancy between the hedonic level of the current stimulus and the AL. For example, if the person eats a pizza that tastes better than what he has been accustomed to in the past, he is likely to evaluate the pizza positively and therefore experience satisfaction eating it. If it tastes worse than what he has been accustomed to eat, then he is likely to judge the pizza as "bad" and thus experience dissatisfaction. The amount of satisfaction or dissatisfaction he experiences is determined by the degree of discrepancy between how the current pizza tastes and his AL. Specifically, if the pizza were better than his past expectations, he should feel very satisfied. If the pizza were as good as what he expected, he might feel satisfied. In contrast, if the pizza were below his expectations, he might experience dissatisfaction.

Here is another example dealing with income. Suppose a company executive rewards and punishes employees through merit raises. One can predict the amount of satisfaction or dissatisfaction experienced by the employees by computing a simple difference between an employee's last pay and his new pay. Employees who made more money in relation to their last pay are likely to feel more satisfied than those who made less money, and their degree of satisfaction is likely to be proportional to the magnitude of the difference between their current pay and their last pay.

Social science researchers noted that civilian prisoners adapt well to prison life, but some of those who are approaching release time become quite agitated. One explanation is they anticipate their life out of prison and compare the anticipated life of out prison to what they grew accustomed in prison. That is, the experience of life in prison became their adaptation level. For some, life out of prison is full of uncertainties and possible adversities (Buskel & Kilman, 1980).

The Adaptation-Level Principle of Re-evaluation: Satisfaction
experienced in a life domain can be increased (and dissatisfaction can be
decreased) by comparing perceived events in that domain to referents
having hedonic values lower than the hedonic value of the perceived
events.

Niven (2000, p. 77), a social psychologist and a happiness researcher,
recommends:

Your happiness is relative to a scale you yourself have created. If you measure
your satisfaction right now against the two or three greatest moments in your life,
you will often be unhappy because those moments can't be duplicated. If you
measure today's satisfaction against tough days you've had, you have all the
reason in the world to appreciate this moment.

Myer (1993, p. 65), in his book *The Pursuit of Happiness*, made reference
to an illustration provided by another psychologist (Shelley Taylor), which
makes the point about re-evaluation clear. Here is the illustration.

Shelley Taylor further illustrates with a Jewish fable about a farmer who seeks a
rabbi's counsel because his wife nags him, his children fight, and his
surroundings are in chaos. The good rabbi tells him to go home and move the
chickens into the house. "Into the house!" cries the farmer. "But what good will
that do?" Nevertheless, he complies and two days later returns, more frantic than
before. "Now my wife nags me, the children fight, and the chickens are
everywhere, laying eggs, dropping feathers, and eating our food. What am I to
do?" The rabbi tells him to go home and bring the cow into the house. "The
cow!" cries the distraught man. "That can only worsen things!" Again, the rabbi
insists, the man complies, and then returns a few days later more harried than
ever. "Nothing is helping. The chickens are into everything and the cow is
knocking over the furniture. Rabbi, you have made things worse." The rabbi
sends the frantic man home to bring in the horse as well. The next day the man
returns in despair. "Everything is knocked over. There is no room for my family.
Our lives are in shambles. What shall we do?" Now the rabbi instructs, "Go
home and take out the horse and cow and chickens." The man does so and
returns the next day smiling. "Rabbi, our lives are now so calm and peaceful.
With the animals gone, we are a family again. How can I thank you? The rabbi
smiles.

23.2 Range-Frequency

Parducci (1968, 1984, and 1995) found that evaluations are influenced by factors other than the mean stimulus level theorised by Helson. Parducci refined Helson's ideas and offered his *contextual theory of happiness*. He theorised that satisfaction in a given domain is determined by a theoretical summation over separate momentary pleasures and pains. The period may be a moment, a day, or a longer period in one's life. Therefore, domain satisfaction of any period is a conceptual summation of these separate hedonic values, positive and negative, divided by the duration of that period. Each hedonic value is determined by a judgement of a stimulus in a context. The hedonic value reflected in that judgement is a direct function of the average of two factors, namely range and frequency of the stimulus in relation to a history of relevant stimuli. Here is an example borrowed and adapted from Parducci's book, *Happiness, Pleasure, and Judgement* (Chapter 8).

Consider the work situation of a salesman who sells door-to-door who earns commissions on sales. After each day, he assesses how much commission he made that day, and as a result of this assessment he feels happy or unhappy. The accumulated average of these feelings of happiness and unhappiness determines his overall satisfaction in his work life domain (assuming that pay is the most important aspect of his job).

What determines his daily feelings of happiness or unhappiness? His judgement of the amount of commission he made that day in relation to the *range* and *frequency* of past commissions. Suppose his most recent 10 days of selling resulted in the following distribution of commissions: $35, $55, $20, $50, $60, $50, $30, $60, $55, and $45. Let us say that the salesman makes $50 in commission. How happy or unhappy will he feel having made $50? According to the contextual theory of happiness, the resultant feeling of satisfaction is an average of two values, namely range and frequency. With respect to the *range* value, the person calculates the location of the $50 commission in the range of commissions for the last 10 days. Because $50 is three-quarters of the way between $20 (the lowest commission in the context) and $60 (the highest), the hedonic value should be .75 (scale is 0 to 1.0). With respect to the *frequency* value, the person calculates the proportion of the commissions in the context falling below $50 (and counting one half of those tied with $50). The resultant value is .44. Taking the average of the range and frequency values [(.75 +. .44) / 2] produces an overall value of .60 (scale is 0 to 1.0). This value, when linearly transformed to a scale from −500 (very, very dissatisfying) to +500 (very, very satisfying), yields a score of +100, which corresponds to a semantic rating category such as "slightly satisfying".

Now assume a history of the following feelings of satisfaction related to the last 10 days: +50, +100, +500, +300, -200, -300, +400, -50, +350, and +50. The cumulative average should be +135. This cumulative average (which corresponds to a semantic category of "slightly satisfying") reflects the overall level of satisfaction in the salesman's work domain.

Of course, this is a great oversimplification of the overall satisfaction the salesman experiences in his work domain. This is because we are considering the pay commission dimension of his job only, thus excluding other work dimensions. However, according to Parducci, other work dimensions can be similarly considered and cumulative average satisfaction values can similarly be derived. Thus, overall satisfaction in the work life domain can be extrapolated as a weighted average across the many dimensions of work that generate hedonic values.

To reiterate, Parducci maintained that the hedonic value of an experience is dependent on how it is coded in the range of experiences to which it is compared, as well as on its position in the frequency distribution of these experiences. Thus, positively skewed distributions are detrimental to momentary happiness, and conversely, negatively skewed ones are conducive to momentary happiness.

There is much evidence in the quality-of-life literature to support the principle of *range and frequency* of past affective experiences.

- Inglehart and Rabier (1986) found that recent raises in income positively affect both subjective well being and overall satisfaction.[10]
- Michalos' (1985) multiple discrepancies theory identifies the "have-past possessions" discrepancy as a significant predictor of subjective well being. That is, feelings of life satisfaction can be predicted by taking into account the difference between what a person currently has and what the person had in the past.
- Van Praag (1971) conducted Dutch and Belgian surveys that found evidence that people's satisfaction with current income is a function of the difference between current and past income, i.e., the greater the income increment the higher the satisfaction (cf. van de Stadt, Kapteyn, & van de Geer, 1985).
- Additional evidence concerning the relationship between comparison of recent life accomplishments with past accomplishments and subjective well being come from Strack, Schwarz, and Gschneidinger (1985, Experiment 1). These researchers asked subjects to report

[10] Diener et al. (1993) found that income change does not produce the SWB effect demonstrated by Inglehart and Rabier's (1986) study. However, Hagerty (1999) and Schyns (1998) have criticised Diener et al.'s method and produced their own data that provides support to the past self effect on subjective well being.

either three positive or three negative recent life events. Subjects reported higher ratings of life satisfaction after they recalled the positive events rather than the negative recent events. Other subjects were asked to recall positive and negative past distant events (those that occurred over five years ago). Subjects who recalled negative events provided higher ratings of life satisfaction than those who recalled positive events. The authors explained this finding by arguing that life satisfaction judgements are determined by judging current life events with past distant events. If the current life events are judged more positively than past distant events then life is judged to be positive, and vice versa.

- Elder (1974) conducted a study of U.S. senior citizens, those who lived through the economic depression. The main finding was that those who reported higher levels of subjective well being also reported that they suffered greatly from the economic depression during their adolescent years. Hence, the more the negative past compared to the present, the higher the subjective well being.

The Range-Frequency Principle of Re-evaluation: Satisfaction of a life domain can be increased (and dissatisfaction can be decreased) by comparing perceived events in that domain to referents having hedonic values lower than the hedonic value of the current events in terms of not only the frequency of past outcomes but also the range of outcomes.

According to Parducci, people can develop strategies to maximise their happiness overall and in specific life domains, based on the principle of *range and frequency*. For example, in any life domain such as work, ". . . one ought to stop the upward climb toward higher and higher levels of achievement at that step where the best of the context is experienced relatively often, whatever that best might be" (pp. 144-145). This of course suggests that success and happiness may not go hand-in-hand.

Furthermore, one needs to work hard in every domain to ensure that happiness now will not come at the expense of happiness in the future and happiness in other life domains. For example, the salesman is perhaps better off not working too hard because doing so shifts the context upwardly, i.e., it becomes increasingly difficult to make frequent commissions that are at the upper end of the range, hence to sustain positive feelings about his pay. However, doing so may jeopardise future promotions, perhaps because his supervisor expects him to continue working hard. Not getting that promotion may affect other life domains--perhaps his marriage and friendships with colleagues and associates.

23.3 Adaptation over Time

Helson (1947) had theorised that people adapt emotionally to events. When an event is experienced at first, people react to the event strongly. As time passes the emotional intensity associated with the event is felt less and less intensely. That is, people adapt towards neutrality. The novelty of new events wears of, and therefore the feelings associated with these events wear off too. For example, research has shown that lottery winners were not significantly happier than a control group, and that people with a spinal cord injury were not as unhappy as expected (see Loewenstein & Frederick, in press, for a review). Brickman and Campbell (1971) explored the implications of Helson's adaptation level theory in relation to happiness. They developed the notion of the "hedonic treadmill". This concept refers to the fact that people tend to adapt to changing circumstances to the point of affective neutrality. This notion of the hedonic mill is consistent with Tibor Scitovsky's thesis that comforts are different from pleasures in that comforts are mostly affectively neutral (Scitovsky, 1976). They are neutral because of adaptation. People in modern societies strive to meet their consumption expectations, which over time have become "neutral". Therefore, the best that people can feel is a neutral-type satisfaction (what he calls "comfort") but not elation or a high level of satisfaction (what he calls "joy").

Here is a partial list of suggestive evidence:

- Brickman, Coates, and Janoff-Bulman (1978) showed that lottery winners are no happier than a control group; paraplegics are less happy than controls but still above the midpoint on the scale.
- Satisfaction with standard of living did not increase among Detroit area wives between 1955 and 1971, although real income increased by 40 percent during the same period (Duncan, 1975). This finding suggests that adaptation to improving circumstances causes people to move on a "hedonic treadmill," with small or no gain in actual welfare.
- Headey and Wearing (1991) conducted a major study referred to as the Victorian Quality-of-Life Study in which they found that age was negatively related with positive and negative affect. That is, the older people get the lower positive and negative affect they report.
- Argyle (1987) reported similar findings. The explanation is that people adapt their expectations to life events. Hence, a particular positive (negative) life event may initially elicit strong satisfaction (dissatisfaction) in a particular domain, however in time the same positive (negative) life event experienced at another point in time generates lower levels of satisfaction (dissatisfaction). This is because people's expectations move in the direction of the life event,

i.e., they *adapt*. As people age, they become more adaptive. That is, they have accumulated so much experience with life events that their expectations become increasingly less discrepant from reality. Therefore, they are less likely to experience extreme levels of satisfaction (dissatisfaction) compared to younger people.

* Related theoretical developments include Tversky and Griffin's (1991) endowment/contrast model and Schkade and Kahneman's (1998) focusing illusion effect. The *endowment/contrast* model predicts an event that generated feelings of happiness at time t is incorporated into the context judging future related events. Therefore, a similar event occurring at time t+1 is likely to be judged as less pleasant than the original event experienced at time t. Thus, pleasant stimuli reduce the pleasure associated with subsequent similar stimuli. The theory of the *focusing illusion effect* posits that people tend to predict that they are likely to be happier if they experience a change of circumstance (e.g., move from the Midwest to California). However, when they experience the desired change of circumstance their subjective well being is increased temporarily, falling back to previous levels comparable to the time before the change of circumstance took place.

The Adaptation-over-time Principle of Re-evaluation: Satisfaction resulting from a life event judged much better than what one has been accustomed to decreases toward neutrality over time. Conversely, dissatisfaction resulting from an event judged much worse than what one has been accustomed to decreases toward neutrality over time.

The *adaptation-over-time principle* tells us that intense pleasures and intense pains move toward neutrality over time. That is, feelings of pain and suffering become less and less intense over time. As the saying goes, "time heals wounds." Conversely, intense pleasures and joys loose their strength over time.

How can we use this principle to enhance the quality of our lives? If we feel dissatisfied, then let the passage of time diffuse the dissatisfaction. Let time take its course. But if one feels satisfaction, one should not let time reduce the intensity of the pleasurable feelings. The challenge is to find ways to prevent time from decreasing the positive affect that came from an evaluation of a life event. Find ways to preserve the memory of these positive feelings. Keep the memory of these positive feelings alive. Keep referring back to these pleasurable feelings. Keep them at the forefront of your consciousness.   Keep an album, a journal, and other souvenirs and memorabilia to remind you of these good feelings.

23.4 Sensitisation

Not all hedonic stimuli loose their affective intensity over time through adaptation.   The hedonic intensity of some stimuli increases over time, a phenomenon referred to as *sensitisation* (Thompson & Spencer, 1966).   For example, in the early stages of a marriage, little irritating habits (e.g., smoking, using inappropriate language in certain situations, being tardy for meetings) may be easily tolerated by the newly weds.   However, over time the hedonic intensity of these irritants increase significantly.   In other words, instead of the married couple adapting to their different habits, these minor sources of irritation become *major* sources of irritation.   People become "allergic" to these irritants resulting in major arguments, break-ups, and ultimately divorces.   This is the sensitisation effect at work.

The same sensitisation effect works with hedonically positive stimuli too. For example, research has shown successive experiences with marijuana, high quality wine, food, and culture serves to increase the hedonic intensity of these stimuli.   Frederick and Loewnstein (1999) explained the sensitisation effect using Zajonc's *mere exposure* theory that posits exposure repetition of the hedonic stimulus increases the preference for that stimulus because of increased familiarity.   The more people get to become familiar with a stimulus, the more they develop an appreciation for it.   Thus its hedonic value increases over time.

Berlyne (1970) presented an explanation to help us understand the conflict between adaptation and sensitisation.   He theorised that the extent to which people adapt or become sensitised to a particular hedonically laden stimulus is dependent on whether the stimulus is "simple" or "complex." Sensitisation occurs with complex stimuli, not simple ones.   High quality wines, cheeses, exotic cuisine, opera, and the fine arts are examples of complex stimuli.   Repeated exposure to complex stimuli increases their positive hedonic value merely because people cultivate a sense of appreciation of the stimuli (cf. Bornstein, 1989; Rozin & Vollmecke, 1986). Unfortunately, Berlyne's explanation may explain sensitisation to positive hedonic stimuli, but not negative ones.

Bower (1981) offered another explanation capable of accounting for both positive and negative stimuli.   Bower theorised that an initially slightly negative stimulus may induce a depressed mood.   A depressed mood may cue negative thoughts, which intensify the depressed mood, which in turn induces further negative thoughts and so on.   The result is that an initially mildly negative stimulus becomes very negative over time. The same can be said for positive stimuli too.

The Sensitisation-over-time Principle of Re-evaluation: *Satisfaction in a life domain increases by repeated exposure over time to the same stimuli associated with the life event that initially induced the positive feelings, given that the repeated exposure is experienced with a positive mood. Conversely, dissatisfaction in a life domain increases by repeated exposure over time to the same stimuli associated with the life event that initially induced the negative feelings, given that the repeated exposure is experienced with a negative mood. .*

The *sensitisation* principle reiterates what most parents believe about children and cultural events. They feel justified to drag their children to the symphony, the opera, or any other cultural event. Even though their children are not likely to enjoy the event, in time they will grow to develop a taste for it. Or at least this is what most parents hope will happen. Well, the sensitisation principle tells us in that *it depends*. It depends on the person's mood at the time the child initially experiences the event. So the advice is to cultivate your pleasures, but make sure you are in a good mood when you first try the exotic stimulus or event. Don't slam the door on things you initially think are not enjoyable (e.g., classical music, opera, the theatre, fine dinning, educational events, fine arts, political conversation, poetry, a Shakespearean play). These leisure activities can enrich your life, *once you get sensitised to them*. The many things that are enjoyable in life are usually cultivated over time. But again, make sure that you experience them while you are in a good mood.

The same principle tells us to beware of the sensitisation caveats. Minor irritants can become major sources of stress over time. How should we stop the minor irritants from becoming major irritants in our lives? To prevent the sensitisation of negative life events from becoming catastrophes, stop the sensitisation effect by doing the following. First, anticipate the event before it occurs. Find out when the event occurs and in what situational context. Second, before the onset of that event, make sure that you are in a pleasant mood. Surround yourself with environmental cues that induce a good mood. For example, start listening to music you enjoy, sip on a good cup of coffee, and read something that you think you may enjoy, or get on the phone and socialise with a good friend. Third, allow yourself to experience the negative event while you are in a good mood. Experiencing the event while you are in a good mood prevents the event from snowballing into a major irritant. Actually, this situation may lead you to experience the event less negatively. You can also use a re-appraisal strategy to take the sting out of the negative event all together. But this is the subject of a later chapter.

RE-EVALUATION BASED ON SELF-CONCEPT

As described in the previous chapter, one can re-evaluate oneself in ways to increase positive affect (or decrease negative affect) in a particular life domain. In the previous chapter the focus was on using this strategy by manipulating expectancies based on one's personal history. In this chapter I will describe a similar strategy, however the focus here will be on manipulating expectancies based on one's self-concept. Specifically, I will describe how people enhance their subjective well being by re-evaluations in relation to their ideal self, social self, deserved self, minimum tolerable self, predicted self, competent self, and aspired self. I will also address the issue of self-concept integration and how it affects subjective well being.

24. WHAT IS RE-EVALUATION BASED ON SELF-CONCEPT?

The re-evaluation strategy based on the self-concept is illustrated in figures 16 and 17. Note that essentially the same figure shown in the previous chapter is used here to illustrate the strategy I call *re-evaluation based on self-concept*. This is because the only thing that is different about this strategy is the use of a different standard of comparison in re-evaluating the life domain. In the previous chapter the standard of comparison was expectancies based on personal history; in this chapter the standard of comparison is expectancies based on the self-concept. The top part of the figure shows the same person (as in Jay) who is satisfied with his family life, somewhat dissatisfied with his work life, and very dissatisfied with his leisure life. The bottom part shows the effect of using the re-evaluation strategy. Here, Jay focused on the leisure domain and managed to change how he feels about his leisure life. He did so by replacing the standard of comparisons within that domain with a self-concept standard in a way to induce satisfaction--more on this shortly.

As we described in the previous chapter, Jay feels very dissatisfied with his leisure life because he spent his summer vacation with his family at his in-laws. He does not get along with his in-laws, but he did it to please his wife. He now re-evaluates his leisure life by comparing the image of himself as presented to his in-laws with his social self. His social self dictates that he would like to be seen by his in-laws as a caring person who does not hold any grudges. He feels this is precisely the image he managed to uphold during the visit at his in-laws. This evaluation made him feel good about the vacation. He was able to gain the approval of his in-laws by presenting himself in ways that matches his social self.

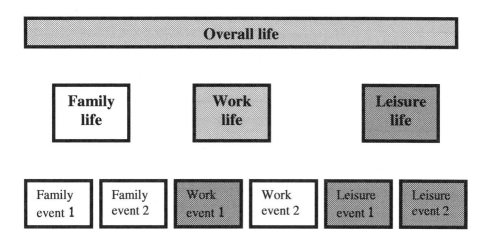

Figure 16. [Re-evaluation based on Self-concept--Before]

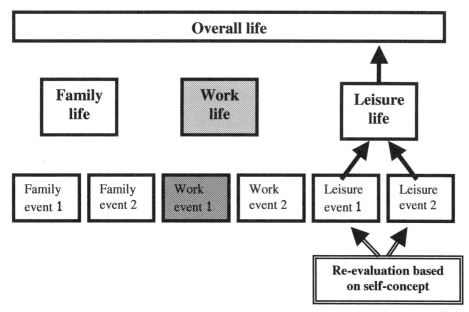

Figure 17. [Re-evaluation based on self-concept--After]

The Self-concept Principle of Re-evaluation: People feel satisfied about themselves when they compare themselves against self-expectations and discover that their actual self is better or equal to what they expect of themselves. Conversely, they feel dissatisfied about themselves when they compare themselves against what they expect of themselves and find that they had performed less than what they expected. Positive self-evaluations boost subjective well being, while negative self-evaluations reduce subjective well being.

The *self-concept principle* advocates that we should evaluate ourselves positively. Positive self-evaluations can play a major role in boosting our subjective well being. Negative self-evaluations play an adverse role on our perceived quality of life. How do we manage to evaluate ourselves positively? By choosing the right self-referent or self-expectancies. This is what we will discuss in the sections below.

25. FACTORS AFFECTING RE-EVALUATIONS BASED ON THE SELF-CONCEPT

Social psychologists have long recognised that the self-concept is not a unidimensional construct. The self-concept is multidimensional in that in the mind of every person there may be multiple selves (Brewer & Nakamura, 1984; Garza & Herringer, 1987; Hoelter, 1985; Markus, 1977; McCall & Simmons, 1978). The self-concept is divided in terms of psychological *life domains*. Thus, a person may have a self-concept in relation to education, family, health, job, friends, and romantic relationships, among others. In other words, the psychological world of a person is divided into life domains, and within each life domain the person has certain self-related beliefs and values (Burke & Tully, 1977; Campbell, Converse, & Rodgers, 1976; Griffin, Chassin, & Young, 1981; Scott & Stumpf, 1984). In addition to segmenting life experiences into life domains, people also have a self-concept of their overall life, a global domain that captures one's emotional state as a function of one's global feelings about one's major successes and failures in life.

People engage in self-evaluations within all life domains. That is, they evaluate themselves in a specific context of a life domain. For example, a person may evaluate his or her actual job achievements to date against his or her ideal image of what he or she wants to achieve. Thus, self-evaluation can be viewed as a comparison process in which the actual self is compared to the ideal self within a given life domain (Sirgy, 1986). Positive self-evaluations result in satisfaction, whereas negative self-evaluations reflect dissatisfaction (e.g., Campbell, Converse, & Rodgers, 1976; Gecas, 1982; James, 1890; Masters, Furman, & Barden, 1977; Scott & Stumpf, 1984). Therefore, satisfaction with a particular life domain comes in part from self-evaluations within that domain.   Specifically, positive self-evaluations produce feelings of satisfactions, whereas negative self-evaluations generate feelings of dissatisfaction.

In the quality-of-life literature, my colleagues and I (Meadow et al., 1992; Sirgy et al., 1995a) have argued that evaluations of one's overall life may be made in relation to different standards of comparison. For example, one can evaluate his or her life in relation to *friends*, *relatives*, *associates*, *people of similar position*, and so on. One can evaluate one's life against one's life *ideal* goals, or perhaps against one's conception of what he or she *deserves* from life. Perhaps the self-evaluation may be based on what one feels that he or she could have accomplished realising his or her *personal strengths and weaknesses*, and so on.   Thus, we developed the *Congruity Life Satisfaction* measure using different standards of comparisons and conducted several studies to demonstrate the validity of the measure. We showed that positive self-evaluations using a variety of standard of comparisons explain a significant amount of variance in overall life satisfaction.

Similarly, Michalos (1985) advanced the notion that life satisfaction may be due to a comparison of one's lot *with a number of standards*. These may involve comparisons with one's past, social comparisons, and comparisons with one's needs. His ideas have become known as *multiple discrepancies theory* in the quality-of-life literature.

Building on this literature, I will make the distinction among several forms of standard of comparisons. These are ideal self, ideal social self, deserved self, and minimum tolerable self, past self, predicted self, competent self, and aspired self.

25.1 The Ideal Self

Personality psychologists have long asserted that people have an image of themselves in relation to certain life domains, namely an *actual self-image*. For example, in the context of the material life domain, a person may see himself as "poor". In contrast to the actual self, people have a desired image of what they want to become or what they aspire to be. This is known as the *ideal self-image*. In the context of the material world, a person may want to become "rich". The concepts of actual and ideal self are well known to personality psychologists as reflected by the huge literature on self-concept and self-esteem.   Psychologists have traditionally defined the self-esteem motive as the motivational tendency to change one's perception of the self (actual self) toward one's aspired images or standards one has for oneself (ideal self) (e.g., Cohen, 1959; Coopersmith, 1967; Rogers & Dymond, 1954; Rosenberg, 1979; Sirgy, 1986).

Here is an example to help illustrate the theoretical argument. We have a man, let us call him Tom, who has an ideal self-image of being "filthy rich". The image of him rubbing elbows with the economic elite is a childhood wish. Before we go further, I would like to make the distinction between the ideal self and the achievement self (aspired self and competent self). We will address the achievement self in a later section. However, it will suffice to say that the achievement self is not necessarily the ideal self. The achievement self is the image a person tries to achieve in life by engaging in achievement-related tasks for the specific purpose of achieving this image. An ideal self-image, on the other hand, is simply a "wish" image, in the same manner that children express their magical wishes—wishes are not necessarily grounded in reality.

One can argue that an experience of positive self-evaluation with an ideal self-image is very unlikely. Can you imagine not only having to realise one's dream of becoming rich but also perhaps exceed the wish? What would be better than rich? I guess "filthy rich" would be better than rich. Evaluating oneself better than one's ideal image of "filthy rich" is very unlikely. A positive disconfirmation experience, if and when it occurs (although very unlikely), is likely to produce feelings of great satisfaction, elation, and joy. Imagine Tom winning a multi-million dollar lottery and now thinking of himself as not simply rich, but "filthy rich". He is likely to feel ecstatic. A confirmation experience also is likely to bring about high satisfaction and joy, but perhaps not as much compared to a positive disconfirmation experience. Although one would expect dissatisfaction resulting from negative disconfirmation, this may not be the case with negative disconfirmation with an ideal self-image. It is hard to imagine that people do experience much dissatisfaction with ideal expectations. Can you imagine he would feel really bad because he did not strike it rich? Not likely! This is because ideal expectations are not realistic and reflect a "wish list". The point of all of this is to help the reader understand that subjective well being is influenced by self-evaluations involving an ideal self-image.

Here is some work that provides suggestive evidence of positive and negative self-evaluations based on the ideal self.

- Michalos' (1985) multiple discrepancies theory identifies the "have-want" discrepancy as a significant predictor of subjective well being. Data related to have-want discrepancy pertaining to income is significantly correlated with overall life satisfaction (Lance, Mallard,

& Michalos, 1995) and pay satisfaction (Rice, Phillips, & McFarlin, 1990).

- Higgins and colleagues (Higgins, Grant, & Shah, 1999; Higgins, Shah, & Friedman, 1997; Strauman, 1989; Strauman & Higgins, 1987) have theorised and empirically demonstrated that actual-ideal discrepancies tend to generate negative affect such as depression (compared to actual-ought discrepancies which generate social anxiety).

- People do not find themselves in situations in which they evaluate themselves against their ideal self. They pursue these situations. Thus, they choose restaurants, housing, cars, and other products and services guided by the matching of the product-user image and their ideal self-images (Sirgy, 1982). Hence, people anticipate how they would evaluate themselves given their actions and situations against their ideal self, and if the anticipated self-evaluations are positive they become motivated to take purchase and use these products and services.

- Diener (1984), in his seminal review article, has concluded based on the available evidence at the time that " . . . high self-esteem is one of the strongest predictors of SWB (p. 558)." Campbell, Converse, and Rodgers (1976), in their classic large-scale study of life satisfaction, found that satisfaction with the self produced the highest correlation with life satisfaction compared to other satisfaction in other domains. How can one explain this relationship? Self-esteem is very much based on self-evaluations in which the actual self is compared against the ideal self. Recall that domain satisfaction is partly determined by comparing the actual self with other self-concepts such as the ideal self and the social self (we will explain the social self shortly). These self-evaluations feed directly into self-esteem. Positive self-evaluations enhance self-esteem, whereas negative self-evaluations deflate self-esteem.

The Ideal Self Principle of Re-evaluation: *Satisfaction in a life domain can be increased (and dissatisfaction can be decreased) by evaluating specific events in that domain against an ideal self that is likely to generate positive self-evaluations. Positive self-evaluations are experienced given the perception of low discrepancy between the actual and ideal self.*

The *ideal self-principle* argues that we should be careful how we use our ideal self in evaluating our everyday actions and outcomes. Self-evaluations with the ideal self, in most cases, are likely to generate negative affect. This is because, in most, cases, the actual self is likely to fall short from the ideal. Remember, the greater these discrepancies the greater the dissatisfaction. And in most cases, most people have inflated ideal self-images, images of themselves that are difficult and unrealistic to attain (Sirgy, 1998). Hence, the message is to get to know yourself. Get to know what ideal images you have of yourself. If these ideal self-images are high and inflated, then avoid making self-evaluations using these as a standard of comparison. This is because you may evaluate yourself to fall short. But on the other hand, if you anticipate that your actual self may come close of your ideal, then you should evaluate yourself against your ideal self. Positive self-evaluations should ensue. These feelings, in turn, should contribute significantly and positively to your subjective well being.

If you anticipate that your actual self falls quite short from your ideal self, then try to evaluate your actual self against other standards. What other standards can one use, the reader might ask? Perhaps the answer might be in the social self, the deserved self, the minimum tolerable self, the competent self, or the aspired self. These will be discussed below.

25.2 The Social Self

The social self is part of the self-concept that focuses on the public self. People have beliefs about how they like others to see them. They behave in ways to impress others. They are motivated to gain the approval and avoid the disapproval of their significant others (Sirgy, 1986).

Kitayama and Markus (2000) highlighted the fact that the social self differs significantly from one culture to another. For example, in North America, the social self that generates social approval from others is that of a self who has and is willing to express self-esteem and participates in mutually approving relationships. Having and willing to express self-esteem are typically manifested in culturally shared images, ideals, norms, and practices associated with self-efficacy, control, personal choice and initiative. Participating in mutually approving relationships is typically manifested through social exchange, trust, fairness, and decency. In contrast, in East Asian cultures, the social self that generates social approval is different from the social self that generates social approval in North America. Specifically, what generates social approval in East Asia is a self who is having and willing to express self-critical attitudes and participate in mutually sympathetic relationships. These relationships, in turn, are manifested through self-control, effort, social roles, filial piety, community values, warm-heartedness, empathy, perspective taking, and balance (Ying and Yang).

Consider the following example. Oliver has grown up under the shadow of his father, who is quite an eccentric. His father is very demanding of everyone in the family, including Oliver. Much of Oliver's life has been devoted to doing things to please his father. He feels that he cannot gain his father's approval. Oliver is now in college. Of course, he went to college to please his father. It was unthinkable for him to do otherwise. Now he is looking back and evaluating his life. Let us suppose that Oliver experienced a positive disconfirmation with his social self-image. He wants his father to see him as successful. His father just recently met Oliver and expressed to Oliver how proud he is of his son. His father was so forthcoming with his praise and flatteryThis was unexpected. How do you think Oliver feels? Such a positive disconfirmation is likely to produce feelings of high satisfaction.

Now suppose instead of his father being so forthcoming with praise and flattery, he was simply subdued in his expression of his approval of his son doing well in college. A confirmation experience, in this instance, is likely to bring about a modest amount of satisfaction--perhaps not as much compared to a positive disconfirmation experience.

Now imagine a situation involving negative disconfirmation. His father was supposed to come and visit him on campus, but failed to show up. Oliver calls him up and finds out that his father completely forgot about the planned campus visit. And worse, his father scolds Oliver for being away from his family and abandoning his family responsibilities because he is in college. Oliver is likely to feel a great deal of dissatisfaction.

Suggestive evidence of how positive self-evaluations involving the social self enhance subjective well being include:

- One study has shown that people actively seek to disconfirm others' mistaken impressions of them. Doing so enhances their subjective well being (Swann & Hill, 1982).
- Another study has shown that people are more likely to seek social feedback if they believe it will confirm their self-conceptions. Again doing so enhances their subjective well being (Swann & Read, 1981a, 1981b).
- Research has shown that most people seek feedback when feedback is likely to be positive. Doing so enhances their subjective well being (Brown, 1987).
- Studies have shown that people form relationships with others who see them as they see themselves. Doing so confirms their social self-

image and enhances their subjective well being (Secord & Backman, 1965; Swann, 1983).

- The evidence also suggests that people tend to be unhappy in relationships in which they are not seen as they want to be seen (Laing, Phillipson, & Lee, 1966).

The Social Self Principle of Re-evaluation: Satisfaction in a life domain can be increased (and dissatisfaction can be decreased) by evaluating specific events in that domain against a social self that is likely to generate positive self-evaluations. Positive self-evaluations are experienced given the perception of low discrepancy between the actual and social self.

What advice does the *social-self principle* provide us? Compare your accomplishments with the expectations that others have of you, if and only if these expectations are reasonable to meet. Not all others (those who matter to you) have the same level of expectations of your achievements. For example, your brother and sister may have a more realistic set of expectations than your parents. This is typical of most families. Parents tend to invest in their children. They invest themselves emotionally, financially, and in every other way. Because of their vested interest, they tend to expect a lot more from their children than siblings. If you are having a hard time living up to your parents' expectations but you meet the expectations of your brother or sister, then evaluate your accomplishments against the expectations of your brother or sister, not your parents'. Doing so is likely to make you feel better about your life.

25.3 The Deserved Self

The *deserved self*, refers to expectations about oneself that reflect one's sense of equity. One may feel that she deserves to be live in comfort and luxury; another may feel he deserves to be treated with dignity and respect. Consider the following scenario. Katherine is a middle-level manager in an insurance firm. She works very hard at her job and she takes her job seriously. She feels that she is as good as most of the other middle-level managers in the company. Recently, she reads a company memorandum that was supposed to be confidential, but it was leaked out accidentally to middle management. The salaries of all middle-level managers were reported in this document. She noted that she makes significantly more than most other middle-level managers. How is she likely to feel about her work life having seen this report? She is likely to feel pretty good! This is a positive disconfirmation experience.

Now let us change things a little and consider the scenario in which she finds out that she is making about the same as most other middle-level managers. In other words, her actual situation matches her deserved self. This is a confirmation experience with deserved expectations. She is likely to feel satisfied in her work life. A confirmation experience also is likely to bring about only moderate satisfaction, lower than that of a positive disconfirmation experience. In contrast, if she finds out that she makes significantly less than most middle-level managers in her company, she is likely to feel dissatisfied. She feels she deserves to make at least as much as most other middle-level managers. That is, she is feeling dissatisfaction in her work domain because she experiences a negative disconfirmation experience in relation to her deserved self.

Suggestive evidence for this type of social judgement and its effect on satisfaction comes from studies conducted in an organisational context. For example, Clark and Oswald (1996) and Drakopoulos and Theodossiou (1997) computed a "deserved income expectation" based on demographic factors such as age, education, years on the job, and hours worked. Both studies found a negative relationship between job satisfaction and the discrepancy between deserved and actual income.[11]

Michalos' (1985) multiple discrepancies theory identifies the "have-deserve" discrepancy as a significant predictor of subjective well being. Data related to the have-deserve discrepancy pertaining to income is significantly correlated with overall life satisfaction (Lance, Mallard, & Michalos, 1995).

The Deserved-self Principle of Re-evaluation: *Satisfaction in a life domain can be increased (and dissatisfaction can be decreased) by re-evaluating specific events in that domain against a deserved self that is*

---

[11] Diener et al. (1993) hypothesised that people make social judgements based in part on their educational levels so that the more education someone has the more money and material possessions he or she deserves. Thus, people with less education should be happier (controlling for the direct positive effects of education on subjective well being), since they would be exceeding what they deserve. However, the data did not support the hypothesis. Other studies failed to confirm the deserved expectation hypothesis. For example, Campbell (1981) has even found that lower income people with a college education are happier than non-college educated respondents of the same income level, while college education had no influence on subjective well being among the high-income respondents (see Veenhoven, 1991a, for other examples).

likely to generate positive self-evaluations. Positive self-evaluations are experienced given the perception of low discrepancy between the actual and deserved self.

The *deserved-self* principle recommends that we evaluate ourselves against our sense of what we deserve when two conditions are present: (1) our sense of what we deserve is reasonable and low, comparatively speaking, and (2) the outcome is likely to meet or exceed what we think we deserve. Otherwise, making self-evaluations using deserved expectations are likely to make us feel worse about life. So be careful how you make these self-evaluations. Self-evaluations with deserved expectations, just like ideal expectations, can cause a great deal of damage to our psyche and subjective well being. The reason is that in most cases our deserved self-image (just as our ideal self-image) is likely to be inflated and difficult to meet. Many of us feel underpaid, underappreciated, and underloved because we think we deserve better. Although it is nice to think of ourselves as deserving more, this comes at an expense of reducing our sense of subjective well being.

25.4 The Minimum-needs Self

Satisfaction and dissatisfaction with *minimum-needs expectations* tend to have a slightly different pattern of satisfaction/dissatisfaction than deserved expectations. Consider the case of Melinda. Melinda is a single mother caring for two teenagers. She works full time in a local bank as a bank teller. She budgets carefully to make sure that her monthly income stretches till the end of the month. She figures she needs a net minimum of $2,000/month to get by. Her bank teller job provides her with $1,500/month (net). She finds out that another job just opened up as a manager of a small clothing store, and her friend who knows the owner recommended Melinda to the owner. The job pays a net of $2,200/month. She jumps at the opportunity and she gets the job. How is she likely to feel about her work/personal finances domain? She may feel somewhat satisfied, perhaps relieved. Her experience can be characterised as a positive disconfirmation with minimum needs expectations. How about if the new job pays $2,000/month net? How will she feel? The prediction is "barely satisfied". This of course is a confirmation experience based on minimum needs expectations. What happens if she remains in her old job? She is likely to experience moderate-to-high dissatisfaction. This is negative disconfirmation.

Michalos' (1985) multiple discrepancies theory identifies the "have-need" discrepancy as a significant predictor of subjective well being. Data related to have-need discrepancy pertaining to income is significantly correlated with overall life satisfaction (Lance, Mallard, & Michalos, 1995). Higgins and colleagues (e.g., Higgins, Grant, & Shah, 1999; Strauman, 1989; Strauman & Higgins, 1987) have theorised and empirically demonstrated that actual-ought discrepancies tend to generate negative affect such as social anxiety (compared to actual-ideal discrepancies which generate depression). In this case, the concept of the "ought self" is highly akin to our concept of the minimum-needs self.

The Minimum-needs Principle of Re-evaluation: Satisfaction in a life domain can be increased (and dissatisfaction can be decreased) by re-evaluating specific events in that domain against a minimum-needs self that is likely to generate positive self-evaluations.

The *minimum-needs principle* begs more attention. This is because positive self-evaluations are more likely with minimum-needs expectations than expectations related to the ideal self, social self, and deserved self. Minimum-needs expectations are usually low, comparatively speaking. Therefore, it is easier to meet these expectations, inducing positive self-evaluations. So figure out your minimum needs and do not hesitate to compare life events and outcomes against your minimum needs. As a matter of fact, the advice is to compare your actual self against your minimum-needs self as often as you can. It is quite likely that you will feel better about your life doing so.

25.5 The Predicted Self

People can experience either positive or negative self-evaluations with predictice expectations. Predictive expectations are beliefs that reflect an anticipated or future self based on past experience.

Consider the case of Tony. Tony went to medical school. His career aspiration has been to become a surgeon since he was a child. Both of his parents are surgeons. They expected Tony to follow in their footsteps and become a surgeon too. Their expectations of him became so internalised that he always expected that one day he will become a surgeon too. Tony is now in his forties. He looks back at his life and evaluates himself. He thinks of himself as a renowned surgeon. In other words, he exceeded his parents' (as well as his own) predictions of his accomplishments in his career. He feels very good (high satisfaction) about his career. This is a state of positive disconfirmation. However, note that positive disconfirmations with a predicted self may generate different levels of satisfaction based on the degree of positivity of the predicted self and the degree of positivity of the actual self. These predictions are akin to those made in relation to self-evaluations using the actual self as a standard of comparison.

Michalos' (1985) multiple discrepancies theory identifies the "have-predicted possessions" discrepancy as a significant predictor of subjective well being. Data related to have-relevant others discrepancy pertaining to income is significantly correlated with overall life satisfaction (Lance, Mallard, & Michalos, 1995). Have-relevant others in relation to income denotes the perceived difference between one's level of income and what others have in terms of income. These "others" are similar to the person who is making the evaluation in some way, e.g., colleagues at work. Higgins, Vookles, and Tykocinski (1992) have shown that actual-predicted self (or what they called the "future self") results in negative self-evaluations, and the nature of these negative feelings was characterised as "chronically unfulfilled hopes," "feelings of despondency," and "feeling discouraged and hopeless."

Scheier and Carver (1985) developed a theory of optimism to explain the positive relationship between the personality trait of optimism and subjective well being. They argued that optimists tend to have a higher level of subjective well being than pessimists because optimists tend to *expect favourable outcomes in their lives.* If they expect positive outcomes, they are likely to work hard to attain these goals, which in turn increases the chances of goal attainment. Goal attainment, in turn, increases subjective well being. The notion of setting the kind of goals that are high but realistic is very much consistent with our notion of goal setting based on expectations of an ideal self-image tempered by predictive, past, and ability-based expectations. Thus, a goal characterised as high but achievable is more likely to be set by optimists than pessimists. Specifically, one can explain the relationship between optimism/pessimism and subjective well being as follows: Optimists are more likely to set high and achievable goals in one or more life domains than pessimists. Optimists' set goals may be based on expectations based on their perceptions of past performance (likely to be higher than that of pessimists), anticipated performance (likely to be higher than that of pessimists), and their strengths and weaknesses (likely to be higher than that of pessimists). Conversely, pessimists' goals may be based more on their perceptions of past performance (likely to be lower than that of optimists), anticipated performance (likely to be lower than that of optimists), and their strengths and weaknesses (likely to be lower than that of optimists). The high goals set by optimists, once attained, are likely to generate high level of satisfaction in those domains, which in turn spill over to the most superordinate domain of overall life causing the optimists to experience high levels of subjective well being. In contrast, the low goals set by pessimists, once attained, are likely to generate only moderate levels of satisfaction in those domains, which in turn spill over to the most superordinate domain of overall life causing the pessimists to experience only moderate levels of subjective well being.

The Predicted Self Principle of Re-evaluation: *Satisfaction in a life domain can be increased (and dissatisfaction can be decreased) by re-evaluating specific events in that domain against a predicted self that is likely to generate positive self-evaluations.*

The principle of the predicted self urges self-evaluations when and if the probability of reaching the predicted self is high. In most cases, people tend to have a good sense of what outcomes they predict in their lives. If these predictions are used as a self-referent in evaluating the events and outcomes in their lives, then they are likely to feel good about themselves. However, it should be noted that this could happen only if the person perceives that he or she is making progress towards the predicted self. Thus, this principle, just like the minimum-needs principle, promises that it can deliver quality of life if and when it is used often. So go ahead and use it and use it often. You may feel better about your life doing it.

25.6 *The Competent Self*

Higgins, Vookles, and Tykocinski (1992) have shown that actual-competent self (or what they called the "can self") results in negative self-evaluations, and the nature of these negative feelings was characterised as "feelings of weakness," "lacking proficiency, potency, and vigour," and "feeling ineffective." Of course, this happens when one's perceived level of competence falls short of one's ideal level of competence.

Furthermore, research has indicated that expectancies of control relate to subjective well being. The typical finding is that those who have *expectancies of control* report greater subjective well being than those who have low expectancies (see Diener, 1984; Diener, et al. 1999). Grob, Stetsenko, Sabatier, Botcheva, and Macek (in press) explained this relationship by arguing that high-expectancy individuals tend to expect to succeed and therefore work harder at making things work and achieve their goals. Therefore, this finding recommends people who have high expectancies of control to evaluate their actual self in relation to their competent self. This is because these people are likely to work hard and reduce any discrepancy they may perceive between their actual self and their competent self. Thus, moving towards one's achievement-related goals is likely to induce positive self-evaluations, which in turn should serve to enhance subjective well being.

Here is a question that can further illustrate the power of expectancies of control. Answer this question: Who is happier, stay-at-home moms or moms who work outside the home? Haw (1995) has compared these two population segments and found that both groups experience happiness if they felt *competent* at what they were doing.

The Competent Self Principle of Re-evaluation: *Satisfaction in a life domain can be increased (and dissatisfaction can be decreased) by re-evaluating specific events in that domain against a competent self that is likely to generate positive self-evaluations when goals related to the competent self are attained (or at least progress towards the attainment of these achievement-related goals).*

The message we can take away from this study is positive self-evaluations based on one's ability can go a long way toward enhancing our subjective well being.

25.7 The Aspired Self

Irwin (1944) observed that aspiration levels are highly correlated with real and expected achievements, though aspirations are generally somewhat higher than real and expected achievements. Diener (1984) referred to "telic" theories of subjective well being explaining how life goals, goal attainment, and progress towards goals play a role in subjective well being. Emmons and Diener (1985) found that aspiration level alone does not account for subjective well being among college students. Instead, subjective well being was significantly influenced by the extent to which the goals were set realistically and were congruent with subjects' personal resources (Diener & Fujita, 1995).

One can argue that it is not the level of aspiration that matters much but the extent to which these aspirations are realised. When people set high and unrealistic aspirations, the chances are that they are not likely to be realised. Therefore, people who set their goals unrealistically high (incongruent with their personal resources) are likely to experience low levels of subjective well being.

The Aspired Self-Principle of Re-evaluation: Satisfaction in a life domain can be increased (and dissatisfaction can be decreased) by re-evaluating specific events in that domain against an aspired self that is likely to generate positive self-evaluations.

25.8 Self-concept Integration

Note that we described how satisfaction can be experienced in a given life domain through self-evaluations using a variety of self-concept standards such as the ideal self, the social self, the deserved self, the competent self, etc. What happens when these self-evaluations conflict with one another-- one self-evaluation involving one type of self-concept standard generates satisfaction but a different self-evaluation results in dissatisfaction? This situation is referred to as _self-concept differentiation_ or a fragmentation of the self-concept. The situation in which different self-evaluations involving different self-concept standards generates similar positive self-evaluations is referred to as _self-concept integration_.

How is the person's subjective well being affected by self-concept differentiation? Donahue and her colleagues (1993) found that self-concept differentiation is associated with poor emotional adjustment, whereas integration is related with healthy adjustment. Van Hook and Higgins (1988) tested the hypothesis that conflict between the ideal self and the minimum-needs self (what Higgins and colleagues refer to as the "ought self") generates "confusion-related symptoms" in the form of confusion, muddledness, uncertainty about self and goals, identity confusion, indecision, distractibility, and rebelliousness. These findings point to a strategy of integration to enhance subjective well being. The integration strategy is to adjust the level of the different self-referents to ensure that the use of these self-referents would generate positive self-evaluation. For example, tone down the ideal and the deserved selves to ensure a higher level of positive self-evaluations. Adjust the predicted self and the competent self with reality and in such a way to ensure that the actual self is least discrepant. Doing so helps achieve self-concept integration.

The Principle of Self-concept Integration: Satisfaction in a life domain can be increased (and dissatisfaction can be decreased) by ensuring that self-evaluations are performed using self-concept standards likely to generate consistent positive self-evaluations.

The principle of *self-concept integration* is difficult to implement, but nevertheless is an important one. It calls for consistency in positive self-evaluations using different self-referents. The advice then is to repeatedly and consistently over time make self-evaluations using only those self-referents that can generate satisfaction. Self-evaluations using self-referents that have the potential to generate dissatisfaction should be avoided as much as possible. This is one way to ensure consistency. Another way is to reassess those self-referents that are responsible for negative self-evaluations and change those referents. For example, if you believe that your expectations based on your ideal and deserved self are constantly getting you into trouble (inducing much dissatisfaction), then perhaps you need to revisit those self-referents. Are your deserved expectations realistic? Perhaps not! Then tone them down. Are your ideal expectations sky-high? Then bring them down to earth.

RE-EVALUATION BASED ON SOCIAL COMPARISON

As described in the two previous chapters, one can re-evaluate oneself in ways to increase positive affect (or decrease negative affect) in a particular life domain. In the previous two chapters we focused on using this strategy by manipulating expectancies based on one's personal history and self-concept. In this chapter I will describe a similar strategy, however the focus here will be on manipulating expectancies based on social comparisons. I will describe how this strategy works and explain how people experience subjective well being guided by three motives, namely self-enhancement, self-improvement, and self-identification. Then I will describe an offshoot principle of social comparison dealing with fictitious occurrences.

26. WHAT IS RE-EVALUATION BASED ON SOCIAL COMPARISON?

See an illustration of this strategy in figures 18 and 19. Note that essentially the same figure shown in the previous two chapters is used here to illustrate the strategy we call *re-evaluation based on social comparison*. This is because the only thing that is different about this strategy is the use of *significant others* as a different standard of comparison in re-evaluating the life domain. In the previous two chapters the standard of comparison were expectancies based on personal history (Chapter 8) and self-concept (Chapter 9). In this chapter the standard of comparison is expectations based on significant others. This type of evaluation is commonly known in social psychology as *social comparison*.

We will use the case of Jay's leisure life described in the last two chapters. The top part of the figure shows Jay satisfied with his family life, somewhat dissatisfied with his work life, and very dissatisfied with his leisure life. The bottom part shows the effect of using a social comparison strategy. Remember that Jay feels very dissatisfied with his leisure life. This is because he had to spend his summer vacation with his in-laws. He does not get along with his in-laws, but he did it to please his wife. He now re-evaluates his leisure life by comparing his last vacation at his in-laws with his neighbour's last vacation. His neighbours are Tim and Caroline, a nice couple in their 60's with no children. Tim and Caroline went on a cruise to Alaska last August. This was supposed to be their 30-year wedding anniversary. They were looking forward to a wonderful vacation. But the vacation turned into a disaster. The cruiseship ran into an iceberg, which damaged part of the ship. It was almost like the Titanic. People had to be evacuated from the ship by raft boats. Tim suffered a stroke while he was being evacuated. Now he is recovering from that stroke. The damage was severe, the doctor told his wife, Caroline. The end result was that the vacation was an utter disaster. So Jay compares his family vacation with Tim's and Caroline's. He feels somewhat blessed that his vacation was uneventful. At least there were no disasters and he and his family enjoyed themselves a little, despite the in-laws.

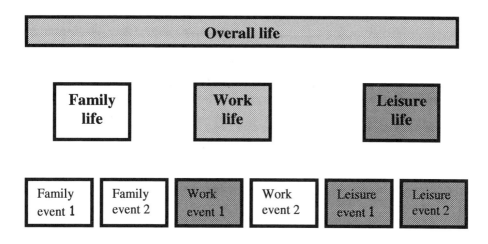

Figure 18. [Re-evaluation based on Social Comparison--Before]

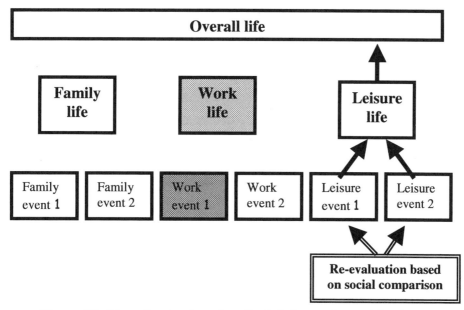

Figure 19. [Re-valuation based on Social Comparison--After]

Much research in subjective well being has suggested that social comparison plays an important role in subjective well being (see Diener & Fujita, 1996, for a review of the literature). For example, Michalos (1991) studied the role of the comparison gap between oneself and others among college students and the effect of that gap on life satisfaction and happiness. The social comparison measure was based on asking students how they compared to other students. Michalos found that the social comparison gap was one of the strongest correlates of life satisfaction and happiness. Upward social comparison (comparison of oneself with another who is better off) tends to generate dissatisfaction, whereas downward comparison (comparison of oneself with another who is worse off) generates satisfaction.

Similarly, Michalos (1993) found a significant social comparison effect in a variety of life domains. The social comparison effect was a significant predictor of satisfaction with health, religion, education, and recreation in every nation studied (cf. Saris, 2001).

Further evidence concerning the principle of social comparison comes from data related to "have-relevant others" discrepancy pertaining to income. Have-relevant others discrepancy refers to the comaprison of one's level of income to the income of others who are significant to the person making the comparison in some ways such as work colleagues and associates. Lance, Mallard, and Michalos (1995) found that have-relevant others discrepancy is significantly and negatively correlated with overall life satisfaction.

The Principle of Social Comparison: Satisfaction in a life domain can be increased (and dissatisfaction can be decreased) by evaluating life events in that domain to similar others (e.g., relative and friends, neighbours, professional associates and colleagues, people of the same age, same sex, same race or ethnic background, same handicap, same home place, and same social class).

Based on the principle of *social comparison*, Niven (2000) provides good advice:

Many of our feelings of satisfaction or dissatisfaction have their roots in how we compare ourselves to others. When we compare ourselves to those who have more, we feel bad. When we compare ourselves to those who have less, we feel grateful. Even though the truth is we have exactly the same life either way, our feelings about our life can vary tremendously based on who we compare ourselves with. Compare yourself with those examples that are meaningful but that make you feel comfortable with who you are and what you have (p. 9).

27. FACTORS AFFECTING RE-EVALUATION BASED ON SOCIAL COMPARISON

There are many sources of standard of comparisons used to evaluate one's happiness. These include comparisons with relatives and friends, associates or colleagues who have similar professional positions, people of the same age, gender, and ethnic status, and people who share some disability or handicap (Meadow et al., 1992; Sirgy et al., 1995). Why do people compare their lives to others? Festinger (1954) initially proposed that people compare themselves to similar others, because doing so allows them to get to know more about themselves. People gain more knowledge about themselves in relation to others who are "just like themselves". Thus, a student compares his grade on the last test with the grades of his classmates. Doing so allows the student to assess his skills and competencies in relation to his peer group.   This motive has been referred to by many social psychologists as the *self-assessment* motive (e.g., Diener et al., 1993). In my own previous research on the self-concept, I have made reference to this motive as the "need for self-knowledge" and discussed it extensively (Sirgy, 1986). Thus, we compare ourselves to others to know more about how we stand in relation to others. Subjective well being is not affected by the self-assessment motive.   However, the self-assessment motive conjoins with other motives to influence subjective well being. These other motives are *self-enhancement*, *self-improvement*, and *self-identification* (cf. Schwarz & Strack, 1999). We will discuss the QOL research in relation to these three motivational states.

27.1 Self-enhancement

Besides the self-assessment motive, a second motive in social comparison is the need for *self-esteem*. Social psychologists refer to this motive as the "self-enhancement motive." A *downward comparison* is a comparison of one's own life against another person or group who is less fortunate. Thus, a downward comparison serves to enhance self-esteem because the outcome generates positive affect reflective of positive self-evaluation.

Here is suggestive evidence of the effect of downward social comparison on subjective well being:

- Michalos' (1985) multiple discrepancies theory identifies the "have-relevant others" discrepancy as a significant predictor of subjective well being. Have-relevant others discrepancy scores pertaining to income were significantly correlated with overall life satisfaction (Lance, Mallard, & Michalos, 1995).   Thus, upward social comparisons were shown to generate feelings of dissatisfaction, whereas downward comparisons generated feelings of satisfaction. This finding is consistent with the self-enhancement explanation.

- A classic study of need deprivation with soldiers in World War II found that the morale in a unit tended to be low if its circumstances were significantly worse than those of a comparable unit (Stouffer, 1949). Research has shown women whose morale is high but are paid much less than men for the same work. The explanation was that morale and satisfaction was high for women because women compare themselves to other women rather than to men (Crosby, 1982).

- Easterlin (1974) hypothesised that people tend to compare themselves only with the people next door. Therefore, people in poor countries do not compare themselves with people in rich countries. Easterlin was able to empirically demonstrate that people in poor countries are also as happy as people in rich countries. This is because people compare themselves with others in their own countries not other countries. However, other quality-of-life researchers have taken issue with Easterlin's data and his interpretation of the data. For example, Veenhoven (1991a) re-analysed Easterlin's data and was able to show high correlations between national wealth and subjective well being. Additional evidence supporting the claim that there is a positive relationship between national wealth and subjective well being was generated by Cummins (1998), Diener, et al. (1993), Diener, Diener, and Diener (1995), and Schyns (1998). In 1995, Easterlin (1995) then dropped his claim that rich countries are not much happier than poor ones.

- So why is socio-economic status related to subjective well being? One plausible explanation is higher socio-economic status persons may engage in downward social comparisons. This type of social judgement may be responsible for positive self-evaluations and satisfaction in important life domains, which in turn play a significant role in enhancing subjective well being. This explanation is consistent with Argyle's (1994) explanation, which states that high socio-economic people tend to be treated with greater respect, which boosts their self-esteem. People with high socio-economic status also hold more interesting and challenging jobs, which may be the cause of greater job satisfaction.

- Haring, Stock, and Okun (1984) conducted a meta-analysis of 65 effects from 34 U.S. studies, and found a moderate positive correlation between socio-economic status and subjective well being.

Headey and Wearing (1991) conducted a major study in which they found that socio-economic status was positively related to positive affect and negatively related to negative affect. A composite measure of family income, occupational status of the main breadwinner, and the respondent's level of formal educational attainment measured socio-economic status. These three factors were equally weighted in the composite index.

- Studies in social psychology (e.g., Tesser, 1980; Tesser & Campbell, 1980; Tesser, Campbell, & Smith, 1984; Tesser & Paulhus, 1983) have shown that people select friends in self-serving ways. Specifically, they choose to befriend those with inferior abilities on tasks relevant to their own abilities. In contrast, they befriend those who have superior abilities but on tasks less relevant to them. Thus, they can enhance the self by associating with their friends--their friends have exceptional abilities. They do so without detracting from their own positive self-evaluations--they do not engage in upward social comparison with their friends because their friends' abilities are irrelevant to them.

The Self-enhancement Principle of Re-evaluation: People compare positive events in their life with others that have experienced similar but negative events. This downward social comparison generates satisfaction, which in turn enhances subjective well being. Downward social comparison serves to satisfy the self-enhancement motive by inducing positive self-evaluations.

Here is advice that comes in the form of a story from the Orient. This story is told by Mark Epstein, a psychiatrist who blends Western and Eastern thinking (Epstein, 1995, p. 44).

Kisagotami was a young woman whose first child died suddenly somewhere around his first birthday. Desperate in her love for the child, Kisagotami went from house to house in her village, clasping the dead child to her breast and asking for medicine to revive her son. Most of her neighbours shrank from the sight of her and called her mad, but one man, seeing her inability to accept the reality of her son's death, directed her to Buddha by promising her that only he had the medicine she sought. Kisagotami went to Buddha and pleaded with him for medicine. "I know of some," he promised. "But I will need a handful of mustard seed from a house where no child, husband, parent, or servant has died." Slowly, Kisagotami came to see that hers was not a unique predicament. She put the body of her child down in a forest and returned to Buddha. "I have not brought the mustard seed," she told him. "The people of the village told me, 'the living are few, but the dead are many'." Buddha replied, "You thought that you alone had lost a son; the law of death is that among all living creatures there is no permanence." . . . The Buddah helped Kisagotami find happiness not by bringing her dead child back to life, but by changing her view of herself.

27.2 Self-improvement

A third motive is to set goals in life to improve oneself and ultimately enhance one's self-esteem *in the future*. This motive is referred to as the *self-improvement* motive. People engage in downward or upward comparisons. An upward comparison is self-deflating because the outcome is dissatisfaction. Here, the person compares himself with another person or group who is more fortunate. Although the resulting emotion is life dissatisfaction, people do engage in upward comparisons to set future goals. For example, a low-income person compares himself with a high-income person. Doing so, the low-income person sets his aspirations to work hard to generate more income—so that he can become like the high-income person, i.e., the role model.

Some studies (e.g., Diener et al., 1993) have failed to provide evidence for the self-enhancement effect due to at least two effects, namely inspiration and identification confounds. The i*nspiration* confound (or what is referred to here as the "self-improvement motive") can best be exemplified by the case of cancer patients who gain solace from comparisons with those much sicker than themselves but look to those doing better than themselves for models of hope and recovery (Kruglanski & Mayseless, 1990). As Lyubomirsky and Ross (1997) have put it, "a peer's success can be a source of either envy and self-doubt or of inspiration and motivation, and a peer's misfortune may make one feel either fortunate to have escaped such a fate or afraid that a similar fate awaits in the future" (p. 1141).

Research has shown that people afflicted with a handicap or with a significant illness such as cancer compare themselves with others who are similarly afflicted, and that these social comparisons influence their subjective well being (e.g., Buunk, Collins, Taylor, Van Yperen, & Dakof, 1990; Dunning, Meyerowitz, & Holzberg, 1989; Pelham & Wachsmuth, 1995). Upward and downward comparisons tend to conflict. For example, a cancer victim comparing himself with another cancer victim who is worse off may make him feel better about himself; however, at the same time, he may feel depressed thinking that he will become as debilitated as the other victim. Conversely, comparing himself to a victim who is better off may make him feel unhappy; however, such comparisons may instill a sense of hope about his condition causing a boost in spirits.

Research also has shown that people usually identify themselves with others of their own social class (e.g., Centers, 1947). Thus, they compare themselves with people of the same class, not with people who are lower than them and neither with people higher than them. They do this perhaps because comparisons with people of higher status would make them feel bad about themselves. But then comparing themselves with lower class people should make them feel good about themselves. Right? Not really! This is because people think that it is more desirable to compare themselves with an aspirational group than a non-aspirational one. Identifying oneself with an aspirational group gives the person a sense of purpose in life. They would like to belong to that referent group. This aspirational group membership serves as a life goal. Pursuing and progressing towards the attainment of this goal enhances one's sense of subjective well being.

The Self-improvement Principle of Re-evaluation: People compare negative events in their life with others that have experienced similar events with a positive outcome. This upward social comparison generates satisfaction, which in turn enhances subjective well being. Upward social comparison serves to satisfy the self-improvement motive by allowing the person to predict a positive future for one's condition based on the positive condition of the significant other.

The *self-improvement* principle provides good advice for people who have experienced predicaments in their lives. Whatever the predicament (e.g., cancer, divorce, death of a loved one, lay off at work), compare yourself with others who have had a similar predicament but managed to overcome the predicament and experience a happy ending. Comparing yourself with these kinds of people gives you hope that your predicament will pass and life will be better. The hope serves to enhance your quality of life.

27.3 Self-identification

With respect to the *self-identification*, this motive can be illustrated best by a person comparing his inferior sports performance to that of his home team's performance. On the one hand, he may feel dissatisfied with his performance compared to his home team; however, he may take pride by identifying with his home team's success. Cialdini (1976) called this social phenomenon "basking in reflected glory". One can think that this phenomenon also is a form of social comparison. What people do is "put themselves in other people's shoes" and experience the pleasure or joy that others experience. For example, a person hears that his colleague at work received a promotion and a healthy raise. He feels good knowing that his colleague is promoted and making more money, perhaps much more so than he makes. These feelings may occur as a direct function of thinking of himself in the position of his colleague and "basking in his glory". Or perhaps his colleague is incorporated in his expanded sense of self. Thus, he compares his expanded sense of self (i.e., his colleague as part of self) with less fortunate others, and, in doing so, feels good about his "expanded self." One can easily argue that the identification confound is a reflection of the "self-enhancement motive."

> *The Self-identification Principle of Re-evaluation: People compare negative events in their life with others that have experienced similar events with a positive outcome. This upward social comparison generates satisfaction, which in turn enhances subjective well being. Upward social comparison serves to satisfy the self-identification motive by allowing the person to identify with those others who have experienced positive events. This self-identification with those positive others induces positive self-evaluations, which in turn enhances subjective well being.*

The principle of *self-identification* urges us to identify with successful referent groups. Doing so allows us to experience positive affect. For example, if your home football team is on a winning streak, feel good about that. Bask in the glory of your team. Feel proud of the team. Talk about the success of your home team to others, especially those others who also identify with the home team. This type of self-identification should boost the quality of your life.

27.4 Fictitious Occurrences

People judge their current life occurrences against fictitious occurrences of "what might have been". Consider the following scenario. A woman watches a show on television. In that show, one of the main characters contracted breast cancer. That fictitious character's health began to fail rapidly. She was been pronounced terminally ill with six months to live. The subject confronted with this information may feel quite sad about her fictitious character. However, in judging her own life she may feel "blessed". That is, her subjective well being is likely to increase as a result of comparing her health with what "might have been" (as in being struck by breast cancer).

Another person who had to change travel arrangements learns that the airline he was originally booked on crashed and all passengers on board were killed. He feels like he had another chance in life. His subjective well being is likely to increase as a function of comparing his current situation with "what might have been" (killed by that plane crash).

Of course, other fictitious occurrences can result in lower ratings of subjective well being. Consider the following scenario. A friend just won a $5 million lottery. Although the person in question may feel good about his friend winning the lottery he may feel bad about his own life. This is because he may compare his current situation with "what might have been" if he were to win that $5 million jackpot.

Roese and colleagues (Roese, 1997; Roese & Olson, 1995a, 1995b) have argued and empirically demonstrated that fictitious occurrences can be used as a standard of comparison in judging one's circumstances, thus affecting subjective well being.

> *The Principle of What Might Have Been of Re-evaluation*: *Satisfaction of a life domain can be increased (or dissatisfaction can be decreased) by comparing one's situation against negative "what-might-have-been" fictitious occurrences.*

The *what-might-have-been* principle prompts us to focus on events that are unfortunate. This is easy because the news media is saturated with negative events, e.g., murder, robbery, air plane accidents, highway accidents, business bankruptcies, major layoffs at work, and so on. Whenever we are exposed to any major negative event, ask yourself, "what if that had happened to me?" The answer, of course, is "thank goodness it is not me." These self-verbalisations can make you feel good about your life.

27.5 Integration of Social Comparison Judgements

Note throughout this chapter we described how people make social comparisons which conflict with one another. For example, making a doward social comparison may enhance subjective well being by satisfying the need for self-enhancement. However, doing so may frustrate the need for self-improvement and therefore may decrease subjective well being. In contrast, making an upward social comparison may decrease subjective well being because of the frustration experienced in relation to the need for self-enhancement. The same upward comparison may enhance subjective well being because the person may be able to meet the needs of self-identifcation and self-improvement.

Can social comparison judgements be made in ways that *consistently* generate subjective well being? This can be achieved if one chooses to engage in upward social comparisons that can satisfy both the needs of self-identification and self-improvement with very little decrements of subjective well-being resulting from failing to satisfy the need for self-enhancement. But at the same time, the person can compensate for any decrement of subjective well being from failure to satisfy the need for self-enhancement by engaging in related downward social comparisons.

Consider the following example. Tiffany is a physiological psychologist who has been doing important research on Alzheimers. Her research has received much attention, and she feels that she is well recognized by her peers in the scientific community. Her aspirational group is the highly renowned and distinguished scientists in her field. She compares her level of distinguished research with the credentials of the highly successful people in her profession, and she feels good because she identifies with them. She is well accomplished but did not receive the highest honors and distinctions she hopes to earn eventually. Hence, there is room for improvement. She feels proud being a physiological scientist. She feels proud being connected with an elite group of scientists making important breakthroughs and helping discover ways to control and possibly cure Alzheimers. Hence, her subjective well being is enhanced through satifying both needs for self-identification and self-improvement. She compares herself with her graduate students who are trying hard to become what she is already. This is a downward comparison adding to her sense of subjective well being. In this situation, subjective well being is maximized by satisfying the three needs (self-enhancement, self-improvement, and self-identification) *conjointly*.

The Principle of Integrated Social Comparisons: Subjective well being could be enhanced by making social comparison judgements that satisfy the needs of self-enhancement, self-identification, and self-improvement, simultaneously or conjointly.

The principle of *integrated social comparisons* is important. This is because it highlights the irony involved in making social comparison judgements. A person makes one type of social comparison that results in both positive and negative affect. The goal is to make judgements that increase positive affect and decrease negative affect. To do so the advice is to engage in a social comparison with a status group (an aspirational group). You should be able to identify with the people in that group and may feel like emulating the most successful in that group. Doing so satisfies the needs for self-identification and self-improvement. Then find people within the same reference group who look up to you and aspire to become like you. This can be a good source of self-enhancement. Making social comparison judgements that satisfy the three needs of self-enhancement, self-identification, and self-improvement can go a long way to enhance your subjective well being.

GOAL SELECTION

In this chapter I will describe how subjective well being can be enhanced by selecting important and value-laden goals. Attainment of important and value-laden goals makes a significant contribution to subjective well being by creating positive affect related to significant events in life domains. Specifically, this chapter describes goal selection and the factors people should consider in goal selection to enhance their quality of life. I will describe factors that people need to consider in deciding to focus on bringing more joy to their lives rather than simply decreasing dissatisfaction. I also will describe other factors that people need to consider in goal selection, factors to help them select goals that are achievable or goals that are candidates for successful completion.

28. WHAT IS GOAL SELECTION?

However, before describing the specifics of goal-oriented action, let us for a moment try to understand how goal-selection is used as a strategy to increase overall life satisfaction or decrease dissatisfaction. Figures 20 and 21 describe this process in a graphic manner. The top part of the figure shows a person, let us call her Maggie, feeling happy with her family life (the box is white fill-in), somewhat dissatisfied with her work life (the box is a grey fill-in), and very dissatisfied with her leisure life (the box is dark grey fill-in). Maggie takes action in her leisure domain in an attempt to decrease the negative affect in that domain and possibly generate positive affect. Doing so is likely to spill over to the most superordinate domain, namely overall life, and contribute to the enhancement of subjective well being. This action is represented in the boxes underneath the leisure domain box and subsumed within the leisure domain. Note that these boxes are not shaded, i.e., their valence is positive. For example, Maggie discovers a passion in handicraft such as pottery and basket weaving. She now attends a night class (two nights per week) in handicraft and is feeling very artistic and creative doing so. She also is beginning to thoroughly enjoy aerobic exercise. She exercises three nights a week. She gets a great work out; she loves the instructor, the music, and the people who go to that fitness centre. Moreover, she feels good about staying in shape and loosing weight. These two actions in the leisure domain have managed to change the valence in the leisure domain completely—form negative to positive. The positive affect from the leisure domain, in turn, spills over to the most superordinate domain of overall life, thus increasing life satisfaction. However, the key to understanding the focal point of this chapter is goal selection. Maggie has selected goals that made a difference in her leisure life. Selecting the right goals that can make a difference is the main focus of this chapter.

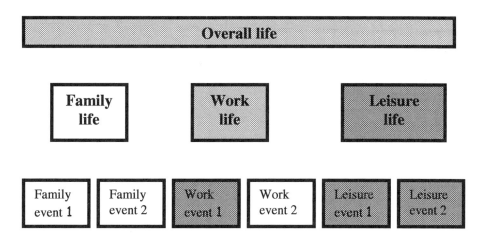

Figure 20. [Goal Selection--Before]

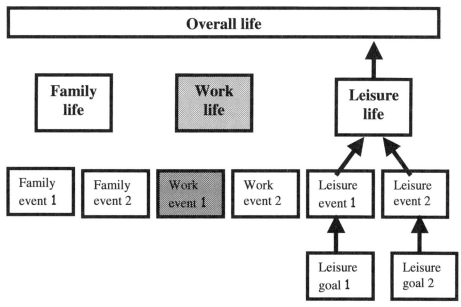

Figure 21. [Goal Selection--After]

The Goal Selection Principle: Subjective well being can be enhanced by being highly selective in pursuing the kind of goals in which goal attainment s likely to induce positive emotions, e.g., joy, affection, pride.

This *goal selection* principle urges people to be careful and selective in the goals they choose to pursue in life. There are some goals in life not worth pursuing. This is because their attainment does not contribute to one's subjective well being. They may simply bring comfort. Tibor Scitovsky, a renowned economist, has attracted much attention in his famous book *The Joyless Economy* (1976). His main thesis is that Americans (and people from highly developed economies) have decreasingly experienced joy and increasingly experienced comfort. This is partly due to the fact that we increasingly have chosen goals related to the good life and material comfort. These goals do not have the capacity to generate feelings of joy, pride, and affection. The best they can do (if and when they are attained) is to decrease one's level of discomfort. The remainder of this chapter is devoted to exploring the factors that one needs to consider in making decisions to pursue certain goals in life. How can a person know which goals to pursue to experience happiness in life?

29. FACTORS AFFECTING THE SELECTION OF GOALS THAT BRING JOY AND HAPPINESS

Goal selection is quite important in enhancing subjective well being. Selecting goals that are likely to generate a high dose of positive affect when attained is crucial to one's quality of life. So how can we judge the extent to which a goal is likely to contribute significantly to subjective well being when attained? Research in subjective well being has demonstrated the effect of several factors. These include goal meaningfulness, intrinsic versus extrinsic goals, high- versus low-level goals, goals related to basic versus growth needs, and approaching desired states versus avoiding undesired states.

29.1 Goal Meaningfulness

Studies of older Americans have found that one of the best predictors of happiness is the extent to which people have meaningful goals. The goals define their purpose in life (Lepper, 1996). Goals that reflect a sense of purpose in life play an important role in subjective well being and attaining such goals is likely to generate substantial gains in quality of life.

For example, once people retire they loose their sense of worth, and their life satisfaction plummets. This is because their work-related goals are very much connected to their identities of who they are. To maintain their sense of identity and hold on to meaningful goals related to work, many retired people choose to volunteer their services for good causes. Crist-Houran (1996) has analysed volumes of past research on volunteering. Most studies show that volunteering contributes to happiness by creating an increased sense of purpose in life.

The Meaningfulness Principle of Goal Selection: Selecting meaningful goals in important life domains generates substantial satisfaction in these domains upon attainment. This satisfaction is likely to contribute significantly to subjective well being.

Based on the principle of *goal meaningfulness*, the reader should realise that it is very important to select goals that are meaningful. To make an attempt to enhance your satisfaction with life, re-examine all your daily habits, regular chores, and structured activities. Ask yourself why you engage in those activities. Behind every activity is a personal goal. We do not do things for the "heck of it"; we engage in activities because these activities help us achieve certain goals. What are these goals? Try to articulate them. You can identify your goals by first focusing on the important domains of your life, e.g., work, family, social, leisure, community, health, etc. Within each domain, try to identify your structured activities—those tasks and chores you take on regularly. Make a list of them and identify the personal goals related to each. Then go down that list of goals. Question yourself about these goals. Are these goals meaningful to your life at large? Answering this question will help you identify personal goals you find meaningful. Hold on to these goals. Find additional structured activities that tie in to these goals. Goals you find as less meaningful should prompt you to action. Either reduce or eliminate those structured activities related to your less-meaningful goals. In essence, re-organise your life activities based on a "meaningfulness" type of goal assessment.

Frisch (in press, Chapter 5) recommends the use of the *ideal obituary technique* to help identify meaningful lifetime goals. This technique allows a person to write their own obituary focusing on how they would like to be remembered in death. The goals identified by an ideal obituary should help identify meaningful goals for those who seem to be floundering without real direction in life.

29.2 *Intrinsic versus Extrinsic Goals*

Kasser and Ryan (1993, 1996, 1998; Kasser, 1997; Kasser, et al. 1995) distinguished between intrinsic and extrinsic goals. Examples of intrinsic goals include having good social relationships with loved ones, making a significant contribution to the community, helping others in need, personal growth, maintenance of good health, among others. In contrast, examples of extrinsic goals include the desire to make money, the desire to control people, to attain social recognition, etc. (cf. Deci & Ryan, 1987; Sheldon & Kasser, 1995; Sirgy, 1998). According to Kasser and Ryan, intrinsic goals tend to contribute more to subjective well being than extrinsic ones (cf. Carver & Baird, 1998).

Other quality-of-life researchers such as Cantor and Sanderson (1999) have echoed this notion that attainment of intrinsic goals generates greater positive affect--leading to subjective well being--compared to extrinsic goals. Other evidence supporting this notion comes from a study conducted by Murray and Peacock (1996). These researchers have found that number of friends, closeness of friends, closeness of family, and relationships with co-workers and neighbours account for 70 percent of the variance in personal happiness. Furthermore, Diener and Fujita (1995) found that the availability of material resources was significantly less important to happiness than the availability of personal resources such as friends and family.

Therefore, one can argue that intrinsic goals are likely to be more satisfying than extrinsic goals. This is because intrinsic goals tend to be more related to growth needs (and therefore attaining intrinsic goals contributes to satisfaction), whereas extrinsic goals are more related to basic needs (and therefore attaining extrinsic goals serves to decrease possible dissatisfaction).

> *The Intrinsicness Principle of Goal Selection: Subjective well being can be increased (or dissatisfaction can be decreased) by selecting intrinsic than extrinsic goals in that domain. Attainment of intrinsic goals induces more positive affect in that domain than extrinsic goals.*

The message pertaining to the principle of *goal intrinsicness* is loud and clear. Choose goals that are more intrinsic and less extrinsic. For example, if you are in a job strictly for the money, then you are "barking up the wrong tree". Investing yourself in the pursuit of an extrinsic goal such as making money can do only so much to bring you joy and happiness. You have to go beyond the extrinsic goals. Make sure that your job gives you meaning in life too. You should wake up in the morning and feel like going to work.

This should be because your work makes a difference in your life or someone else's. Do you have a relationship with a significant other? Are you with your significant other or spouse because of love, passion, companionship, and commitment? These are intrinsic goals. These are the kind of goals that bring true joy in life. If you are maintaining your relationship with your significant other because of extrinsic goals such as financial security, power, or status, then again you are "barking up the wrong tree". Give up these extrinsic goals and replace them with intrinsic ones, if you can.

29.3 High- versus low-level Goals

Carver and Scheier (1982, 1990) have theorised that goals can be structured hierarchically. Some goals are abstract, whereas others are concrete, and still other goals may be in-between. An abstract goal can only be implemented by transforming these goals into concrete goals. That is, abstract goals are strategic goals; concrete goals are tacticle or operational goals. Strategic goals have to be oprrationalised into tactical goals for implementation.

For example, a goal such as learning French can be attained by systematically and methodically working and attaining a hierarchy of subordinate goals. Thus, a low-level goal such as memorising a list of 20 vocabulary words feeds into other higher-level goals such as practising the use of these memorised words in different situations, which in turn becomes increasingly instrumental to learning French. Although the attainment of every goal in the goal hierarchy generates a certain degree of satisfaction, satisfaction is experienced more intensely with the attainment of higher-level than lower-level goals (cf. Cantor & Sanderson, 1999).

The High-Level Principle of Goal Selection: Subjective well being can be increased (or dissatisfaction can be decreased) by selecting more high-level than low-level goals. Attainment of high-level goals induces more positive affect in that domain than low-level goals.

The principle of *high-level goals* is very important. Are you familiar with the ecologist's distinction between the "forest" and the "trees"? One's sense of ecology can come from understanding the natural dynamics of the forest, not the trees. But the dynamics of the "trees" make up the forest. An ecologist can easily become so engrossed with the study of trees that he may fail to see the forest. The trees are equated with low-level goals, whereas the forest is equated with high-level goals.

Let us use an example we can all relate to. Karen and Gabe are parents with a 16-year old daughter. They both are conscientious parents, but their parenting styles are different. They are conscientious because they both try hard to achieve family harmony and well being. That is, family harmony and well being is a high-level goal for both Karen and Gabe. Karen has the ability to stay focused on the "forest" without getting lost in the "trees". Gabe, on the other hand, has trouble staying focused on the "forest". The daughter, as most 16-year old teenagers, tends to be mindless at times. For example, many times she has forgotten to report in when she is late beyond her curfew hours. Gabe has been fast to punish his daughter thinking that good parenting requires contiguous action. That is, to teach his daughter to become responsible, she has to be grounded for a few days. This punishment will ensure learning and a future sense of responsibility. Gabe has grounded his daughter on many occasions in the past because of her mindless behaviour. Karen disagrees with Gabe's rush to punishment. She thinks that although repeated punishment is likely to quell this behaviour, punishment is likely to adversely affect the maintenance of the higher-level goal, i.e., family harmony and well being. She opts to respond in a way to quell the misbehaviour (decrease the future tendency of not reporting in after hours) in ways not to jeopardise family harmony and well being. She has a heart-to-heart chat with her daughter. She relays to her daughter how she and her father worry too much when she does not report in after-hours. The strategy is to foster a sense of responsibility by getting her daughter to experience feelings of guilt and remorse. This low-level goal is not in conflict with the high-level goal of preserving family harmony and well being. Repeated grounding is likely to create the impression (in the mind of the daughter) that the parents do not trust her. This image of herself as an untrustworthy person is likely to be in direct conflict with family harmony and well being. Achieving the high-level goal offamily harmony and well being most likely should contribute to well being, much more so than achieving the low-level goal of quelling the daughter's misbehaviour. The best that a low-level goal can generate are feelings of relief, i.e., reduction of dissatisfaction. So the moral of this story is to stay focused on higher-level goals and try your best to achieve them through low-level goals that are not in conflict with the higher-levels ones. Connecting the low-level goals with the higher-ones is indeed a challenge that we have to overcome to ensure a positive state of subjective well being.

29.4 Goals Related to Basic versus Growth Needs

There is much evidence in the literature suggesting that subjective well being is composed of two dimensions that are somewhat independent from each other, namely positive and negative affect. The factors affecting satisfaction (positive affect) may be different from the factors affecting dissatisfaction (negative affect). We call the factors affecting positive affect "growth factors", whereas factors affecting negative affect are "hygiene factors"--based on Herzberg's two-factor theory (Herzberg et al., 1957). The two-factor theory suggests that job satisfaction may be influenced by *growth* factors such as recognition and responsibility. That is, the presence of recognition and responsibility at work serves to contribute to additional job satisfaction. Conversely, the absence of these conditions does not contribute to dissatisfaction. In contrast, job dissatisfaction, on the other hand, is affected by *hygiene* factors such as wages and physical working conditions. That is, the presence of these conditions does not contribute to satisfaction, however their absence contributes to dissatisfaction. Hygiene factors are related to lower-order (or basic) needs such as biological and safety needs (*a la* Maslow). In contrast, growth factors are related to higher-order needs such as social, esteem, and self-actualisation needs (again *a la* Maslow). For example, factors affecting job dissatisfaction such as wages and physical safety are indeed directly related to lower-order needs of sustenance and physical safety, whereas factors such as recognition and responsibility are directly related to higher-order needs. I believe that the two-factor theory developed to explain job satisfaction is generalisable to all other life domains to explain satisfaction in general.

Here is suggestive evidence supporting the effect of hygiene and growth factors on positive versus negative affect.

- Diener and Lucas (1999), based on a review of the literature, have concluded that positive affect seems to be more influenced by the environmental factors (e.g., given an achievement award) than negative affect. Conversely, negative affect seems to be more influenced by biological factors (e.g., enurticism) (cf. Baker et al., 1992).
- The distinction between positive and negative affect was demonstrated also by a study conducted by Diener, Horwitz, and Emmons (1985). The study compared the very rich with average middle-class Americans. The study found no difference in the levels of positive affect between the rich and the middle class but found that the rich experienced significantly less negative affect.
- Costa and McCrae (1980) and Headey and Wearing (1989) found that negative evaluations of life (perceived in terms of "hassles") seem

independent from positive evaluations (perceived in terms of "uplifts").

*   Furthermore, research on mood shows that daily negative mood but not positive mood is associated with somatic complaints (DeLongis et al, 1982; DeLongis, Folkman, & Lazarus, 1988; Watson & Pennebaker, 1989).

These findings combined are consistent with the notion that negative affect (i.e., dissatisfaction) can be induced by failure to meet lower-order needs such as biological and safety needs. Fulfillment of biological and safety needs do not contribute much to positive affect (i.e., satisfaction).

The Growth Needs Principle of Goal Selection: *Subjective well being can be increased by selecting goals related to the satisfaction of growth needs (higher-order needs such as social, esteem, and self-actualisation). Dissatisfaction can be decreased through selection of goals related to the satisfaction of basic needs (lower-order needs such as biological and safety needs).*

What is the message behind the *growth needs* principle? Enhancing overall life satisfaction is a two-edge sword. We have to enhance satisfaction on the one hand and reduce dissatisfaction on the other. Applying Herzberg's two-factor theory suggests that we can do a better job at enhancing overall life satisfaction by realising that the sources of dissatisfaction are likely to be different from the sources of satisfaction. We need to acknowledge the independence of positive affect from negative affect. The sources of dissatisfaction with life may lie in life domains mostly related to lower-order needs such as health, family, residential, and economic. Activities within these domains are not likely to contribute much to enhance positive affect; however, they can play an important role in reducing negative affect. In contrast, life domains such as leisure and recreation, social, work, cultural, educational, and aesthetics, can play an important role in increasing positive affect. Therefore, we need to participate in a diversity of life domains, some of which can serve to reduce negative affect, while others serve to enhance positive affect. Doing so helps maintain a high level of quality of life.

29.5 Approach of Desired States versus Avoidance of Undesired States

Gollwitzer (1993) has demonstrated that approaching goals and attaining them produce higher levels of subjective well being than avoiding undesired goals. For example, a person may experience higher levels of well being working toward making friends than avoiding being lonely (cf. Cantor & Sanderson, 1999; Emmons, Shepard, & Kaiser, 1994; Higgins et al., 1994). Perhaps this may be due to the fact that avoiding being lonely serves mostly to reduce negative affect, whereas making friends serves to generate positive affect. In a study of marital conflict, Simpson (1990) has shown that passive avoidance of problems between couples significantly reduces contentment. To maintain happiness, he recommends, difficulties must be faced rather than avoided.

This notion of goal approach or attainment is the converse of the concept of avoidance in the coping literature (Carver, Scheier, & Weintraub, 1989; Roth & Cohen, 1986). Avoidance is a coping strategy that serves to reduce the experience of dissatisfaction in a particular life domain. For example, a student will avoid enrolling in a difficult course as a way to prevent the experience of failure and dissatisfaction in the academic life domain. But it should be noted that while most coping strategies serve to reduce negative affect in a particular life domain, they also reduce the possibility of positive affect. This avoidant style of coping reduces the incidence of negative life events. This outcome serves to lessen the overall negativity in life quality. By the same token, an avoidant coping style also reduces the number of positive life events and therefore reduces positive life quality. Thus, a person who adopts an avoidant coping style may have an okay life (a good "negative life quality") but also a poor "positive life quality."

The Approach Principle of Goal Selection: Subjective well being can be increased (or dissatisfaction can be decreased) by taking action to approach and attain a desirable state of affairs rather than action to avoid an undesirable state of affairs.

The *goal approach* principle urges people to become engaged in life. Participate in life by pursuing goals that can lead to positive affect. Do not walk away from life by avoiding the things that scare you. Do not let the things that scare you overwhelm your life. If you cannot help it, then the next best thing is to limit the avoidance behaviour to that one thing that scares you. Do not let this one thing generalise into an avoidant tendency that makes you avoid most things in life. Life's pleasures can only be experienced with attainment of pleasurable things, not avoidance of things that can be the source of displeasure. The avoidant tendency can best help you reduce dissatisfaction with life; it cannot make you happy with life.

29.6   Goals Related to Intensity versus Frequency of Positive Affect

Should a person select to pursue a leisure goal that provides frequent but small doses of satisfaction or a leisure goal that is less frequent but provides large doses of satisfaction?   Diener, Sandvik, and Pavot (1991) have demonstrated that intense and frequent positive experiences are related to subjective well being because they are easily evoked from memory when a person is asked to evaluate his life.   However, they also demonstrated that frequent positive experiences are more related to long-term well being than intense ones.

The Frequency Principle of Goal Selection: Subjective well being can be enhanced by selecting goals that allow the person to experience positive affect repeatedly and in small doses rather than sparsely and in large doses.

The *frequency* principle teaches us that we should be careful in the way we seek pleasurable experiences from life.   Instead of Bungee jumping, parachute diving, or going on a safari expedition, we should engage in a lot of small but daily pleasures.   Examples, sip a nice cup of coffee in the morning while reading the paper listening to classical music, watch your favourite show on prime-time television every night or so, go to your neighbourhood theatre every weekend with your significant other and munch on some popcorn while watching the show, have a nice romantic dinner and make love every chance you get, go to a nice exotic restaurant and socialise with friends as often as you can, and so on. Get the picture?   Small doses of frequent pleasures are much better than large doses of non-frequent pleasures.

29.7   Goals Related to Cultural Norms

Oishi, Diener, Suh, and Lucas (1999) argued that personal values (e.g., power, achievement, hedonism, security) moderate the extent to which domain satisfaction contributes to overall life satisfaction.   Both culture and stage of development cycle (i.e., age) influence personal values.   For example, these quality-of-life researchers hypothesised that life satisfaction is more strongly related to personal achievements and self-esteem in individualist cultures than in collective cultures.   That is, the pursuit of achievement and self-esteem goals can bring high levels of subjective well being in cultures that value these goals.   These cultures are individualistic, not collectivistic.   The results of the study found support for the cultural value-as-a-moderator hypothesis, in which domains affect subjective well being most strongly when they are consistent with cultural norms and values.

Here are other examples that further demonstrate the moderation effect of culture in the most generic sense. For example, let us look at the *cultural* differences between men and women. Past research has shown that marital status and happiness are related in that married people are happier than unmarried ones, and this relationship is moderated by gender. More specifically, married women are happier than married men are and unmarried people in general (e.g., Lee, Seccombe, & Shehan, 1991; Wood, Rhodes, & Whelan, 1989). Why? Perhaps because the cultural norm is women should find happiness in the home, whereas men find fulfilment at work. This norm bestows status and prestige on women who are married (e.g., Inglis & Greenglass, 1987; Shostak, 1987). Women are socialised to value marriage more than men are. They are more concerned about their appearance and fear of aging due to the pressure they feel to attract a man for marriage (e.g., Tannen, 1994). Women's identities are tied with family identities (e.g., Gerson, 1993; Thorne, 1992). This is commonly referred to in the gender socialisation literature as a "hierarchy of gender identities."[12]

In his literature review article, Diener (1984) examined much of the evidence relating employment to subjective well being and concluded that employment does indeed have a significant impact on subjective well being of both men and women in general. That is, those who are unemployed report lower levels of subjective well being than those who are employed. The exception is the homemakers segment of the population. There is no significant difference between homemakers' subjective well being and the subjective well being of the employed. One explanation is that culture endows men with the norm that man's identity is directly connected with their jobs. "Who they are" is articulated by what jobs they have. Hence, the work domain is most salient compared to other life domains. This is not the case for homemakers. They choose to define themselves in terms of their family. Hence, the family domain is likely to be most salient compared to other life domains. Unemployment for men has a devastating effect on subjective well being because their self-evaluations using a variety of self-concept and social comparison referents generate dissatisfaction in the work domain, which in turn spills over to overall life.

---

[12] Some readers may feel offended reading this. The reaction is typically that this is male chauvinism *par excellence*. To those readers I do apologise. I am a feminist. However, having said this I believe that there is some semblance of truth to this research. Cultural norms pertaining to gender identity are changing rapidly. Hence, this "reality" has to be qualified by making reference to the historical era, the country in question, the subcultural context, etc.

The Cultural Norms Principle of Goal Selection: Selecting goals consistent with cultural norms can enhance subjective well being because achieving those goals brings about social recognition and therefore heightened satisfaction. Achieving goals inconsistent with cultural norms, on the other hand, may not be as rewarding because of the lack of social recognition.

The *cultural norm* principle advises us to be cognisant of the extent to which our goals are consistent with cultural norms, and the extent to which our own identities are linked to these norms. A woman who defines herself as a homemaker and a mother in a manner consistent with the prevailing norms of the community is not likely to be able to experience much joy and happiness outside of the home. This is because her home life is the most important part of her life and it overrides the importance of all other life domains. Such identities and strong cultural norms are found in many Moslem countries. The same cultural norms are changing in many of the Judeo-Christian countries, especially the countries of the West. Women in those countries no longer define themselves as homemakers only; they are homemakers *and* career women, some are career women, *period*; and some are homemakers, *period*. The cultural norms of the West have changed to allow multiple identities for women and the freedom to choose these identities. So the message is to select personal goals that do not conflict with cultural norms of your own community. Goals that are consistent with cultural norms are likely to be more valued and considered more important. Therefore, the attainment of goals that are consistent with cultural norms is likely to be highly satisfying compared to goals that are inconsistent with the norms.

29.8 Goals Related to Deprived Needs

Ahuvia and Friedman (1998) have argued that economic deprivation is a strong factor influencing materialism (the tendency to value money and material possessions). Poor people who attain wealth become so happy. This is because economic deprivation heightens the need intensity for money and material possessions. This argument can be extended to non-economic needs too. That is, need deprivation heightens the intensity of any need. In turn, those life domains and subdomains in which this need can be met increase in importance. As a result, satisfying the deprived need generates a great deal of satisfaction in those important life domains. This satisfaction, in turn, contributes significantly to life satisfaction (cf. Abramson & Inglehart, 1995; Inglehart, 1977, 1990).

People who are starving for love feel that happiness is being in love. When they finally fall in love, they feel like they are in heaven. Those who are sick think that being healthy is the most important condition to overall well being. When they eventually get cured, they become happy. When people are constantly hungry, they may think that food and nutrition is the most important thing in life. When they finally get to eat well, they become highly satisfied. People who are existentially hopeless are likely to emphasise the sense of meaning or purpose in life to be the most important thing in life. When they finally discover meaning in their life events, they discover happiness too.

The Need Deprivation Principle of Goal Selection: *Selecting goals that reflect deprived needs can enhance subjective well being. The attainment of these goals induces intense positive affect because of heightened involvement in those life domains through which these needs are met.*

The *need deprivation* principle advises us to introspect and identify needs that we think we have not met, but we feel the motivation to meet them still. How is your need for esteem? Do you feel the need to be recognised for your achievements and successes at work? Then select those work-related goals (e.g., work hard at a task you know is directly related to some award) that may help you attain such goals. Attainment of such goals will bring you much pleasure in life.

29.9 Achievement versus Non-achievement-Related Goals

Personal goals can be achievement or non-achievement oriented. For example, a person may set a goal of making a job promotion, and he succeeds. He feels very good about his work life domain as a direct function of goal attainment in relation to the job promotion. In contrast, a person may feel that his community is indeed a beautiful place. He feels quite satisfied with his community, and these feelings spillover, thus enhancing his overall subjective well being. In evaluating his work life, the person may have used his job-related goals, which are achievement goals. The outcomes are perceived to be a direct result of his actions. But evaluating his community did not involve any achievement goals. He feels he is simply lucky to live in a beautiful town. The question is: which domain satisfaction is likely to be more fulfilling, work life or community life? One can easily argue that satisfaction in life domains in which people feel they control their own destiny is likely to be more intense and meaningful than satisfaction in domains in which people feel little control.

> *The Achievement Principle in Goal Selection: Selecting achievement-oriented goals rather than non-achievement goals can enhance subjective well being. The attainment of these goals induces intense positive affect because of heightened involvement in those life domains involving achievement goals.*

The advice from the *achievement* principle is clear. Select goals that you can call your own. Select goals that make you feel proud when these goals come to fruition. A person whose life goal is to live in sunny Southern California does not have a challenging goal. There may be little achievement involved in attaining this goal besides moving there. Well, perhaps this may be an achievement goal to some! Compare this situation to going to graduate school and completing a Masters degree in your field of speciality. Now that is an achievement goal! Obtaining a Masters degree is much more fulfilling than moving to sunny Southern California. Right?

29.10 Autonomy in Goal Setting

Subjective well being has something to do with the extent to which personal goals are selected *autonomously*. Cantor and Sanderson (in press) have argued that "Well being should be enhanced when individuals are able to pursue their distinct personal goals in ways that are intrinsically-valued and autonomously chosen" (p. 5). That is, goals that are essentially determined by others, not the individual himself, are not likely to be important goals. Thus, the subjective well being experienced from goal attainment is very much dependent on whether the goal was selected autonomously or whether the person was pressured by others to take on that goal. Goals chosen freely and autonomously are more intrinsically satisfying than goals set by others.

Readers who are professors can relate to this case in point. Being a professor at a large research university, I have chaired, co-chaired, and participated on countless doctoral dissertation committees. The temptation is great to simply give students ideas for their dissertation research and help them closely conduct the research. The reward for professors usually comes in the form of co-authoring the resultant publication(s) based on the dissertation research. For many years I had to fight off the temptation of doing this. Actually, I have developed an explicit policy about this. *Doctoral students should take ownership of their own dissertations.* They should not rely heavily on the mentoring and guidance from their dissertation chairperson and members of their dissertation committee. They should be the sole authors of their dissertation research. Doing so is extremely important in instilling in them a passion for research and the rewards that come from taking ownership of their research. Taking ownership of their research and succeeding does contribute significantly to their subjective well being. Relinquishing that ownership to others diminishes the significance of the accomplishment. It diminishes the passion, the pride, and the feelings of joy they can take from completing their dissertation. If doctoral students were to complete their dissertation without feeling passion for the research, then their professors who chaired their dissertation committees may have failed them. The professors may have failed their students because their students are not likely to make future significant research contributions to the discipline and may end up as "teachers", not "scholars". Being a "teacher" is fine, of course. But if these students have the research talent and end up giving up research because they did not develop the passion for it, then this is most unfortunate. And the blame lies in part with the professors who failed to allow their students to take ownership of their dissertation in the first place. Over the many years I have been in academe I have seen many "casualties". I have to admit that on some occasions I have contributed to this problem, and I am guilty as charged. However, I have become increasingly cognisant of the problem, and I have been making an effort over the years to correct it. I hope professors who read this will think about this issue.

The Autonomy Principle of Goal Selection: *Selecting goals autonomously, i.e., without the interference or cajoling of others, can enhance subjective well being. The attainment of autonomous goals induces intense positive affect because of heightened involvement in those life domains involving those goals.*

We can all relate (some of us more than others) to the *autonomy* principle. We often heard how parents force their children to do things they do not want to do. Parents force them to take unwanted hobbies. They cajole them into certain competitive sports they don't enjoy. They convince them that going to college is "a must". There are no "if's and but's" about that. The result is that children often select goals "forcibly". They may not feel happy when they accomplish goals that are selected by their parents. They do not feel that these goals are their own. They do not take ownership of these goals. Therefore, little pride can be felt when these goals come to fruition. Consider the story of Tony. Tony felt little joy when he recently graduated from medical school. He comes from a family of doctors—his father, mother, grandparents, aunts, and uncles. Heck, even his baby brother recently enrolled in a medical school. Imagine the social pressure! He did not have much of a choice. It is either this or getting disowned by his family.

So the message to parents and all of us who interject ourselves in the lives of our loved ones: back off! Don't push too hard. Allow your loved ones to select their own goals. You can give them advice and support. That is the best you can do. Make sure that they take ownership of their own goals. Let them take "ownership" of their lives by selecting their own goals in life, goals that reflect their own interests and passions.

29.11 Flow

Argyle (1999) reviewed much of the evidence linking leisure with subjective well being. He concluded that there is indeed a strong relationship between the two constructs. He injected the *flow* principle to explain how certain kinds of challenging leisure activities (e.g., competitive sports) contribute to subjective well being much more compared to passive forms of leisure activities such as watching television. The flow principle is based on the work of Csikszentmihalyi and his colleagues (e.g., Csikszentmihalyi, 1975, 1982; Csikszentmihalyi & Csikszentmihalyi, 1988; Csikszentmihalyi & Kubey, 1981; Kubey & Csikszentmihalyi, 1990; Massimini, Csikszentmihalyi, & Carli, 1987; Massimini, Csikszentmihalyi, & Delle Fave, 1988).

Csikszentmihaly and his colleagues have theorised that subjective well being can be induced by a state of "flow". Flow is a psychological state produced by the person's perception that his skills match the challenges presented in a given situation. When skills are perceived to be greater than challenges, the person is likely to feel bored. When the challenge presented in a given situation is perceived to be higher than one's own skills, the person is likely to feel anxious. When both challenges and skills are perceived as low, the person is likely to feel apathetic.

The Flow Principle of Goal Selection: Subjective well being can be enhanced by selecting goals in life domains requiring a certain level of skill matching the person's skill level. Doing so enhances positive affect, which in turn contributes to subjective well being.

The *flow principle* recommends that we choose our goals in a way to match our skills. Goals unmatched to our skill levels are either not likely to be attained, or if attained might not generate much satisfaction.

An offshoot of the flow principle is the principle of skillful winning. Anyone who played competitive sports may attest to the "flow" experience that is experienced when playing against a player who has a comparable skill level. The competition is intense and the victory is particularly sweet. Playing against a player (team) unmatched in skill can produce feelings of boredom (when the opposition's skill level falls significantly below the party in question) and anxiety (when the opposition's skill level is significantly higher). This example alerts us to the distinction between evaluating the situation before the onset of the event and evaluating the same situation after the event (cf. Omodei & Wearing, 1990). The concept of pleasure derived from a flow experience is different from pleasure derived from achievement. Murray (1938), one of the founders of motivational psychology, made a similar distinction among three types of pleasures related to need satisfaction: (a) activity pleasure, (b) achievement pleasure, and (c) effect pleasure. Murray's definition of *achievement pleasure* corresponds closely to the concept of flow. With respect to *achievement pleasure,* focus on the example of a player facing a competitor who is much more skilful than he is. It is very likely that he will feel quite anxious, but if he beats the competitor he is likely to feel much happier than if that competitor has a comparable skill level. This is because this type of situation may lead the person to generate predictive expectations based on the skill level of himself and his competitor. In the situation in which the competitor is perceived to be more skilful, the person predicts that he will lose. Winning in light of a loss prediction generates intense positive affect.

The Skillful Winning Principle of Goal Selection: Subjective well being can be enhanced by winning competitive events requiring a certain level of skill matching the person's skill level. Doing so generates positive affect, which in turn contributes to subjective well being.

To reiterate, the *flow principle* recommends that we choose our goals in a way to match our skills. The principle of skilful winning recommends a similar matching in competitive situations. Goals unmatched to our skill levels are either not likely to be attained (if skill level is too high), or if attained might not generate much satisfaction (if skill level is too low). So select your goals to match your skill level.

30. FACTORS AFFECTING THE SELECTION OF GOALS LIKELY TO BE ATTAINED

In the preceding section we discussed factors that can help people select goals that are capable of bringing happiness to their lives. That is, the focus was on the goals likely to generate positive emotions once attained. In this section we will discuss selecting the kind of goals that are likely to be attained. Factors that affect goal completion include setting goals to adapt to changes, feedforward, goal-motive congruence, goal-cultural value congruence, goal-resources congruence, goal-skills congruence, and goal realism.

30.1 Setting Goals to Adapt to Changes

One study dealt with attorneys who have experienced a distinct transition--career became less important and family became more important (Adams, 1983). Those who recognised the change and reorganised their goals accordingly expressed significantly higher levels of life satisfaction than those who failed to recognise the change and failed to adapt their goals.

The Adaptation Principle of Goal Selection: Selecting goals to reflect changes in circumstances can decrease dissatisfaction in a life domain. The new goals consistent with the new circumstances may also serve to increase satisfaction in the long run. Doing so should enhance subjective well being.

The *adaptation* principle urges us to be flexible. Our goals should be malleable. We have to be ready to change our goals to reflect the realty of our changing circumstances in life. Take for example a college student in the U.S. who is playing on the football team and his life goal has been to do well so he can join a National Football League (NFL) team and play professional. One day, he is injured. The injury, according to his medical doctors, is likely to hamper his physical performance on the field. However, this player was not ready to give up football. He persisted and eventually saw his athletic performance dwindling; his chances to play professional football gradually evaporated; and his academic standing in college was significantly undermined.

The advice from the adaptation principle is that instead of holding on to his life goal of becoming a professional player, he should face up to reality. The new reality dictated that becoming a professional football player is no longer possible. Hanging on to this goal is likely to create much unhappiness in his life. He should have changed that goal to meet his new life circumstances. He should have selected another goal that is more reflective of his current and future physical conditions. Perhaps, he could have focused on becoming a physical education teacher or coach.

Niven (2000) puts it this way: "People who cannot attain their goals become consumed with disappointment. You must let your goals evolve with your life circumstances. Update your goals over time as you consider your changing priorities and resources (p. 59)."

30.2 Feedforward

Cantril (1965) found that older people are more satisfied with their past and current life, but less satisfied with what they anticipate to happen to them in the future. Life satisfaction is not only heavily influenced by the events of the past in various life domains, but also by what they anticipate in the future. The extent to which people feel their goals are likely to be met is an important factor in life satisfaction. If goals are projected to be unattainable, one way to deal with this adversity is to set goals projected to be attainable. This is what is called "feedfoward".

Feedback is based on past trial-and-error learning. In other words, people receive feedback about whether certain actions were successful in increasing positive affect (or decreasing negative affect), and they make adjustments to planned action based on the feedback. *Feedforword* is somewhat different. It is based on anticipating the future. The past may or may not be a guide. In other words, people tend to conjure up a mental situation to anticipate actual outcomes (Frederick & Loewenstein, 1999). A person decides which action to take based on the positive or negative affect imagined as a result of a contemplated action. Thus, goal setting is heavily influenced by feedforward—anticipating consequences from alternative goals and task accomplishments.

The Feedfoward Principle of Goal Selection: Goals likely to be attained are selected by conjuring up scenarios visualising alternative ways to achieve those goals. Goals that are selected should reflect the person's confidence in goal attainment.

The *feedforward* principle suggests that we need to put much thought in selecting our goals. Our goals should not be selected in whimsical fashion. Our goals should not be selected impulsively based on what feels good at the moment. The feedforward principle urges us to think about each goal in the important life domains and conjure up possible scenarios related to goal

.

attainment. Can these goals be attained? If so, through what course of action? What are the likely consequences of the contemplated course of action? What about alternative courses of action? What are the likely consequences of those? Which is the course of action likely to generate consequences that are most positive and least negative. Thus, goals and actions designed to generate most pleasure with the least pain should be selected. This is what is meant by the use of feedforward in goal selection.

30.3 Goal-Motive Congruence

Brunstein, Schultheiss, and Grassman (1998) found that subjective well being is not only dependent on goal attainment but also on the extent to which the realised goals are congruent or incongruent with personal motives. Their study revealed that commitment to motive-incongruent goals led to a reduction in emotional well being. A typical example is one that most college professors are familiar with--the college student whose motives are not congruent with educational goals. Many students are strongly motivated by social and love (romantic) needs. These needs sometimes interfere with the setting and attainment of good grades. Partying late nights interferes with completing important homework assignments and attending morning classes. Thus, educational goals are said to be incongruent with the social and love needs of many college students. This goal-motive incongruence may cause students to perform poorly in college classes, thus preventing them from attaining their educational goals--obtaining decent grades in their classes. Failing to obtain decent grades leads to dissatisfaction in the education domain.

The Motive Congruence Principle of Goal Selection: Subjective well being can be increased (or dissatisfaction can be decreased) by selecting goals consistent with needs. Doing so increases the likelihood of goal attainment, domain satisfaction, and subjective well being.

What can we learn from the *goal-motive congruence* principle? Select goals that are consistent with your motives. Find out the motive underlying the goal you are trying to achieve. Is it motivated by biological needs, safety needs, social needs, or esteem needs? Is the need underlying the goal a strong one? If yes, then this is the kind of goal that is likely to be attained. This is because it is not likely that other competing goals are strong enough to override the focal goal.

30.4 Goal-Cultural Value Congruence

Malatesta et al. (1986) have shown that classical conditioning, instrumental learning, and imitation effects influence subjective well being. For example, mothers teach their children how to behave to conform to cultural norms. Such conformance leads the children to experience positive affect and non-conformance leads to negative affect. In one study, Malatesta and her colleagues found a linear increase in positive affect (and a proportional decrease in negative affect) as a function of age among children from age two and a half months to age seven and a half months. This is evidence of socialisation effects on subjective well being. This finding can be explained through the concept of *goal-cultural value congruence*. By learning what is acceptable and not acceptable, children become increasingly successful at goal attainment. Goal attainment enables them to experience more positive than negative affect, thus making systematic and incremental contribution to their subjective well being.

Oishi, Diener, Suh, and Lucas (1999) found that satisfaction with travel predicted subjective well being more in wealthy than poor countries. They explained that goals related to leisure activities are more accepted in wealthy countries much more so than poor ones.

Cantor and Sanderson (in press) argued that subjective well being is not only dependent on goal attainment but also on the extent to which these realised goals are congruent or incongruent with cultural values. People who are successful in attaining personal goals that are valued by their culture or subculture are likely to experience higher levels of subjective well being than those who attain goals that are incongruent with those of their culture or subculture.

The Cultural Value Congruence Principle of Goal Selection: *Subjective well being can be increased (or dissatisfaction can be decreased) by selecting goals consistent with cultural (and/or subcultural) values. Doing so increases the likelihood of goal attainment and subjective well being.*

The *goal-cultural value congruence* principle advises us to select goals that are consistent with cultural norms. Goals consistent with cultural norms are likely to be attained with less difficulty than goals inconsistent with cultural norms. If you belong to a cultural group you identify with, select your goals in a manner consistent with the norms of that group. You will find fewer obstacles on the way to achieve your goal, and you will feel better about yourself and your life after achieving that goal.

30.5 Goal-Resources Congruence

The concept of "resources" as used here is not restricted to financial resources. Cantor and Sanderson (1999) specified three dimensions of resources: (a) personal resources such as health, traits, strategies, and abilities, (b) social resources such as social networks and social support, and (c) material resources such as money, power, and status. Cantor and Sanderson (in press) theorised that subjective well being is not only dependent on goal attainment but also on the extent to which the goals that are realised are congruent or incongruent with one's own personal resources. Those who have resources that match their goals are more likely to attain these goals and thus experience higher levels of subjective well being than those who do not match their goals with their resources. Diener and Fujita (1995) tested this hypothesis. Indeed, resources predicted subjective well being better when goals and resources were matched than when they were not. Much evidence is available to support the principle of goal-resource congruence (see Cantor & Sanderson, 1999 for a review of much of the evidence).

Diener (1984) and Diener et al. (1999) in their literature review articles acknowledged an overwhelming amount of evidence showing a positive relationship between income and subjective well being. One of the most plausible explanations referred to by Diener and colleagues is the goal-resource congruence principle. That is, goal attainment (a major source of satisfaction and therefore subjective well being) is facilitated by the availability of resources, e.g., economic resources. Argyle (1999) reviewed the research literature and arrived at a similar conclusion:

> . . . richer people have a higher standard of living, better food, housing, transport, education, and leisure, access to medicine—resulting in better health, even better mental health and a more competent personality (through being able to afford therapy)—and the higher self-esteem resulting from the respect given to the rich. . . . Money is good for marriage, since it enables the newly wedded to have a place of their own instead of living with one of the families, and marriage is a major source of happiness. . . . Furthermore, relative income rather than, or as well as, actual income, makes people happy. . . . In conclusion, it looks as if comparisons are most important for pay, especially when employees know exactly what they and members of other groups of workers are paid (pp. 358-359).

Cummins (2000b) also has reviewed the quality-of-life literature on the effect of personal income on subjective well being and found substantial support for the notion that income plays a significant role in subjective well being. He explains this finding by arguing that personal income plays an important role in enhancing three personality-like factors that may induce feelings of subjective well being. These personality-like factors are environmental control, self-esteem, and optimism. Monetary resources serve to help the individual to exert control over his environment. Income serves to help the individual attain his goals. For example, if a person likes to socialise with his friends (because friendship is important in his life and he experiences a great deal of satisfaction in that domain), then monetary means to help him socialise would facilitate goal attainment. Goal attainment provides the individual with feelings of optimism, i.e. perceptions that future goals can also be attained. Hence, the lesson here about money is that money by itself does not buy happiness, but how one uses money to help with the attainment of important goals is a key to happiness.

The Resources Congruence Principle of Goal Selection: Subjective well being can be increased (or dissatisfaction can be decreased) by selecting goals consistent with available resources. Doing so increases the likelihood of goal attainment and subjective well being.

The advice of the *goal-resources congruence* principle is simple and straightforward. Personal and financial resources can go a long way to help you accomplish your goals. If your resources are limited, then select goals you can accomplish given your limited resources. Give up or replace those goals that you cannot complete with the resources you have.

30.6 Goal Realism

Vallacher and Wegner (1989) have argued that individuals experience greater satisfaction when they strive to attain goals that are realistic and attainably feasible than if these goals are not realistic and feasible. In other words, people who typically are habituated to engage in easy tasks tend to be happier if their goals are not set high; and conversely those who tend to engage in difficult tasks tend to be happier if their goals are set at a higher level. Thus, satisfaction is maximised when their characteristic striving (low versus high-level strivings) matches the level of challenge of their daily life tasks (easy versus difficult tasks) (cf. Cantor & Sanderson, 1999; Sirgy, 1998).

Argyle (1999), in his review of the literature on age, maintained that much of the evidence points to the notion that the elderly experience a higher level of well being than the non-elderly. Argyle has explained this pattern of findings by maintaining that older people tend to have lower (and therefore more realistic) aspirations, thus decreasing the goal-achievement gap.

The Realism Principle of Goal Selection: Subjective well being can be increased (or dissatisfaction can be decreased) by selecting realistic goals rather than unrealistic ones. Realistic goals are more likely to be attained, and therefore generate positive affect, than unrealistic goals. Doing so enhances subjective well being.

The *goal realism* principle recommends that we select goals that we think have a good chance of being realised. Goals that are too difficult to achieve should be abandoned, because such goals are likely to generate dissatisfaction.

30.7 Goal Conflict

A study by Wilson, Henry, and Peterson (1997) showed that life satisfaction is associated with the consistency of life goals. The greater the consistency among goals regarding career, education, family, and geography, the greater the life satisfaction. Goal compatibility, consistency, or lack of conflict accounted for 80 percent of the variance in life satisfaction.

Cantor and Sanderson (1999) have argued that people who attempt to pursue conflicting goals simultaneously are not likely to end up attaining either goal; hence, they may experience dissatisfaction with goal non-attainment. For example, a college student finds out that she is "on probation" because her grade point average (GPA) has dipped below 2.0. She becomes highly motivated to spend more time studying and exert more effort in the academic domain. She also notes that her relationship with her boyfriend is crumbling. So she vows to spend more time with her boyfriend, without changing anything else in her life to accommodate the extra time devoted for studying and her boyfriend. The goal of raising her GPA by devoting more time and effort to studying and the goal of saving her relationship are in direct conflict. She cannot do both simultaneously. The outcome is likely that she would fail to raise her GPA and save her relationship with her boyfriend.

Much evidence is available that is consistent with this principle. Research has shown that goal conflict is associated with negative affect, neuroticism, depression, stress, psychosomatic complaints, and life dissatisfaction (e.g., Emmons, 1986; Emmons & King, 1988; Sheldon & Kasser, 1995).

The Conflict Principle of Goal Selection: Subjective well being can be increased (or dissatisfaction can be decreased) by selecting goals in one or more life domains that do not conflict with one another. Doing so increases the likelihood of goal attainment and subjective well being.

Niven (2000) has provided the following advice in relation to the *goal conflict* principle:

The four tires of your car have to be properly aligned; otherwise the left tires will be pointed in a different direction from the right tires and the car won't work. Goals are just like that. They all must be pointed in the same direction. If goals conflict with one another, your life may not work. (p. 7)

GOAL IMPLEMENTATION AND ATTAINMENT

In this chapter I will describe how subjective well being can be enhanced by taking action that attains personal goals. The previous chapter described how goals are selected. This chapter focuses on how goals are attained. I will describe also strategies to enhance the likelihood that action will lead to goal attainment, i.e., factors that can facilitate implementation to increase the likelihood of goal attainment. Examples include goal commitment and goal feedback.

31. WHAT IS GOAL IMPLEMENTATION AND ATTAINMENT?

Figures 22 and 23 are designed to describe goal implementation and attainment in a graphic form. The top part of the figure shows Maggie's situation, the person described in the previous chapter (see figures 20 and 21). Maggie is feeling happy with her family life (the box is white fill-in), somewhat dissatisfied with her work life (the box is a grey fill-in), and very dissatisfied with her leisure life (the box is dark grey fill-in). Maggie takes action in her leisure domain in an attempt to decrease the negative affect in that domain and possibly generate positive affect. In the previous chapter, reference was made to the fact that she selects two new leisure goals—handicrafts and aerobics. The question that we need to ask here is *to what extent these two new goals are likely to be realised*. What are the facilitators and inhibitors that may affect goal implementation and attainment. Goal attainment, of course, in the leisure domain is likely to change the valence in the leisure domain completely—from negative to positive.

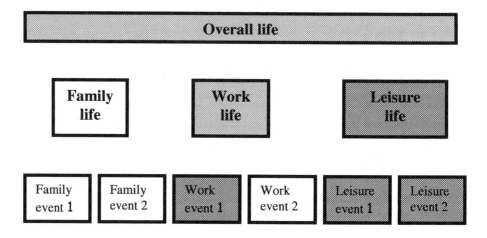

Figure 22. [Goal Implementation and Attainment--Before]

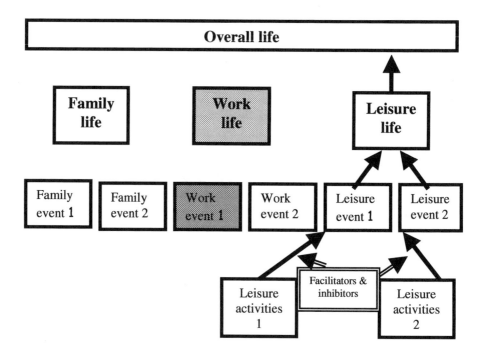

Figure 23. [Goal Implementation and Attainment--After]

Satisfaction in any life domain can be viewed in terms of goal consumption. People who set goals, take action in pursuit of these goals, and attain them feel satisfied. Failing to attain their goals leads to dissatisfaction. Cantor (1994) has maintained that life satisfaction comes from goal attainment, and people who have developed effective strategies to attain their goals tend to experience higher levels of subjective well being than those who have less effective strategies of goal attainment. Therefore, the primary determinant of domain satisfaction is essentially goal attainment, which in turn serves to satisfy activated needs.

The Principle of Goal Implementation and Attainment: Satisfaction in a life domain can be increased (or dissatisfaction can be decreased) by taking action to implement and achieve important goals set in that domain. Doing so contributes to subjective well being.

The message here is very clear. Satisfaction is only experienced when people take action toward accomplishing their goals and experience the fruits of their accomplishments. Most parents get on their children's cases for not doing things that are important. That is, most parents tend to encourage and cajole their children into setting certain goals for themselves (e.g., goals related to academics, sports, and other extra curricular activities) and doing things to attain these goals. Boredom and laziness are the greatest enemies of subjective well being. Children who are not socialised to use their time wisely become troubled. They get into trouble. They become easily alienated from their parents and society. Staying active and focused on accomplishing important goals is the key to the good life.

32. FACTORS AFFECTING GOAL ATTAINMENT

In this section the focus will be on identifying and describing factors that affect goal attainment and the experience of satisfaction derived from goal attainment. These are recognition of goal attainment, goal concreteness, and progress toward goal attainment.

32.1 Recognition of Goal Attainment

It should be noted that it is not goal attainment that contributes to subjective well being but the *recognition of that attainment*. In other words, the satisfaction from goal attainment can only be experienced when the person recognises that they have attained the goal. Research on highly educated professionals has shown that those who are less satisfied with life never *recognised* their own accomplishments (Thurman, 1981). Instead, they focused on the goals yet to be attained, and they judged themselves accordingly. Therefore, goal attainment contributes to subjective well being only if and when the person comes to recognise it. Goal attainment without focal attention by the person does little for subjective well being.

> *The Principle of Recognition of Goal Attainment: Focusing attentionon one's accomplishments in a life domain can increase satisfaction in that domain. A good sense of appreciation of one's accomplishments can be a significant factor in enhancing subjective well being.*

Supposedly the Thanksgiving holiday (a holiday in the U.S.) is designed to do exactly that--help people focus on their accomplishments. They count their blessings for the things they have, *not* the things they are missing from their lives. So the advice we take from the *recognition of goal attainment principle* is to count our blessings. Every once in a while we should revisit a particular life domain and take stock of our accomplishments within that domain. Savor those accomplishments and take pride in them. The recognition of accomplishments is a big factor in our feelings of pride and happiness.

Frisch (in press, Chapter 6) recommends the use of the *B.A.T. Exercise.* This technique forces people to focus on their **B**lessings, **A**ccomplishments, and **T**alents. Instructions provided are as follows: "In order to increase your sense of self-esteem and optimism, make yourself aware of your Blessings or the things that you are thankful for in life, your Accomplishments or the things which you care about, and your Talents or the skills and abilities you possess in every part of life. Make yourself aware of these things, by writing down as many as you can."

Another technique based on the principle of recognition of goal implementation and attainment is the *success log* (Frisch, in press, Chapter 6). This technique involves keeping a daily record of success experiences. Thus, those who are able to maintain a daily record of success experiences are likely to recognise their accomplishments and celebrate them.

32.2 *Goal Concreteness*

Although abstract goals are likely to be more meaningful, people do not know when they have attained these goals. They are hard to measure, and therefore you do not know if and when the goal is achieved. In contrast, concrete goals are measurable goals. One can gauge the extent to which he or she is making progress towards that goal. There is some research that supports what social psychologists call "concrete thinking." Lindeman and Verkasalo (1996) have conducted a study and found that perceptions that life is meaningful and therefore worthwhile, increases significantly with concrete thinking. Concrete thinking is thinking in exact, measurable terms. Concrete thinking may be contrasted with "fuzzy thinking". Concrete thinkers are very conscious of the measurable aspects of their abstract goals. Therefore, they can effectively gauge their progress toward their goals.

The Concreteness Principle of Goal Implementation and Attainment: Abstract goals translated concretely in measurable terms are likely to result in greater domain satisfaction than abstract goals that are non-measurable. This is because satisfaction can only be experienced when the person recognises goal attainment. Recognition of goal attainment is facilitated by goal concreteness, thus contributing to subjective well being.

The reader may note that the principle of *goal concreteness* is not in direct conflict with the principle of high-level goals. On the one hand, we recommend that goals should be high (not low), but then we turn around and recommend that goals should be concrete (not abstract). Abstract and high-level goals can produce a great deal of joy once attained. But attainment of these abstract and high-level goals will be not be recognised if they are not translated in concrete and measurable ways. The principle suggests that if we set a high-level goal, then we need to define this goal concretely. The high-level goal has to be defined in measurable terms so the person would know when the goal is attained. Therefore, the catch is *measurement*.

Remember the story of Karen and Gabe. Both are parents with an adolescent daughter. Both have a high-level goal of family harmony and well being. How do they know when they experience family harmony and well being? If they were to derive any satisfaction from this goal, they have to know when they are at a point in which their family is at harmony and the family at large functions well as a unit. When asked, Karen has a concrete way of defining family harmony and well being. She says, "my family is at harmony when my husband and I go for several months without a major disagreement about how to discipline our daughter, and when our daughter does not rock the boat or misbehaves. In my mind, family well being is when we spend enough time doing things together, we share our daily stories, and feel connected to one another." In Karen's mind, her high-level goal of family harmony and well being is concrete. She knows when the family is experiencing harmony and well being at any given moment. This is what goal concreteness is all about!

32.3 Progress toward Goal Attainment

There is some research that suggests people get much pleasure and enjoyment pursuing goals in an attempt to meet their needs. That the pleasure derived from making incremental *progress* towards need fulfilment is intense and possibly equally or more intense than the pleasure derived from goal attainment *per se*.

Hsee and Abelson (1991) found that the rate of progress towards the realisation of one's goals was more predictive of affect than goal attainment. Therefore, satisfaction in a given domain can be affected not only by goal attainment (or the realisation of goal attainment) but also by perceptions of significant progress toward goal attainment. A study of college students conducted by McGregor and Little (1998) found that students were happier when they felt they were making progress towards achieving their goals compared to students who did not feel they were making progress.

The Progress Principle of Goal Attainment: *Action directed toward goal attainment within a life domain contributes to increases in satisfaction in that domain in two ways: (a) The action increases the likelihood of goal attainment inducing positive affect in that domain, which in turn contributes to subjective well being. (b) The action itself induces positive affect by prompting the anticipation of goal attainment, which in turn contributes to subjective well being.*

The *progress* principle gives away strong advice. This advice is to take stock of not only *fait-a-accompli* events but also the progress you make toward your goals. Recognise your progress and celebrate it. Pat yourself on the back for noting the progress you make towards important goals. Take pride in these accomplishments, even though the end goal has not been achieved. Savour your past accomplishments and think of them as making good progress toward your ultimate goals. Never think of these accomplishments as failures to attain the ultimate goal. They represent hope and anticipation of final goal attainment.

33. FACTORS AFFECTING GOAL IMPLEMENTATION

Much research has suggested that goal attainment can be facilitated by increasing one's commitment to the goal and learning from trial and error to enhance the likelihood of task completion. We will describe these factors in some detail next.

33.1 Goal Commitment

Research has shown that satisfaction experienced in particular life domains is dependent on goal commitment. That is, the person has to be committed to the set goal. He or she has to allocate resources and engage in systematic action in an attempt to achieve the set goal. Brunstein (1993) found that the effect of goal achievement on subjective well being is moderated by goal commitment. That is, a goal attainment is facilitated when the person is commited to the goal and does what he or she can to consummate the goal. If people drop out in the middle of a task designed to achieve a goal, then the result is task non-completion. The goal cannot be attained given that the task is not completed, and thus satisfaction cannot be experienced.

Another study of families conducted by Henry and Lovelace (1995) has produced findings consistent with the goal commitment principle. The study showed that regularity in household routines significantly improved daily personal satisfaction. That is, routinized work is a reflection of goal commitment, and thus facilitates goal attainment.

Yet another study by Turner (1994) has shown that the difference between those who have happy personal relationships and those who have unhappy relationships does not lie in personal conflicts but in goal commitment. Agreements to resolve marital conflict have to *follow through*. Those who did follow through with agreed-upon changes after marital counseling were more satisfied with their marital relationships than those who did not.

Yet another study by Emmons, Cheung, and Tehrani (1998) showed how personal goal strivings contribute to subjective well being. They focused on spiritual strivings and measured this construct by asking respondents to write how they go about meeting their religious goals. Examples of spiritual strivings (see Emmons, 1999, p. 102) include statements such as "praise God everyday whether my situation is good or bad," "spend time reading the Bible every morning," "volunteer my time and talent in my church," "say my prayers daily," and " take a Sabbath." Higher levels of personal goal strivings mean greater goal commitment. This measure of spiritual strivings was positively and significantly correlated with measures of subjective well being.

Speaking about religion and religiosity, Buddha once said,

". . . The thoughtless man, even if he can recite a large portion of the law, but is not a doer of it, has no share in the religious life. . . . . The follower of the law, even if he can recite only a small portion of it, . . . possesses true knowledge and serenity of mind; he . . . has indeed shared in the religious life (Krieger, Reynolds, & Neill, 1997, p. 81)

The Commitment Principle of Goal Implementation: *Action reflective of goal commitment (e.g., persistent effort even in light of failure outcomes) in the context of a life domain contributes to subjective well being by enhancing the likelihood of goal attainment in that domain. Goal attainment is a major source of domain satisfaction and subjective well being.*

The *goal commitment principle* tells us that you cannot bring joy to your life by wishing things only. These wishes have to come true, and for them to come true, you have to pursue them and pursue them vigorously. In other words, you have to be committed to your goals. Without a strong commitment to your goals these goals are not likely to materialise. So stick to your goals and do not give up in light of failure. Repeated attempts and hard work will get you there. And once you get there you will see that it was worth it after all.

33.2 Feedback

Action designed to enhance positive affect in a life domain is based on feedback, i.e., past learning. The simple fact that people learn from their mistakes allows them to adjust their actions by selecting actions that are more likely to produce positive affect based on trial and error learning. Most important is the adaptation of goals to life circumstances. After repeated failure people tend to adjust the goals to make them "more realistic." This means, that people learn strategies by trial and error. Strategies that are not successful are abandoned and new strategies are implemented. This trial-and-error learning helps select effective strategies that result in goal attainment.

The Feedback Principle of Goal Implementation: Trial-and-error learning facilitates task completion and therefore the experience of satisfaction that follows from task completion and goal attainment. Trial-and-error learning entails trying out different ways to accomplish the task, those that lead to task completion are identified and reinforced.

The *trial-an-error learning* principle is a very basic principle from the psychology of learning. This principle recommends that we learn from our mistakes. Our mistakes can show us how to achieve our goals. Use this learning wisely to help you in the future accomplish your important life goals.

RE-APPRAISAL

This chapter describes re-appraisal as a strategy that people can use to enhance their subjective quality of life. The chapter describes what re-appraisal is and how the strategy can be implemented through at least four different ways. These are active teaching, spirituality, emotional support, and passage of time.

34. WHAT IS RE-APPRAISAL?

Figures 24 and 25 illustrate the process of re-appraisal graphically. The top portion of the figure (Figure 24) shows a person who is moderately satisfied with his life. He is happy with his family life, moderately satisfied with his work life, and dissatisfied with his leisure life. He recalls positive events in his family life, some positive and some negative events in his work life, and mostly negative events in his leisure life. Figure 25 shows the process of re-appraisal. He re-appraised the negative events at work causing him to feel good about those events. Now he feels much better about his work life, which in turn made a contribution to increasing satisfaction with life overall. The focal point of the re-appraisal is shedding new meaning on the negative events at work (events 1). Suppose the person in question, let us call her Kathryn, is a medical researcher and a professor of medicine at a renowned medical school. Her research has focused on diabetes. She has conducted a program of research showing how changes in lifestyle (diet, exercise, stress management, leisure activities, etc.) can reduce the symptoms of diabetes in a mature population. She has published much of this research in medical speciality journals related to diabetes. However, she thinks that success and recognition for her research is likely to come from publications in the most renowned medical journals such as the *New England Journal of Medicine* and the *Journal of the American Medical Association*, not in the medical speciality journals related to diabetes. She has tried to get her research published in these journals with no success. These journals typically publish research considered "pioneering" and "path breaking," which is not characteristic of her research. Therefore, she feels bad about this aspect of her work life.

She re-appraises this particular set of events.   She realises that her publications in the diabetes journals are likely to be more impactful than publications in the most prestigious general journals of medicine. This is because physicians who specialise in the treatment of diabetes are more likely to regularly subscribe to diabetes-related medical journals than the most prestigious medical journals. Hence, her research is likely to reach the targeted audience in a more timely and effective way. This re-appraisal has made her feel much better about her work life, which, in turn, made her feel better about her life overall.

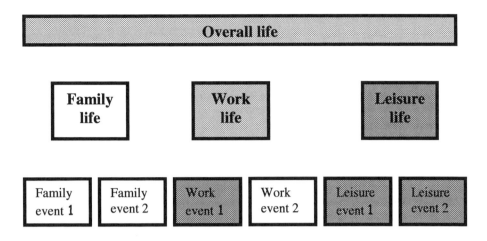

Figure 24. [Re-appraisal--Before]

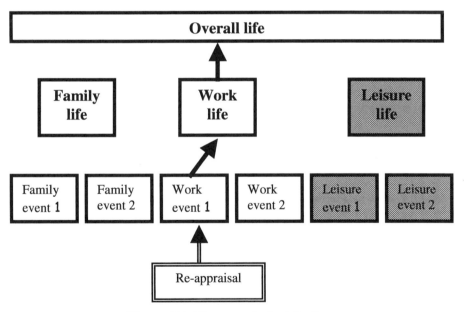

Figure 25. [Re-appraisal--After]

There is much evidence in the literature suggesting that the way people interpret their life circumstances has a lot to do with the way they feel about life.

- Theories of coping are based on the idea that in order to cope with problems, happy people initiate thoughts and behaviours that are adaptive and helpful in solving their problems. In contrast, unhappy people cope in more destructive ways. For example, happy people are more likely to see the bright side of things, pray, and tackle their problems head on, whereas unhappy people are more likely to blame others and themselves and avoid working on their problems (McCrae & Costa, 1986). In other words, how happiness may be influenced by the valence of one's thoughts.

- People might increase their subjective well being by controlling their thoughts. For example, studies have shown that on average religious people are happier than nonreligious people (e.g., Ellison, 1991; Myers, 1992; Pollner, 1989). This may be due to the fact that religious people believe in a larger meaning or force in the universe. In other words, thoughts about one's place in the large scheme of things influence subjective well being.

- Studies have shown that one can heighten subjective well being by being optimistic about one's future (Scheier & Carver, 1993). In other words, thinking about the future in positive or negative terms influence subjective well being.

- The attributional theory of depression (Beck, 1967) asserts that depressed people are more likely to believe that negative events are caused by global and stable causes, and that negative events are very likely to continue to happen to them. Depressed people think about the world in self-defeating ways. Agains, this illustrates how negative thoughts can affect subjective well being.

- Quality-of-life researchers (Larsen, Diener, & Croponzano, 1987) found that one can dampen or amplify one's emotions by what one thinks, and thereby experience more or less intense emotions. Again, this demonstrates the power of thought and appraisals on subjective well being.

- Much research has shown that happy people are not more successful than unhappy people. Their life experiences are almost the same. What is different is the way they view the world, the way they appraise life events. Unhappy people tend to *appraise* their life events negatively, while happy people do the opposite (Lyubomirsky, 1994; Lyubomirsky & Ross, 1997; Seidlitz & Diener, 1993). People with high subjective well being are also more likely to perceive "neutral" events as positive. Thus, people with high SWB may not only experience objectively more positive events, but they also seem to perceive events more positively than do people who are low in SWB. The old adage of "some see the glass as half full while others see it as half empty" applies here. Happy people usually appraise their life events positively (they see the glass as half full). Unhappy people appraise events negatively (they see the as glass half-empty).

- Brown and Dutton (1995) found that happy people interpret defeat differently from unhappy people. Happy people usually explain it away. They attribute defeat to an isolated incident that indicates little about their ability. Unhappy people, on the other hand, take defeat quite personally. They focus on it, magnify, and dwell on it. Defeat colours their future vision too. They predict that they will fail in the future because of that defeat (cf. Cheng & Furnham, 2001; Panos, 1997).

- Brebner (1995) maintains that unhappy people see negative things not only in relation to defeat but also in relation to any world event. Unhappy people tend to infer "hidden agendas" in people's actions. For example, if a person acts benevolently towards another, the unhappy person is likely to think the benevolent act is motivated by an ulterior motive, i.e., personal gain. Happy people, on the other hand, see benevolence as motivated by a caring attitude (cf. Scott & McIntosh, 1999).

- What happens when a person receives a job promotion? Happy people feel quite rewarded and look forward to the new responsibilities; unhappy people lament the added responsibilities (Chen, 1996).

- Staats, Armstrong-Stassen, and Partillo (1995) have shown that personal setbacks and triumphs are not by themselves good predictors of life satisfaction. What predicts life satisfaction significantly is the perception of causes and consequences of those events.

- Research by Gross (2000) has shown that re-appraisals tend to reduce negative emotional experiences with little cost. That the re-appraisal strategy is more effective than the suppression strategy. Suppression strategy refers to coping strategy people use by "suppressing" their emotions. They do not allow themselves to "feel". They do this by detaching themselves from life.

The Re-appraisal Principle: Re-interpreting significant negative events can convert negative affect associated with these events into positive affect. This should decrease dissatisfaction in the domain housing these events. Conversely, re-interpreting significant positive events can enhance the positive valence of the events, thereby increasing satisfaction in the domain housing these events. Doing so should help enhance subjective well being.

Frisch (in press) has developed a model of quality-of-life therapy. The model is based on several strategies of change, one of them is attitude change. Changing attitudes involves re-interpreting events and circumstances in one's life. For example, a man believes that he failed in marriage and therefore he is doomed to fail in finding a life partner. Such generalisation is likely to cause a great deal of sadness and grief. Such misinterpretation can be corrected by a convincing argument that failing in one marriage does not mean that he is doomed to fail in establishing a future romantic relationship.

Frisch recommends a variety of psychotherapy techniques to help with attitude change (in press, chapter 4). An example is the *stress diary technique*. This technique guides the client to identify times when he or she is upset. He or she attempts to identify and articulate the feelings and thoughts related to the negative feelings. The diary then guides the person to identify positive responses to the negative thoughts. That is, the client is encouraged to develop realistic and positive counter arguments to the negative thoughts. Counter arguments can be generated by using another technique Frisch calls "questions-in court". This technique forces the client to assess the situation as objectively as possible. Therefore, counter arguments can be generated by examining the credibility of the evidence and discounting that misinterpretation based on lack of evidence or pointing to evidence that can support a contrary interpretation.

Rational-emotive psychotherapy is very much based on the notion that unhappiness can be transformed into happiness through *rational thought* (Ellis, 1962). The underlying assumption of rational-emotive therapy is that people can be happy if and when they think rationally. What does rationality mean in rational-emotive therapy? It is defined through "irrationality." Irrationality is thought that is illogical, biased, prejudiced, and highly personalised. Thus, unhappiness is the result of self-verbalisations determined, not by external circumstances or events, but by the perceptions toward these events. Perceptions of events are influenced by how people interpret those events. Interpretation is subject to those beliefs that are evoked from memory for the purpose of categorising and giving meaning to that event. Certain beliefs used to interpret events tend to lead to irrational thought. Ellis identifies 11 such irrational beliefs.

1. It is essential that one be loved or approved by virtually everyone in his community.
2. One must be perfectly competent, adequate, and achieving to consider oneself worthwhile.
3. Some people are bad, wicked, or villainous and therefore should be blamed and punished.
4. It is a terrible catastrophe when things are not as one wants them to be.
5. Unhappiness is caused by outside circumstances, and the individual has no control over it.
6. Dangerous or fearsome things are causes for great concern, and their possibility must be continually dwelt upon.
7. It is easier to avoid certain difficulties and self-responsibilities than to face them.
8. One should be dependent on others and must have someone stronger on whom to rely on.
9. Past experiences and events are the determiners of present behaviour; the influence of the past cannot be eradicated.
10. One should be quite upset over other people's problems and disturbances.
11. There is always a right or perfect solution to every problem, and it must be found or the results will be catastrophic.

According to Ellis, these beliefs cause distortions in perceptions and irrational thinking. Irrational thinking, in turn, leads to unhappiness. For example, let us focus on the last belief ("there is always a right or perfect solution to every problem, and it must be found or the results will be catastrophic"). This belief causes irrational thinking because, in reality, there is no such perfect solution to any problem. Any problem can be solved through a variety of ways. The effectiveness of any one solution is highly dependent on the theoretical approach used to judge effectiveness. Insistence on finding the perfect solution leads people to judge effectiveness from one narrow perspective. Deviations from standards as specified from that narrow perspective might cause the individual to be extra critical of many events and outcomes. This negativity forms the basis of the negative affect in many life domains, which in turn affects subjective well being adversely.

So how do we change irrational thinking? How can we become more rational? Rational-emotive therapy recommends that we do this by learning to think rationally. Ridding oneself of the irrational beliefs that are the causes for the misinterpretation does this. Thus, the first step is to identify the irrational belief that is causing you to appraise the event in a negative way. Second, replace the irrational belief with its rational counterpart.

Niven (2000) recommends the following:

> When things go poorly, we sometimes start a list of ways we failed, ways we caused the problem. This kind of thinking not only can upset us, it also can keep us from being able to function. The truth is that any situation is the result of some things that are in your control and some things that are out of your control. Don't delude yourself into thinking a bad situation is completely of your making. Remember that it makes more sense to deal with outcomes than with fault (p. 92).

35. FACTORS AFFECTING RE-APPRAISALS

The literature suggests many strategies people use to help them re-appraise negative events. These include re-appraisal through active teaching, re-appraisal through spirituality, re-appraisal through social support, and re-appraisal through the passage of time.

35.1 Active Teaching

Rational-emotive therapy (Ellis, 1962) recommends re-appraisal through active teaching. That is, the counsellor assumes an active teaching role to re-educate the client. S/He identifies the irrational beliefs and demonstrates to the client why these beliefs are irrational and therefore dysfunctional. The self-defeating verbalisations (the irrational beliefs) are brought to the client's attention in a forceful and direct way. The counsellor shows the client how these self-defeating verbalisations cause his or her unhappiness. The counsellor then teaches the client how to re-think, challenge, contradict, and re-verbalise these beliefs to make them more logical and rational. Finally, the counsellor encourages, persuades, and cajoles the client into acting in ways that are consistent with the newly formed rational beliefs.

The Teaching Principle of Re-appraisal: Re-interpreting significant negative events in rational terms can convert negative affect associated with these events into positive affect. This should decrease dissatisfaction witin the domain housing these events. A person (e.g., counsellor) who assumes the role of the teacher can facilitate this re-interpretation. Doing so should enhance subjective well being.

Based on the *teaching-appraisal principle*, we can re-appraise negative events to increase our happiness. To do so we need to solicit the aid of a trusted counsellor, friend, or colleague who we think may help us challenge the beliefs that are causing us to perceive certain events negatively. This person should become our mentor. Again, the key here is trust. We need to select a person we think as credible, because we need to believe in what he or she says is true. Hence trust and credibility are very important. This person should mentor us in the way we see the world, and particularly in the way we interpret those events that are troubling us. Our mentor should be encouraged to challenge our irrational beliefs and teach us to think differently, more rationally, logically, and positively.

35.2 Spirituality

Spirituality refers to a system of beliefs and actions thet reflect an appreciation of "a greater whole". The greater whole can be a belief in God in the religious sense (and actions to abide by the word of God) or merely beliefs and actions reflecting one's true self is a small part "nature", "the planet", "the community", and/or "family". In other words, spirituality motivates the person to focus away from the self and toward a "greater whole".

Folkman (1997) found that among those who were struck by the HIV virus, some coped better than others do. Those who coped better seemed to interpret the affliction spiritually, and therefore they find purpose and meaning in this occurrence. Doing so reduced the potential negative impact on subjective well being (cf. McCrae & Costa, 1986; Emmons, 1999).

Research on the effect of religion on life satisfaction has shown that people who held strong spiritual beliefs tend to be more satisfied with their lives than those who do not hold strong spiritual beliefs. This finding cuts across all religious affiliations (Gerwood, LeBlanc, & Piazza, 1998).

A study by Lipkus, Dalbert, and Siegler (1996), dealing with crime and victimisation, showed that those who believed that there is justice in this world expressed higher levels of life satisfaction than those who did not believe in justice. The subjects were either crime victims or knew of someone close to them who was a crime victim. Swinyard, Kau, and Phua (2001) also found that happiness is positively related to intrinsic and extrinsic religiosity in two samples (US and Singapore). Intrinsic religiosity refers to the extent to which a person has a system of religious beliefs, whereas extrinsic religiosity refers to a system of actions that reflect religious faith.

The Spiritual Principle of Re-appraisal: Re-interpreting significant negative events in spiritual terms can convert negative affect associated with these events into positive affect. This should decrease dissatisfaction within the domain housing these events. Conversely, re-interpreting significant positive events in spiritual terms may enhance the positive valence of the events, thereby increasing satisfaction. Doing so should enhance subjective well being.

Niven (2000) maintains "religion can show us the way in a world in which bad things happen. It can teach us much of what we see is so complex we cannot understand why and how it occurred (p. 43)."

35.3 Social Support

Scheck, Kinicki, and Davy (1997) have investigated how employees re-appraise work stressors and how this re-appraisal affects subjective well being. Specifically, subjective well being was hypothesised to be directly influenced by problem and emotion-focused re-appraisals. *Emotion-focused re-appraisal* involves attempts to reduce the emotional distress associated with the stressful situation through emotional social support. For example, the employee re-appraises the work stressor by discussing it with others to obtain emotional support.

This notion of emotional support coming from others was confirmed by an experimental study conducted with a group of women who expressed dissatisfaction with their life (Hunter & Liao, 1995). One group of women were introduced to others who provided them with emotional support, the other groups were left to deal with their problems on their own. Those who received the emotional support from others were able to re-appraise their life circumstances and showed a marked improvement in life satisfaction compared to the women who did not receive the emotional support.

In contrast, *problem-focused re-appraisals* involve attempts to reduce stress through instrumental social support--activities such as receiving practical help from others. For example, the employee receives help with family or work responsibilities, advice in resolving situations, and/or financial aid. Thus, workers appraise stressors less negatively when they engage in problem- and emotion-focused coping than those who do not take coping action.

The Social Support Principle of Re-appraisal: Re-interpreting significant negative events with the assistance of significant others can reduce the valence of the negative affect associated with these events. This should decrease dissatisfaction within the domain housing these events. Doing so should enhance subjective well being.

David Myers, author of *The Pursuit of Happiness* (1993), has reviewed the literature relating spirituality with subjective well-being and concluded that religiously active people in Europe and the USA are happier than their non-religious counterparts. Religious people also are much less likely to become delinquent, to abuse drugs and alcohol, to divorce, or to commit suicide. They are also physically healthier. Myers explains that religion plays an important role in buffering personal crises. For example, a person who experiences a loss, such as death of a spouse, interprets the loss in ways that is less damaging to the person's subjective well being. Belonging to a church allows that person to seek the *social and emotional support* from church members. The support helps the person re-interpret the loss in ways that preserves satisfaction with life. So the message to those who seek personal growth is get involved with church, synagogue, mosque, temple, or religious *fellowships* that can give you the social and emotional support you'll need in moments of crisis. This support is important to help you adjust to the negative events of your life by giving those events new meaning.

35.4 Time

As the saying goes, "time heals wounds." When bad things happen, sometimes giving it time helps heal the wound. The disappointment becomes less intense, and the distress created by the negative affect dissipates as life takes new directions. Bless, Clore, Schwarz, and Golisano (1996) have shown that happy people are not immune to negative events. They deal with those events by not thinking about them and allowing time to "heal the wounds".

The Time Principle of Re-appraisal: Dissatisfaction in a given domain arising from a significant negative event decreases over time. Thus, domain dissatisfaction can be reduced by allowing time to pass without thinking and dwelling on the negative event. Doing so enhance subjective well being.

The message from the *time-healing* principle is straightforward. Let time help you heal the wound. Passage of time allows emotion to be less intense. Other events take over more importance with the passage of time. So allow time to intervene, if all else fails.

PART IV:

INTER/INTRA-DOMAIN STRATEGIES

The chapter on *balance* (Chapter 14) constitutes the fourth part of the book and serves to tie things together. This chapter focuses on combining the inter- and intra-psychological dynamics of the previous chapters (chapters 4 through 13) to show how subjective well being can be enhanced through balance--balance within life domains and balance between and among domains. Specifically, the balance strategy refers to how people engage in events to generate both positive and negative affect within a given life domain and how they compensate across life domains. Positive affect in a domain serves to enhance subjective well being in the here and now. Negative affect serves to motivate the individual to plan ahead to correct past mistakes and to take advantage of new opportunities. Negative affect is the basis for motivation to strive to attain future goals. People anticipate and desire future happiness.

Psychological principles of balance are developed to help people use balance concretely. The balance principle is further qualified by several factors. These are the satisfaction quota, aggregation, and satisfaction efficiency factors. Additional balance principles are formulated based on these factors.

14

BALANCE

This chapter is about the use of balance as a strategy for personal development. I will describe in some detail this strategy and recommend advice on implementation. I will make a distinction between two balance concepts, within-domain balance and between-domain balance. Then I will describe three additional principles shedding additional light on the principle of balance. These are the quota principle of domain satisfaction, the principle of aggregation of domain satisfaction, and the principle of satisfaction efficiency. I will show how one can use these additional principles to help enhance subjective quality of life.

36. WHAT IS BALANCE?

Figures 26 and 27 show an individual before and after implementing balance. The before situation describes a person who feels very good about his family life (determined mostly by family events that are all positive), moderately negative about his work life (determined by moderately negative and very negative events at work), and very negative about his leisure life (determined by leisure events that have generated intense negative feelings). The principle of balance dictates that subjective well being can be enhanced by creating balance among the life domains (see Figure 27). This means to experience a balance between positive and negative affect *within* and *between* life domains. Balance within a life domain is achieved by experiencing both positive and negative events. Positive events serve a reward function, i.e., goals are attained and resources are acquired. In contrast, negative events serve a motivational function, i.e., these events lead the person to recognise problems and opportunities for further achievement and growth.

Balance between life domains is achieved through compensation (a principle described in some detail in a previous chapter). That is, increasing the salience of positive life domains compensates for negative life domains. And conversely, increasing the salience of negative life domains compensates for positive life domains. Increasing the salience of negative life domains motivates the individual to pay greater attention to that domain. Increasing the salience of negative life domains prompts the individual to engage in corrective action within these domains. The goal is to decrease the negative valence of beliefs related to one's evaluation of the totality of a negative life domain.

Figure 27 shows the individual achieving balance by increasing the salience of both family life and leisure life. Increasing the salience of leisure life serves to motivate the individual to engage in activities to generate positive feelings in that domain. However, increasing the salience of a negative life domain (i.e., leisure life) would generate more dissatisfaction than satisfaction with life overall. Hence, to avoid experiencing dissatisfaction below intolerable levels, this individual has compensated by increasing the salience of family life from which he experiences much joy. Thus, balance is achieved within the three life domains—family, work, and leisure. Balance is also achieved within the leisure and work domains by engaging in leisure and work activities resulting in positive affect.

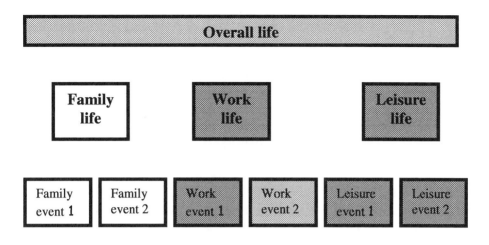

Figure 26. [Balance--Before]

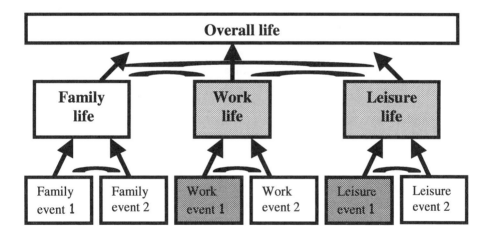

Figure 27. [Balance--After]

Suggestive evidence of the viability of the principle of balance lies in the Ying and Yang notion, which is popular in East Asian cultures. The Ying and Yang concept posits that subjective well being can be achieved by keeping a good balance between positive and negative emotions (Kitayama & Markus, 2000). The adage is to remain calm, undisturbed, and unaroused. Thus, the Ying and Yang is balanced between fulfilment of physical and spiritual needs. Kitayama and Markus report findings from Japan about correlations between positive and negative affect. These correlations were mostly positive and significant (in contrast to negative correlations among U.S. subjects). The authors explain that the East Asian culture dictates that positive events such as achievement and success may generate envy by others and criticism for "showing off." Conversely, negative events may not be perceived as all "bad." Negative events offer opportunity for learning and personal growth. Thus, one can argue that the notion of the Ying and Yang promotes balance *within* life domains. People are encouraged to seek balance in their lives by using the bad to create good; or simply accepting the good with the bad, the positive with the negative, and success with failure.

The Principle of Balance Within Life Domains: *Balance within a life domain contributes to the enhancement of subjective well being in the long run. Balance within a life domain involves action designed to balance positive and negative events within that domain.*

The advice one can take from the *principle of balance within life domains* is simple. Accept a little humility in your life. Do not shy away from making mistakes. Mistakes can be a source of strength. You can learn from these mistakes to continue to grow. Mistakes highlight opportunities for growth. Mistakes offer challenges for the future. Conquests and goal achievements, on the other hand, provide you with "food that nourishes your soul." These personal triumphs help you give meaning to your past. Savour them. Indulge in your accomplishments and appreciate them. Therefore, accept the good with the bad; and acknowledge your successes in light of your failures. Savour the good things that happen to you, and plan the future by learning from your tumbles and falls. Do this with a sense of purpose and balance. Balance is important, because if you dwell so much on your failures, then the future may look all gloom and doom. And if you only dwell on the successes you may cease to grow. Balance gives you a reason to hope for a future that continues to bring meaning to your life.

With respect to balance *across* life domains, there is some evidence suggesting that people are more satisfied with life when the source of the satisfaction derives from *multiple* life domains than a single domain. For example, Bhargava (1995) conducted a study in which subjects were asked to discuss life satisfaction of others. Most subjects inferred life satisfaction of others as a direct function of their satisfaction in multiple domains. They calculated happiness by averaging the satisfaction across several important domains.

Additional evidence comes from a study conducted by Chen (1996). This author found those who believe they will achieve some of their goals and receive satisfaction from multiple domains report higher levels of life satisfaction than those who do not believe that they will achieve these goals.

The Principle of Balance Between Life Domains: Balance between life domains serves to enhance subjective well being. Balance involves increasing the salience of negative and positive life domains. Increasing the salience of a negative domain serves to heighten motivation to take future action to increase satisfaction in that domain. In contrast, increasing the salience of positive life domains serves to generate more positive affect to compensate for the increased negative affect--resulting from the increased salience of the negative life domain.

This strategy has several implications. First, the strategy implies that "putting all your eggs in one basket" may not be effective in enhancing subjective well being. That is, one should not allow one or two life domains to overwhelm one's satisfaction or dissatisfaction with life. It is best to be invested emotionally in several domains. Doing so allows one to compensate for the dissatisfaction of some domains with satisfaction of other domains.

Frisch (in press, chapters 3 and 4) has addressed the issue of "putting all your eggs in one basket" by recounting the story of a patient named Carol. Carol put all her energy into caring for her children. She did not do anything significant in terms of leisure and recreation. She hardly saw any adult friends, although her friends were very important at one point in her life. Frisch assessed Carol's situation as putting all her emotional eggs in the one basket of family life. This is a dangerous strategy because if things go wrong in Carol's family life, she is likely to feel depressed. And this is exactly what happened. She over invested herself in the family domain. To overcome this problem, Frisch's recommends the use of the "happiness pie" and "vision quest" techniques. These techniques are methods to allow psychotherapy clients to establish some meaningful goals and priorities in their life. The therapist asks the client to draw a picture of his or her life in terms of a pie chart. Overall happiness is the pie composed of particular slices that make up overall happiness. Some slices are larger than others because they are more important. The therapist instructs the client to think about 16 areas of life, namely physical health, self-esteem, philosophy of life, standard of living, work, recreation, learning, creativity, helping activities, love relationship, friendships, relationships with children, relationships with relatives, home, neighbourhood, and community. The therapist then asks the client to "draw a picture of what areas seem to dominate your life most now. In other words, where is most of your time and mental energy going?" If the picture drawn turns out to be a pie with one or two life domains (e.g., work), then the therapist guides the client to do some soul searching and develop a new pie that reflects new priorities concerning what the client really wants out of life. The therapist is guided by the balance principle--the more balanced the pie the more likely that the client can experience life satisfaction and happiness. The *vision quest technique* is used as a follow-up to the *happiness pie exercise*. The goal here is to clarify the client's goals and priorities in life. The client is instructed to go over each of the 16 life domains and identify goals the person would like to achieve during one's "limited time on earth." After doing so, the client is urged to select about five goals that are considered to be the most important lifetime goals. For example, Frisch cites how one client identified specific lifetime goals in the area of health, play and friendship, love, work, self-esteem, and spiritual life. He started out by admitting that the only life domain that really mattered was work, work, and more work.

37. FACTORS AFFECTING BALANCE

Let us explore the effect of treating one, several, or many life domains as highly important. We will classify people in three categories, those who "put all their eggs in one basket," those who "put most of their eggs in several but few baskets," and those who "evenly divide all their eggs in too many baskets." Those who "put all their eggs in one basket" are those who invest themselves emotionally in one life domain, and thus their happiness is dependent on how well they do in that domain and that domain only. Let us call these people "the imbalanced types." Those who "put most of their eggs in several but few baskets" are those who regard a small number of life domains (e.g., three or four) as highly important, with the remaining life domains as unimportant. We will call these people "the moderately balanced types." Finally, those who "evenly divide all their eggs into too many baskets" are those who spread themselves too thinly. They are not emotionally involved in life. They choose not to invest themselves in any single domain. They carry on with a certain degree of detachment in all of life's domains. We will call these people "the very balanced types."

37.1 Satisfaction Quota

We theorise that the imbalanced types are likely to have heightened emotional involvement in only one domain. Specifically, the imbalanced types are likely to experience events and outcomes intensely. If things are right in that one most important domain, they feel happy. In contrast, if things are not as expected, then they feel very unhappy. This may be due to the fact that the imbalanced types have been socialised in an environment in which self-worth is defined through accomplishments in one domain and that domain only. Thus, they set goals in that domain higher and more value-laden than those who do not invest themselves much in one domain-- the moderately balanced types and the very-balanced types. The imbalanced types are not likely to experience high levels of subjective well being even though they may experience high levels of satisfaction in their chosen domain. This is because overall life satisfaction requires the satisfaction of a variety of needs. If one adopts Maslow's view of human needs (biological, safety, social, esteem, self-actualisation, knowledge, and beauty), then one can argue that it is highly unlikely that one can adequately satisfy all of the human needs through participation in one domain alone. Subjective well being comes from the satisfaction of a variety of human needs, which can only be satisfied effectively from several life domains.

Take for example this person I call Corey. Corey is entirely focused on achieving wealth in life, at the expense of family, leisure, community, friendship, and love. Corey has achieved high levels of satisfaction from his material life, but he remains not happy with his life at large. Why? This is because the satisfaction stemming from the material domain contributes only so much to overall life satisfaction and happiness. In other words, there may be a *quota* of satisfaction that can be allowed to spillover from a given life domain to overall life. In other words, satisfaction with life overall cannot come from only one source or one life domain. There is a cap of amount of satisfaction in any given life domain that can spillover to the most superordinate domain involving life overall. This is because people have different needs (biological, safety, social, esteem, etc.). It is extremely unlikely to satisfy the full range of human developmental needs in an effective manner through experiences in only one domain.

Consider a person who is workaholic. She may love her job and spends a great deal of time and effort at work. She is very successful in her profession. Her needs for self-actualization, esteem, affiliation, and even safety (economically speaking) may be satisfied from her experiences at work. But what about love, physical intimacy, family, and the need to care for a dependent other like a child? These needs are biologically engrained and cannot be easily met through professional work alone.

This is an important point that brings us back to the notion that subjective well being is not simply cumulative positive minus negative affect-- irrespective of the source. It is the satisfaction of human developmental needs, the full range of needs--not a handful of selected needs. One cannot substitute positive affect related to one need with another need. To illustrate with an arithmetic example, suppose that a person's level of subjective well being is 50 (on a scale varying from -100 to +100). This means that she is relatively happy with life. The source of this moderate degree of happiness come from five key life domains--work, leisure, family, community, and neighborhood. Now let us focus on the work life domain. She has +15 points of satisfaction. The satisfaction quota in the work domain is +10. In other words, only 10 out of the 15 could contribute to subjective well being. She is +5 over the limit in her work domain. This does not mean that she does not feel good about her work life. Yes, she does. But only so much of that satisfaction can contribute to her overall life satisfaction. Why? Because satisfaction from work life may reflect the satisfaction of only a subset of human developmental needs, not the full range of these needs.

Evidence of this phenomenon comes from a body of evidence showing that materialism is negatively correlated with life satisfaction (see Wright and Larsen, 1993, for a meta-analysis of the research findings). Here, materialists can be viewed as imbalanced people in that they regard wealth and material possessions to be most important in life. Materialists who are successful hoarding material wealth may feel successful and happy with their material life. But there is so much happiness that can be extracted from the material domain. Placing undue emphasis on making money is likely to lead them to neglect their family, their place in the community, their social life, and so forth. This neglect is likey to create negative affect in these respective life domains--family, neighborhood, social, leisure, and spiritual life. Negative affect from these other domains in turn adversely affects subjective well being. The overall result is that materialists are likely to be more unhappy than happy with their lives.

The Quota Principle of Balance: *Satisfaction from one life domain can contribute only a limited amount (a quota) to subjective well being. Conversely, dissatisfaction in one life domain can adversely affect subjective well being up to some threshold (or limit).*

What advice can people seeking personal growth take away from the quota principle? Niven (2000) articulates good advice; he recommends: "don't let your entire life hinge on one element" (p. 71). He asserts:

> Your life is made up of many different facets. Don't focus on one aspect of your life so much that you can't experience pleasure if that one area is unsettled. It can become all you think about, and it can deaden your enjoyment of everything else—things you would otherwise love (p. 71).

37.2 Aggregation

Now, let us contrast the life of the *imbalanced* person (Corey) with that of the very-balanced type. Let us call this very-balanced person Joey. Joey can be characterized as follows. He manages his life well. He has things under control. He has his job, wife, children, church, friends, neighbors, community, leisure, politics, and sports, among others. His life is highly regimented. He has his work habits, his habits dealing with his wife and kids. He has his church habit, watching sports, fishing, and so on. However, he is not emotionally invested in any one of these life domains. He is invested only some in each. One can say that this person's life is on "automatic pilot." If things deviate from the set course, his well-established and engrained habits bring him back on track. For example, his goals in relation to his job are quite modest. His father was a baker and was running his own bakery. Joey's father expected his son to work at the bakery and take over someday. Joey is carrying on in his father's footsteps. It has been a tradition within the family. He knows that he is not very smart to be some top executive in a Fortune 500 company. He knows that he can run the bakery, and he does a good job at that.

So we ask, is Joey a happy person? The answer to this question is yes, but his happiness is not likely to be fulfilling. The question arises: Who is likely to feel greater happiness in life, Joey or Corey? The answer is Joey, of course! This is because Joey has more life domains in which he extracts satisfaction from. Even though the satisfaction extracted from each life domain may be small, the aggregate of all the satisfactions from all the domains amounts to a level of overall life satisfaction greater than that of Joey's. Again, we go back to satisfaction of human developmental needs. In Joey's case, he may feel more satisfied with life because he aggregates satisfaction from different life domains. This aggregation of positive affect is likely to reflect satisfaction of different human developmental needs--not constrained to a select few.

The Aggregation Principle of Balance: Aggregating various amounts of satisfaction from various life domains serves to enhance subjective well being. The more satisfaction is experienced from multiple life domains, the higher the subjective well being.

What is the message communicated by the *aggregation* principle? Do not put all your eggs in one basket. To satisfy the full range of developmental needs, you should get involved in life by participating in a variety of domains. The more the better! You can experience personal growth by becoming an active participant in life's diversity. Become fully engaged at work. Get more involved with your family, wife, and kids. Seek out exciting leisure and recreational activities. Get to know your neighbours and be an active citizen in your community. Participate in politics. Be a voter and exercise your civic duties. Enhance your relationships with your friends, co-workers, and relatives. In other words, experience the richness and diversity that life offers.

37.3 Satisfaction Efficiency

Now let us focus on the *moderately balanced* person. Pomerantz, Saxon, and Oishi (1998) conducted a study related to the moderately balanced issue. They were able to show that people with more "very important" goals have higher life satisfaction than people whose goals were not as important. What does this mean? A person investing in fewer domains that are very important to him and succeeds in these domains is more likely to be a happier person compared to a person who either invests himself in too many life domains (with less important goals) or a person who invests himself exclusively in one life domain (with one overriding and very important goal). The person who invests in fewer domains that are important is what I call "moderately-balanced". Let us call this person a name, David.

David has four important life domains in which he emotionally invests himself. Let us say those life domains are work, family, leisure, and health. In relation to work, David has a passion for his job. He is a surgeon. He loves what he does and feels mentally challenged. He feels that that his work counts for something important. His goals and aspirations in regard to his job are high but realistic, and he feels he is making significant progress towards the realisation of these goals. David has a family too—a wife and two children. His relationship with his wife is based on love, respect, and warmth. His wife has her own career, and she feels sufficiently rewarded from her job. Both he and his wife make decent salaries enough to support the material needs of the family. His children, now in their adolescent years, are doing well in school. They have good friends; they are healthy; and they get along great with him and their mother. He loves watching his children learn new things and gets quite excited teaching them about things in life. He loves his kids and cares a great deal about their welfare. In regard to his health, he feels good too. He plays tennis with two of his work colleagues. He feels challenged playing this game and gets a good workout. He tries to eat healthy and takes vitamins on a daily basis. Overall, he feels good about his health. His leisure life is also good. In addition to playing tennis and spending quality leisure time with his wife and children at home, they have exciting family vacations. Each year the family goes to an exotic place. Most of their vacations are quite exhilarating. Furthermore, he and his wife have three close families that they regularly socialise with. One family lives right next door to them. They visit quite often. They get together with the two other families once or twice a month. They host an evening in which the three couples play a game of cards--bridge. They have much fun doing this. In sum, David is a happy man. He is emotionally involved in work, family, leisure, and health, and he feels sufficiently rewarded in these life domains.

The question that needs to be posed here is why David (the more moderately balanced person) is happier than Joey (the very-balanced person)? This is because David has focused on several domains that satisfy most of the human needs (biological, safety, social, esteem, self-actualisation, knowledge, and beauty). There is a principle of *satisfaction efficiency* that plays an important role here. That is, subjective well being is better served through satisfaction from a small set of important life domains than a larger set of domains that are equally important. The intensity of satisfaction experienced in a given life domain is inversely proportional to the amount of effort used to generate that satisfaction. The more effort consumed the less the satisfaction. Investing in life domains that are likely to meet all or most of the human needs is a much more effective strategy than investing oneself in many domains and "spreading one thinly."

Let us go back to Joey. Joey makes enough money to meet his family's economic needs. He works at his father's bakery, and he hopes to own the business after his father retires. He works to earn a living, and he too is looking forward to retirement to devote more time to fishing. As you can guess his leisure life is centred on fishing. He enjoys fishing but it comes at an expense. He travels around 100 miles to reach the lake. It costs him a lot in gas and wear and tear on his pickup truck. The truck is continuously in need of repairs because of this. He pulls a fishing boat with it. He watches sports on television, but the satisfaction he gets from this seems to be minimal. He goes to church but does this irregularly. He does not have close friends from church, so he gets little satisfaction from attending church. He goes to church mostly because of his wife. This makes him happy, plus he feels that he comes closer to God during the church service. He is close to his children, but sometimes they drive him crazy. He feels that he needs to tell them not to do certain things constantly. And this causes quite a bit of family conflict. Nevertheless, he loves his children and feels that he is better off with them than without them. He loves his wife, and he cannot imagine being without her. But then, he sometimes feels the need to be with other women, and he regrets feeling that way. He has been loyal to his wife, and he intends to remain loyal. Lately, it seems that his wife is more demanding of his time and energy. He works hard to make his wife happy, but he feels that he needs to work harder to maintain good marital relations. He has noticed a couple of times during the last few months that his wife was enchanted with his male neighbour. This has created some tension between him and his wife. In relation to his health, he seems to try hard taking care of himself. After work, he goes to the gym and works out for one whole hour. He feels good about staying in shape, but he feels that he works hard at it. His house is in constant need of repairs. He does his best to fix things around the house. His house is a typical blue-collar home in a blue-collar neighbourhood. He feels good about his house, but wishes that he could afford a nicer house in a nicer neighbourhood.

Notice that Joey is somewhat satisfied in many or all of his major life domains—job, leisure/entertainment, family, marital, church, children, house and neighbourhood, and health. However, this satisfaction extracted from all these life domains comes at an expense, hard work. Now compare Joey's situation with that of David's. Remember that David has three or four important life domains in which he is emotionally invested: work, family, leisure, and health. As a surgeon, David feels passionately about his job. His work does not only satisfy his economic needs but also his social, esteem, actualisation, knowledge, and creative needs. He has several physicians he socialises with (including family get-togethers and social outings). He has been recognised as being one of the best surgeons in the region, and he feels very proud of his professional accomplishments. He loves his job and does not feel that it is hard work. He stays in shape by playing tennis with his physician friends at the hospital. He does not feel that he works hard to stay in shape because he really enjoys the game. He is very passionate about his wife and children too. He is very proud of his wife and her accomplishments. She is an attorney. His family gives him the sense of security, the love, the warmth, and being "complete." He does not feel that he has to work hard to keep his marriage going. He is very proud of his children and their accomplishments at school. Again, David does not feel that he has to coach them about things in life to keep them out of trouble. They seem to be doing the right things with very little supervision from the parents. And so on!

The point of contrasting David's life with Joey's is to demonstrate that although Joey is somewhat satisfied with his life, David is much more satisfied. David is happier because he has invested himself in fewer life domains (job, leisure, family, and health), gaining higher levels of satisfaction from these domains, while expending less energy in doing so. Joey, on the other hand, has invested himself in more life domains (job, family, church, house and neighbourhood, leisure, children, spouse, and health). He feels that he has to work hard in each domain to gain an acceptable level of satisfaction. Joey is not efficient in generating satisfaction, whereas David is.

The Satisfaction Efficiency Principle of Balance: Satisfaction from a small set of important life domains generates higher levels of subjective well being than satisfaction from a larger set of domains that are equally important. This is due to the fact that the amount of satisfaction experienced is inversely related to the effort consumed to generate this satisfaction. Thus, satisfaction generated from a small set of domains is likely to involve less effort than satisfaction generated from a larger set of domains.

The *satisfaction efficiency* principle advises us to be efficient in the way we experience satisfaction in all areas of our life. Try to find ways to satisfy much of your developmental needs (biological, safety, social, esteem, knowledge, and aesthetics needs) by being fully engaged in a few areas. Do not spread yourself too thinly. Concentrate your energies in selected areas in which you can derive much satisfaction, the kind of satisfaction that is fulfilling. If you feel that you are working too hard and juggling too many things to maintain a certain level of satisfaction in life, then perhaps you need to simplify your life. Try to re-organise. Find ways to consolidate. Make some tough decisions, and walk away from certain things that consume much energy. Concentrate your energy in the few areas that give you the most pleasure in life.

REFERENCES

Abramson, P. R., & Inglehart, R. (1995). *Value change in global perspective*. Ann Arbor: University of Michigan Press.

Adams, D. (1969). Analysis of a life satisfaction index. *Journal of Gerontology, 24*, 470-474.

Adams, D. (1983). The psychological development of professional Black women's lives and the consequences of career for their personal happiness. Ph.D. dissertation, Wright Institute, Berkley, California.

Ahuvia, A. C., & Friedman, D. C. (1998). Income, consumption, and subjective well-being: Toward a composite macromarketing model. *Journal of Macomarketing, 18*(2), 153-168.

Alderfer, C. P. (1972). *Existence, relatedness, and growth: Human needs in organizational settings*. New York: Free Press.

Allardt, E. (1976). Work and political behaviour. In R. Dubin (Ed.), *Handbook of work, organization, and society*. Chicago: Rand McNally.

Almeder, R. (2000). *Human happiness and morality*. Prometheus Press.

Andrews, F. M., & McKennell, A. C. (1980). Measures of self-reported well-being: Their affective, cognitive, and other components. *Social Indicators Research*, 8, 127-155.

Andrews, F. M., & Robinson, J. P. (1991). Measures of subjective well being. In J. P. Robinson, P. R. Shaver, and L. S. Wrightsman (Eds.), *Measures of personality and social psychological attitudes*, volume 1. (pp. 61-76). San Diego, CA: Academic Press.

Andrews, F. M., & Robinson, J. P. (1992). Measures of subjective well-being. In J. P. Robinson, P. R. Shaver, and L. S. Wrightsman (Eds.), *Measures of personality and social psychological attitudes* (pp. 61-114). San Diego: Academic Press.

Andrews, F. M., & Withey, S. B. (1976). *Social indicators of well-being: America's perception of life quality*. New York: Plenum Press.

Andrisani, P., & Shapiro, M. 1978. Women's attitudes towards their jobs: Some longitudinal data on a national sample. *Personnel Psychology, 31*, 15-34.

Annas, J. (1993). *The morality of happiness*. New York: Oxford University Press.

Annas, J. (1998). Virtue and eudaimonism. In E. F. Paul, F. D. Miller Jr., and J. Paul (Eds.), *Virtue and vice* (pp. 37-55). New York: Cambridge University Press.

Argyle, M. (1987). *The psychology of happiness*. New York: Winstons & Sons.

Argyle, M. (1994). *The psychology of social class*. London: Routledge.

Argyle, M. (1999). Causes and correlates of happiness. In D. Kahneman, E. Diener, & N. Schwartz (Eds.), *Well-being: The foundations of hedonic psychology* (pp. 353-373). New York: Russell Sage.

Argyle, M., & Martin, M. (1991). The psychological causes of happiness. In F. Strack, M. Argyle, & N. Schwarz (Eds.), Subjective *well-being: An interdisciplinary perspective* (pp.77-100). Oxford: Pergamon Press.

Aristotle (1962, 1986 translated). *Nicomachean ethics* (M. Ostwald, Translator). New York: Holt, Rinehart, & Winston.

Austin, J. (1968). Pleasure and happiness. *Philosophy*, 43, 51-62.

Baker, L. A., Cesa, I. L., Gatz, M., & Grodsky, A. (1992). Genetic and environmental influences on positive and negative affect: Support for a two-factor theory. *Psychology and Aging*, 7, 158-163.

Balatasky, G., & Diener, E. (1993). Subjective well-being among Russian students. *Social Indicators Research*, 28, 225-243.

Barak, B., & Rahtz, D. R. (1990). Exploring additional dimensions of quality of life among middle-aged pre-boomers. In H. L. Meadow & M. J. Sirgy (Eds.), *Quality-of-Life Studies in Marketing and Management* (pp. 239-253). Blacksburg, VA: Virginia Tech, Center for Strategy and Marketing Studies.

Baumeister, R. F., & Jones, E. E. (1978). When self-presentation is constrained by the target's knowledge: Consistency and compensation. *Journal of Personality and Social Psychology*, 36, 608-618.

Beck, A. T. (1967). *Depression: Clinical, experimental, and theoretical aspects*. New York: Hoeber.

Becker, E. (1973). *The denial of death*. New York: Free Press.

Benditt, T. M. (1974). Happiness. *Philosophical Studies*, 25, 1-20.

Benditt, T. M. (1978). Happiness and satisfaction--a rejoinder to Carson. *The Personalist*, 59, 108-109.

Bentham, J. (1969). An introduction to the principles of morals and legislation. In M. P. Mack (Ed.), *A Bentham Reader* (pp. 73-144). New York: Pegasus.

Berlyne, D. E. (1970). Novelty, complexity, and hedonic value. *Perception and Psychophysics*, 8, 279-286.

Best, C. J., Cummins, R. A., & Lo, S. K. (2000). The quality of rural and metropolitan life. *Australian Journal of Psychology*, 52(2), 69-74.

Bhargava, S. (1995). An integration-theoretical analysis of life satisfaction. *Psychological Studies*, 40, 170.

Bless, H., Clore, G., Schwarz, N., & Golisano, V. (1996). Mood and the use of scripts. *Journal of Personality and Social Psychology*, 71, 665.

Bornstein, R. (1989). Exposure and affect: Overview and meta-analysis of research, 1968-1987. *Psychological Bulletin*, 106(2), 265-289.

Bower, G. H. (1981). Mood and memory. *American Psychologist, 36*, 129-148.

Bradburn, N. M. (1969). *The structure of psychological well-being*. Chicago: Aldine.

Bradley, G. W. (1978). Self-serving bias in the attribution process: A reexamination of the fact or fiction question. *Journal of Personality and Social Psychology, 36*, 56-71.

Brebner, J. (1995). Testing for stress and happiness: The role of personality factors. In *Stress and emotion: Anxiety, anger, and curiosity*. Washington, DC: Taylor and Francis.

Brewer, W. and G. V. Nakamura (1984). "The Nature and Functions of Schemas." In R. S. Wyer Jr. & T. K. Srull (Eds.), *Handbook of Social Cognition* (pp. 119-159). Hillsdale, NJ: Erlbaum,

Brickman, P., & Campbell, D. T. (1971). Hedonic relativism and the planning of the good society. In M. H. Appley (Ed.), *Adaptation-level theory: A symposium*. New York: Academic Press.

Brickman, P., Coates, D., & Janoff-Bulman, R. (1978). Lottery winners and accident victims, *Journal of Personality and Social Psychology, 36*(8), 917-927.

Bromet, E. J., Dew, A., & Parkinson, D. K. 1990. Spillover between work and family: A study of blue-collar working wives. In J. Eckenrode & S. Gore (Eds.), *Stress between work and family* (pp. 133-151). New York/London: Plenum.

Brown, J. D. (1987). *Evaluating one's abilities: The self-assessment versus self-enhancement debate revisited*. Unpublished manuscript.

Brown, J., & Dutton, K. (1995). The thrill of victory, the complexity of defeat: Self-esteem and people's emotional reaction to success and failure. *Journal of Personality and Social Psychology, 68*, 712.

Brunstein, J. C., Schultheiss, O.C., & Grassman, R. (1998). Personal goals and emotional well being: The moderating role of motive disposition. *Journal of Personality and Social Psychology, 75*, 494-508.

Brief, A. P., & Roberson, L. (1989). Job attitude organization: An exploratory study. *Journal of Applied Social Psychology, 19*, 717-727.

Bukstel, L. H., & Kilmann, P. R., (1980). Psychological effects of imprisonment on confined individuals. *Psychological Bulletin, 88*(2), 469-493.

Bulman, R. J. & Wortman, C. B. (1977). Attributions of blame and coping in the real world: Severe accident victims react to their lot. *Journal of Personality and Social Psychology, 35*, 351-363.

Burke, P. L., & Tully, J. C. (1977). The measurement of role identity. *Social Forces, 55*, 881-897.

Buunk, B.P., Collins, R.L., Taylor, S.E., Van Yperen, N.W., & Dakof, G.A. (1990). The affective consequences of social comparison: Either direction has its ups and downs. *Journal of Personality and Social Psychology, 59,* 1238-1249.

Cameron, P., Titus, D. G., Kostin, J., & Kostin, M. (1973). The life satisfaction of non-normal persons. *Journal of Consulting and Clinical Psychology, 41,* 207-214.

Campbell, A. C. (1976). Subjective measures of well being. *American Psychologist, 31,* 117-124.

Campbell, A. (1981). *The sense of well-being in America: Recent patterns and trends.* New York: McGraw-Hill.

Campbell, A., Converse, P. E., & Rodgers, W. L. (1976). *The quality of American life: Perceptions, evaluations, and satisfactions.* New York: Russell Sage Foundation.

Campbell, J. D. (1986). Similarity and uniqueness: The effects of attribution type, relevance, and individual differences in self-esteem and depression. *Journal of Personality and Social Psychology, 50,* 281-294.

Cantor, N. (1994). Life task problem solving: Situational affordances and personal needs. *Personality and Social Psychology Bulletin, 20,* 235-243.

Cantor, N. & Sanderson, C. A. (1999). Life task participation and well being: The importance of taking part in daily life. In D. Kahneman, E. Diener, & N. Schwartz (Eds.), *Well-being: The foundations of hedonic psychology* (pp. 230-243). New York: Russell Sage.

Cantor, N., & Sanderson, C. A. (in press). Life task participation and well being: The importance of taking part in daily life. In D. Kahneman, E. Diener, & N. Schwartz (Eds.), *Understanding quality of life: Scientific perspectives on enjoyment and suffering.* New York: Russell Sage.

Cantril, H. (1965). *The pattern of human concerns.* New Brunswick, N.J.: Rutgers University Press.

Carson, T. (1978a). Happiness and contentment: a reply to Benditt. *The Personalist, 59,* 101-107.

Carson, T. (1978b). Happiness and the good life. *Southwestern Journal of Philosophy, 9,* 73-88.

Carson, T. (1979). Happiness and the good life: a rejoinder to Mele. *Southwestern Journal of Philosophy, 10,* 189-192.

Carson, T. (1981). Happiness, contentment, and the good life. *Pacific Philosophical Quarterly, 62,* 378-392.

Carver, C. S., & Baird, E. (1998). The American dream revisited: Is it what you want or why you want it that matters? *Psychological Science, 9,* 289-292.

Carver, C. S., & Scheier, M. F. (1982). Control theory: A useful conceptual framework for personality-social, clinical, and health psychology. *Psychological Bulletin, 92,* 111-135.

Carver, C. S., & Scheier, M. F. (1990). Origins and functions of positive and negative affect: A control-process view. *Psychological Review, 97,* 19-35.

Carver, C. S., Scheier, M. F., & Weintraub, J. K. (1989). Assessing coping strategies: A theoretically based approach. *Journal of Personality and Social Psychology, 38,* 668-678.

Centers, R. (1947). The American class structure: A psychological analysis. In T. M. Newcomb and E. L. Hartley (Eds.), *Readings in social psychology* (pp. 481-493). New York: Holt, Rinehart, & Winston.

Chamberlain, K. (1988). On the structure of subjective well-being. *Social Indicators Research, 20,* 581-604.

Chen, N. (1996). Individual differences in answering the four questions of happiness. Ph.D. dissertation, University of Georgia, Athens, Georgia.

Cheng, H. & Furnham, A. (2001). Attributional style and personality as predictors of happiness and mental health. *Journal of Happiness Studies, 2,* 307-327.

Cialdini, R. B. (1976). Basking in reflected glory: Three (football) field studies. *Journal of Personality and Social Psychology, 34,* 366-375.

Clark, A. F., & Oswald, A. J. (1994). Unhappiness and unemployment. *Economic Journal, 104,* 648-659.

Clark, A. F., & Oswald, A. J. (1996). Satisfaction and comparison income. *Journal of Public Economics, 61,* 359-381.

Clark, R. A., & Gecas, V. (1977). *The employed father in America: A role competition analysis.* Paper presented at the 1977 Annual Meeting of the Pacific Sociological Association.

Clark, R. A., Nye, F. I., & Gecas, V. (1978). Husbands' work involvement and marital role performance. *Journal of Marriage and the Family,* 40, 9-21.

Cohen, A. R. (1959). Some implications of self-esteem for social influence. In C. Hovland & I. Janis (pp. 102-120). *Personality and persuasability.* New Haven, CT: Yale University Press.

Coopersmith, S. (1967). *The antecedents of self-esteem.* San Francisco, CA: W. H. Freeman.

Costa, P. T., & McRae, R. R. (1980). Influence of extraversion and neuroticism on subjective well-being: Happy and unhappy people. *Journal of Personality and Social Psychology, 38,* 668-678.

Costa, P. T., & McRae, R. R. (1992). *Revised NEO Personality Inventory (NEOPI-R) and Five Factor Inventory (NEO-FFI) professional manual.* Odessa, Florida: Psychological Assessment Resources.

Costa, P. T., McRae, R. R., & Norris, A. H. (1981). Personal adjustment to aging: Longitudinal prediction from neuroticism and extraversion. *Journal of Gerontology, 36*, 78-85.

Cotgrove, S. (1965). The relations between work and nonwork among technicians. *The Sociological Review*, New Series, *13*, 121-129.

Cottingham, J. (1998). *Philosophy and the good life*. New York: Cambridge University Press.

Crist-Houran, M. (1996). Efficacy of volunteerism. *Psychological Reports, 79*, 736.

Crohan, S. E., Antonucci, T. C., Adelmann, P. K., & Coleman, L. M. (1989). Job characteristics and well being at midlife: Ethnic and gender comparisons. *Psychology of Women Quarterly, 13*, 223-235.

Crooker, K. J., & Near, J. P. (1995). Happiness and satisfaction: measures of affect and cognition? In H. L. Meadow & M. J. Sirgy (Eds.), *Development in Quality-of-Life Studies in Marketing*, volume 5 (pp. 160-166). Illinois: Academy of Marketing Science and the International Society for Quality-of-Life Studies.

Crosby, F. (1982). *Relative deprivation and working women*. New York: Oxford University Press.

Crouter, A. C. (1984). Spillover from family to work: The neglected side of work-family interface. *Human Relations, 37*, 425-442;

Csikszentmihalyi, M. (1975). *Beyond boredom and anxiety*. San Francisco: Jossey-Bass.

Csikszentmihalyi, M. (1982). Towards a psychology of optimal experience. In L. Wheeler (ed.), *Review of personality and social psychology* (Vol. 2). Beverly Hills, CA: Sage.

Csikszentmihalyi, M. (1990). *Flow: The psychology of optimal experience*. New York: Harper Perennial.

Csikszentmihalyi, M. (1997). *Finding flow: The Psychology of engagement with everyday life*. New York: Basic Books.

Csikszentmihalyi, M., & Csikszentmihalyi, I. S. (1988). *Optimal experience: Psychological studies of flow in consciousness*. New York: Cambridge University Press.

Csikszentmihalyi, M., & Kubey, R. (1981). Television and the rest of life. *Public Opinion Quarterly, 45*, 317-328.

Csikszentmihalyi, M., & Wong, M. M. (1991). The situational and personal correlates of happiness: A cross-cultural comparison. In F. Strack, M. Argyle, and N. Schwarz (Eds.), *Subjective well-being: An interdisciplinary perspective* (pp. 193-212). Oxford: Pergamon.

Cummins, R. A. (1993). *Comprehensive Quality of Life Scale for Adults (ComQol-A4)*. (4th edition). Melbourne: Deakin University, School of Psychology.

Cummins, R. A. (1995). On the trail of the gold standard for subjective well-being. *Social Indicators Research, 35*, 179-200.

Cummins, R. A. (1996). The domains of life satisfaction: An attempt to order chaos. *Social Indicators Research, 38*, 303-332.

Cummins, R. A. (1997a). *Comprehensive Quality of Life Scale-Adult: Manual*. School of Psychology, Deakin University-Burwood Campus, Victoria, Australia: Deakin University.

Cummins, R. A. (1997b). Assessing quality of life. In R. Brown (eds.), *Quality of life for people with disabilities* (pp. 116-150). Cheltenham: Stanley Thornes.

Cummins, R. A. (1998). The second approximation to an international standard for life satisfaction. *Social Indicators Research, 43*, 307-334.

Cummins, R. A. (2000a). Normative life satisfaction: Measurement issues and a homeostatic model. In B. Zumbo (Ed.), *Methodological developments and issues in quality of life research*. Amsterdam: Kluwer Academic Publishers.

Cummins, R. A. (2000b). Personal income and subjective well-being: A review. *Journal of Happiness Studies, 1*(2), 133-158.

Cummins, R. A., Eckersley, R., Pallant, J., van Vugt, J., & Misajon, R. (2002). *Developing a national index of subjective wellbeing: The Australian Unity Wellbeing Index*. Unpublished manuscript.

Cummins, R. A., McCabe, M. P., Romeo, Y., & Gullone, E. (1994). The Comprehensive Quality of Life Scale: Instrument development and psychometric evaluation on tertiary staff and students. *Educational and Psychological Measurement, 54*, 372-382.

Danna, K., & Griffin, R. W. (1999). Health and well-being in the workplace.A review and synthesis of the literature. *Journal of Management, 25*(3), 357-384.

Davis, W. (1981a). Pleasure and happiness. *Philosophical Studies, 39*, 305-318.

Davis, W. (1981b). A theory of happiness. *American Philosophical Quarterly, 18*, 111-120.

Day, R. L. (1987). Relationship between life satisfaction and consumer satisfaction. In A. C. Samli (Ed.), *Marketing and quality-of-life interface* (pp. 289-311). Westport, CT: Greenwood Press.

Dea, E. L. & Ryan, R. M. (1984). The dynamics of self-determination in personality and development. In R. Schwarzer (Ed.), *Self-related cognition in anxiety and motivation*. Hillsdale, NJ: Erlbaum.

Deci, E. L., & Ryan, R. M. (1987). The support of autonomy and control of behaviour. *Journal of Personality and Social Psychology, 53*, 1024-1037.

DeLongis, A., Coyne, J. C., Dakof, G., Folkman, S., & Lazarus, R. S. (1982). Relationship of daily hassles, uplifts, and major life events to health status. *Health Psychology, 1*, 119-136.

DeLongis, A., Folkman, S., & Lazarus, R. S. (1988). The impact of daily stress on health and mood: Psychological and social resources as mediators. *Journal of Personality and Social Psychology, 54*, 486-495.

Diener, E. (1984). Subjective well-being. *Psychological Bulletin, 75*(3), 542-575.

Diener, E. (2000). Is happiness a virtue? The personal and societal benefits of positive emotions. Presentation at the Second Annual Positive Psychology Summit, October 13-15, 2000, Washington, DC.

Diener, E., Colvin, C. R., Pavot, W. G., & Allman, A. (1991). The psychic costs of intense positive affect. *Journal of Personality and Social Psychology, 61*(3), 492-503.

Diener, E., & Diener, M. (1995). Cross-cultural correlates of life satisfaction and self-esteem. *Journal of Personality and Social Psychology, 68*, 653-663.

Diener, E., Diener, M., & Diener, C. (1995). Factors predicting the subjective well-being of nations. *Journal of Personality and Social Psychology, 69*, 851-864.

Diener, E., & Emmons, R. A. (1984). The independence of positive and negative affect. *Journal of Personality and Social Psychology, 47*, 1105-1117.

Diener, E., Emmons, R. A., Larsen, R. J., & Griffin, S. (1985). The Satisfaction with Life Scale. *Journal of Personality Assessment, 49*, 71-75.

Diener, E., & Fujita, F. (1995). Resources, personal strivings, and subjective well being: A nomothetic and idiographic approach. *Journal of Personality and Social Psychology, 68*, 926-935.

Diener, E. & Fujita, F. (1996). Social comparisons and subjective well-being. In B. Buunk and R. Gibbons (Eds.), *Health, coping, and social comparison*. Hillsdale, NJ: Erlbaum.

Diener, E., Horwitz, F., & Emmons, R. A. (1985). Happiness of the very wealthy. *Social Indicators Research, 16*, 263-274.

Diener, E., & Larsen, R. J. (1984). Temporal stability and cross-situational consistency of affective, behavioral, and cognitive responses. *Journal of Personality and Social Psychology, 47*, 580-592.

Diener, E., Larsen, R., Levine, S., & Emmons, R. (1985). Intensity and frequency: Dimensions underlying positive and negative affect. *Journal of Personality and Social Psychology, 48*, 1253-1265.

Diener, E., & Lucas, R. E. (1999). Personality and subjective well being. In D. Kahneman, E. Diener, & N. Schwartz (Eds.), *Well-being: The foundations of hedonic psychology* (pp. 213-229). New York: Russell Sage Foundation.

Diener, E., Oishi, S., Lucas, R. E., & Suh, E. M. (2000). Looking up and looking down: Weighting of good versus bad information in life satisfaction judgments. Unpublished manuscript, University of Illinois at Champaign.

Diener, E., Sandvik, E., & Pavot, W. (1991). Happiness is frequency, not intensity, of positive versus negative affect. In F. Strack, M. Argyle, & N. Schwarz (Eds.), *Subjective well-being* (pp. 119-139). Oxford, UK: Pergamon Press,.

Diener, E., Sandvik, E., Pavot, W., & Fujita, F. (1992). Extraversion and subjective well being in a U.S. national probability sample. *Journal of Research in Personality, 26*, 205-215.

Diener, E., Sandvik, E., Seidlitz, L., & Diener, M. (1993). The relationship between income and subjective well-being: Relative or absolute? *Social Indicators Research, 28*, 195-223.

Diener, E., Smith, H., & Fujita, F. (1995). The personality structure of affect. *Journal of Personality and Social Psychology, 69*, 130-141.

Diener, E., & Suh, E. M. (1999). National differences in subjective well-being. In D. Kahneman, E. Diener, & N. Schwartz (Eds.), *Well-being: The foundations of hedonic psychology* (pp. 433-450). New York: Russell Sage.

Diener, E., Suh, E., Lucas, R., & Smith, H. (1999). Subjective well-being: Three decades of research. *Psychological Bulletin, 125*, 276-302.

Donahue, E. M., Robins, R. W., Roberts, B. W., & John, O. P. (1993). The divided self: Concurrent and longitudinal effects of psychological adjustment and social roles on self-concept differentiation. *Journal of Personality and Social Psychology, 64*, 834-846.

Drakopoulos, S. A., & Theodossiou, I. (1997). Job satisfaction and target earnings. *Journal of Economic Psychology, 18*, 692-704.

Dubin, R. (1956). Industrial workers' worlds: A study of the 'central life interests' of industrial workers. *Social Problems, 3*, 131-142.

Dubin, R. (1973). Work and nonwork: Institutional perspectives. In M. D. Dunnette (Ed.), *Work and nonwork in the year 2001* (pp. 54-68). Monterey, CA: Brooks/Cole.

Dubin, R. (1976). Work in modern society. In R. Dubin (Ed.), *Handbook of work, organization, and society*. Chicago: Rand-McNally.

Dubin, R., Headley, R. A., & Taveggia, T. C. (1976). Attachment to work. In R. Dubin (Ed.), *Handbook of work, organization, and society*. Chicago: Rand-McNally.

Duncan, O. (1975). Does money buy satisfaction? *Social Indicators Research, 2*, 267-274.

Dunning, D., Leuenberger, A., & Sherman, D. A. (1995). A new look at motivated inference: Are self-serving theories of success a product of motivational forces? *Journal of Personality and Social Psychology, 69*, 58-68.

Dunning, D., Meyerowitz, J. A., & Holzberg, A.D. (1989). Ambiguity and self-evaluation: The role of idiosyncratic trait definitions in self-serving assessments of ability. *Journal of Personality and Social Psychology, 57*, 1082-1090.

Easterlin, R. A. (1974). Does economic growth improve the human lot? Some empirical evidence. In P. A. David & M. W. Reder (Eds.), *Nations and households in economic growth*, (pp. 89-125). New York: Academic Press.

Easterlin, R. A. (1995). Will raising incomes of all increase the happiness of all? *Journal of Economic Behaviour and Organization*, 2735-2747.

Edwards, R. B. (1979). *Pleasures and pains: A theory of qualitative hedonism*. Ithaca, Cornell University Press.

Efraty, D., Sirgy, M. J., & Siegel, P. (2000). The job/life satisfaction relationship among professional accountants: Psychological determinants and demographic differences. In E. Diener and D. Rahtz (Eds.), *Advances in quality-of-life theory and research*, volume 1 (pp. 129-157), Netherlands: Kluwer Academic Publishers.

Elder, G. H. (1974). *Children of the Great Depression*. Chicago: University of Chicago Press.

Ellis, A. (1962). *Reason and emotion in psychotherapy*. New York: Stuart.

Ellison, C.G. (1991). Religious involvement and subjective well-being. *Journal of Health and Social Behavior, 32*, 80-89.

Emmons, R. A. (1986). Personal strivings: An approach to personality and subjective well-being. *Journal of Personality and Social Psychology, 51*, 1058-1068.

Emmons, R. A. (1999). *The psychology of ultimate concerns: Motivation and spirituality in personality*. New York: The Guilford Press.

Emmons, R. A., Cheung, C., & Tehrani, K. (1998). Assessing spirituality through personal goals: Implications for research on religion and subjective well-being. *Social Indicators Research, 45*, 391-422.

Emmons, R. A., & Diener, E. (1985). Factors predicting satisfaction judgements: A comparative examination. *Social Indicators Research, 16,* 157-167.

Emmons, R. A., & King, L. A. (1988). Conflict among personal strivings: Immediate and long-term implications for psychological and physical well-being. *Journal of Personality and Social Psychology, 54,* 1040-1048.

Emmons, R. A., Shepherd, N. R., & Kaiser, H. A. (1994). Approach and avoidance strivings and psychological and physical well-being. Poster presented at the 102nd Annual Convention of the American Psychological Association, Los Angeles (August).

Epstein, M. (1995). Opening up to happiness. *Psychology Today, 28*(4), 42-46.

Ferrans, C. E., & Powers, M. J. (1985). Quality of life index: Development and psychometric properties. *Advances in Nursing Science, 8*(1), 15-24.

Fishbein, M., & Ajzen, I. (1975*). Belief, attitude, intention, and behavior.* Reading, MA: Addison-Wesley.

Fogarty, M. P., Rapoport, R., & Rapoport, R. N. (1971). *Sex, career, and family.* Beverly Hills, CA: Sage.

Folkman, S. (1991). Coping and emotion. In A. Monat & R. S. Lazarus (Eds.), *Stress and coping: An anthology* (pp. 207-227). New York: Columbia University Press.

Frederick, S. & Loewenstein, G. (1999). Hedonic adaptation. In D. Kahneman, E. Diener, & N. Schwartz (Eds.), *Well-being: The foundations of hedonic psychology* (pp. 302-329). New York: Russell Sage.

Frey, D. (1978). Reactions to success and failures in public and private conditions. *Journal of Experimental Social Psychology, 14,* 172-179.

Friedman, M. M. (1993). Social support sources and psychological well-being in older women with heart disease. *Research in Nursing and Health, 16,* 405-413.

Frisch, M. B. (1992). Use of the Quality-of-Life Inventory in problem assessment and treatment for cognitive therapy of depression. In A. Freeman & Dattilio (Eds.), *Comprehensive casebook of cognitive therapy* (pp. 27-52). New York: Plenum.

Frisch, M. B. (1993). The Quality of Life Inventory: A cognitive-behavioral tool for complete problem assessment, treatment planning, and outcome evaluation. *Behavior Therapist, 16,* 42-44.

Frisch, M. B. (1994a). *Quality of Life Inventory^{TM} (QOLI^{TM}).* Minneapolis, MN: National Computer Systems.

Frisch, M. B. (1994b). *Manual for the Quality of Life Inventory^{TM} (QOLI^{TM}).* Minneapolis, MN: National Computer Systems.

Frisch, M. B. (1998). Quality of Life Therapy and assessment in health care. *Clinical Psychology: Science and Practice, 5*, 19-40.

Frisch, M. B. (1999). Quality of life assessment/intervention and the Quality of Life Inventory™ (QOLI™). In M. R. Maruish (Ed.), *The use of psychological testing for treatment planning and outcome assessment* (2nd edition) (pp. 1227-1331). Hillsdale, NJ: Lawrence Erlbaum.

Frisch, M. B. (2000). Improving mental and physical health care through quality of life therapy and assessment. In E. Diener and D. Rahtz (Eds.), *Advances in Quality of Life Theory and Research*, volume 1 (pp. 207-241). New York: Kluwer Academic Publishers.

Frisch, M. B. (2001). *Quality of Life Therapy: A new approach to cognitive therapy for depression and related problems*. Rome: Sorveno.

Frisch, M. B. (in press). *Quality of Life Therapy: Interventions to improve the quality of life of patients with emotional or physical problems*. New York: Wiley.

Frone, M. R., Yardley, J. K., & Markel, K. S. (1997). Developing and testing an integrative model of the work-family interface. *Journal of Vocational Behaviour, 50*, 145-167.

Furnham, A. (1991). Work and leisure satisfaction. In F. Strack, M. Argyle, and N. Schwarz (Eds.), *Subjective well-being* (pp. 235-260), Oxford, U.K.: Pergamon Press,

Garza, R. T., & Herringer, L. G. (1987). Social identity: A multidimensional approach. *Journal of Social Psychology, 127*, 299-308.

Gauthier, D. P. (1967). Progress and happiness: a utilitarian consideration. *Ethics, 78*, 77-82.

Gecas, V. (1982). The self-concept. In R. H. Turner and J. F. Short (Eds.), *Annual Review of Sociology*, volume 8 (pp. 1-33). Palo Alto, CA: Annual Reviews.

George, J. M., & Brief, A. P. (1990). The economic instrumentality of work: An examination of the moderating effects of financial requirements and sex on the pay-life satisfaction relationship. *Journal of Vocational Behaviour, 37*, 357-368.

George, L. K., & Landerman, R. (1984). Health and subjective well-being: A replicated secondary data analysis. *International Journal of Aging and Human Development, 19*, 133-156.

Gerson, K. (1993). *No man's land: Men's changing commitments to family and work*. New York: Basic Books.

Gert, B. (1988). *Morality: a new justification of the moral rules*. New York: Oxford University Press.

Gerwood, J., LeBlanc, M., & Piazza, N. (1998). The purpose in life test and religious denomination. *Journal of Clinical Psychology, 54*, 59.

Glatzer, W. (1984). Lebenszufriedenheit und alternative Masse subjektiven Wolhlbefindens. In W. Glatzer and W. Zapf (eds.), *Lebensqualitat in der Bundersrepublik.* Frankfurt: Campus Verlag.

Gollwitzer, P. (1993). Goal achievement: The role of intentions. In W. Stroebe & M. Hewstone (eds.), *European review of social psychology,* vol. 4 (pp. 141-185). New York: Wiley.

Goldstein, B. & Eichhorn, R. L. (1961). The changing protestant ethic: Rural patterns in health, work, and leisure. *American Sociological Review, 26,* 557-565.

Goldstein, I. (1973). Happiness: the role of non-hedonic criteria in its evaluation. *International Philosophical Quarterly,* 13, 523-534.

Greenberg, J., & Pyszczynski, T. (1985). Compensatory self-inflation: A response to the threat to self-regard of public failure. *Journal of Personality and Social Psychology, 49,* 273-280.

Greenberg, J., Pyszczynski, T., & Solomon, S. (1986). The causes and consequences of a need for self-esteem: A terror management theory. In R. R. Baumeister (Ed.), *Public self and private self* (pp. 189-212). New York: Springer-Verlag.

Greenley, J. R., Greenberg, J. S., & Brown, R. (1997). Measuring quality of life: A new and practical survey instrument. *Social Work, 42,* 244-254.

Greenwald, A. G. (1980). The totalitarian ego: Fabrication and revision of personal history. *American Psychologist,* 35, 603-618.

Griffin, J. (1986). *Well-being: its meaning, measurement, and moral importance.* Oxford: Claredon Press.

Griffin, N., Chassin, L., & Young, R. (1981). Measurement of global self-concept versus multiple role-specific self-concepts in adolescents. *Adolescence, 16,* 49-56.

Grob, A., Sttsenko, A., Sabatier, C., Botcheva, L., & Macek, P. (in press). A cross-national model of subjective well-being in adolescence. In F. D. Alsaker & A. Flammer (Eds.), *European and American adolescents in the nineties: Tell what they do, and I'll tell who they are.* New York: Erlbaum.

Gross, J. (2000). Emotion regulation: Making the most of our emotion. Presentation at the Second Annual Positive Psychology Summit, October 13-15, 2000, Washington, DC.

Guttman, J. (1982). A means-end chain model based on consumer categorization processes. *Journal of Marketing,* Spring, 60-72.

Haavio-Mannila, E. (1971). Satisfaction with family, work, leisure, and life among men and women. *Human Relations, 24,* 585-601.

Hagerty, M (1999). Unifying livability and comparison theory: Cross-national time-series analysis of life satisfaction. *Social Indicators Research, 47*(3), 343-356.

Haller, M. & Rosenmayr, L. (1971). The pluridimensionality of work commitment. *Human Relations, 24,* 501-518.

Harackiewicz, J. M., Sansone, C., & Manderlink, G. (1985). Competence, achievement orientation, and intrinsic motivation: A process analysis. *Journal of Personality and Social Psychology, 47,* 287-300.

Haring, M. J., Okun, M. A., & Stock, W. A. (1984). A quantitative synthesis of literature on work status and subjective well-being. *Journal of Vocational Behaviour, 25,* 316-324.

Haw, C. (1995). The family life cycle. *Psychological Medicine, 25,* 727.

Haybron, D. M. (2000). Two philosophical problems in the study of happiness. *Journal of Happiness Studies, 1,* 207-225.

Headey, B., & Wearing, A. (1988). The sense of relative superiority: Central to well-being. *Social Indicators Research, 20,* 497-516.

Headey, B., & Wearing, A. (1989). Personality, life events, and subjective well-being: Toward a dynamic equilibrium model. *Journal of Personality and Social Psychology, 57,* 731-739.

Headey, B., & Wearing, A. (1991). Subjective well-being: A stocks and flows framework. In F. Strack, M. Argyle, & N. Schwarz (Eds.), *Subjective well-being* (pp. 49-73). Oxford, UK: Pergamon Press.

Headey, B., & Wearing, A. (1992). *Understanding happiness: A theory of subjective well being.* Melbourne: Longman Cheshire.

Headey, B., Kelley, J., & Wearing, A. (1993). Dimensions of mental health: Life satisfaction, positive affect, anxiety and depression. *Social Indicators Research, 29,* 63-82.

Heckhausen, J. & Schultz, R. (1995). A life-span theory of control. *Psychological Review, 102,* 234-304.

Helson, H. (1947). Adaptation-level as frame of reference for prediction of psychological data. *The American Journal of Psychology, 60,* 1-29.

Helson, H. (1948). Adaptation level as a basis for a quantitative theory of frames of references. *Psychological Review, 55*(6), 297-313.

Helson, H. (1964). *Adaptation-level theory: An experimental an systematic approach to behaviour.* New York: Harper and Row.

Henry, C. & Lovelace, S. (1995). Family resources and adolescent family satisfaction in remarried family households. *Journal of Family Issues, 16,* 765.

Herzberg, F. (1966). *Work and the nature of man.* Cleveland: World.

Herzberg, F., Mausner, B., Pederson, R., & Capwell, D. (1957). *Job attitudes: Review of research and opinion.* Pittsburgh, PA: Psychological Services.

Higgins, E. T., Grant, H., & Shah, J. (1999). Self-regulation and quality of life: Emotional and nonemotional experiences. In D. Kahneman, E. Diener, & N. Schwartz (Eds.), *Well-being: The foundations of hedonic psychology* (pp. 244-266). New York: Russell Sage.

Higgins, E. T., Roney, C. J. R., Crowe, E., & Hymes, C. (1994). Ideal versus ought predilections for approach and avoidance: Distinct self-regulatory systems. *Journal of Personality and Social Psychology, 66,* 276-286.

Higgins, E. T., Shah, J., & Friedman, R. (1997). Emotional response to goal attainment: Strength of regulatory focus as moderator. *Journal of Personality and Social Psychology, 72,* 515-525.

Higgins, E. T., Vookles, J., & Tykocinski, O. (1992). Self and health: How "patterns" of self-beliefs predict types of emotional and physical problems. *Social Cognition, 10,* 125-150.

Hill, T. E., Jr. (1999). Happiness and human flourishing in Kant's ethics. In E. F. Paul, F. D. Miller Jr., and J. Paul (Eds.), *Human flourishing* (pp. 143-175). New York: Cambridge University Press.

Hoelter, J. W. (1985). The structure of self-conception: Conceptualisation and measurement. *Journal of Personality and Social Psychology, 49,* 1392-1407.

Hsee, C. K., & Abelson, R. P. (1991). Velocity relations: Satisfaction as a function of the first derivative of outcome over time. *Journal of Personality and Social Psychology, 60,* 341-347.

Hunter, M. & Liao, K. L. (1995). Problem-solving groups for mid-aged women in general practice. *Journal of Reproductive and Infant Psychology, 13,* 147.

Inglehart, R. (1977). *The silent revolution: Changing values and political styles among Western publics.* Princeton, NJ: Princeton University Press.

Inglehart, R. (1990). *Culture shift in advanced industrial society.* Princeton, NJ: Princeton University Press.

Inglehart, R. (1997). *Modernization and post-modernization: Cultural, economic, and political change in 43 societies.* Princeton, NJ: Princeton University Press.

Inglehart, R., & Rabier, J-R. (1986), Aspirations adapt to situations—but why are the Belgians so much happier than the French? A cross-cultural analysis of subjective quality of life. In F. M. Andrews (Ed.), *Research in the Quality of Life.* Ann Arbor, MI: Institute for Social Research.

Inglis. A., & Greenglass, E. R. (1989). Motivation for marriage among women and men. *Psychological Reports, 65,* 1035-1042.

Irwin, F. W. (1944). The realism of expectations. *Psychological Review*, *51*, 120-126.

Jacobs, J. (1985). The place of virtue in happiness. *Journal of Value Inquiry*, *19*, 171-182.

Jacques, J. M. & Chason, K. J. (1977). Self-esteem and low status groups: A changing scene? *Sociological Quarterly*, *18*, 399-412.

James, W. (1890). *Principles of psychology*. New York: Holt.

Janoff-Bulman, R. (1989). Assumptive worlds and the stress of traumatic events: Applications of the schema construct. *Social Cognition*, *7*, 113-116.

Judge, T. A., & Hulin, C. L. (1993). Job satisfaction as a reflection of disposition: A multiple source causal analysis. *Organisational Behaviour and Human Decision Processes*, *56*, 388-421.

Judge, T. A., & Locke, E. A. (1993). Effect of dysfunctional thought processes on subjective well-being and job satisfaction. *Journal of Applied Psychology*, *78*, 475-490.

Judge, T. A., & Watanabe, S. (1993). Another look at the job satisfaction-life satisfaction relationship. *Journal of Applied Psychology*, *78*, 939-948.

Kabanoff, B. (1980). Work and nonwork: A review of models, methods, and findings. *Psychological Bulletin*, *88*, 60-77.

Kahneman, D. (1999). Objective happiness. In D. Kahneman, E. Diener, and N. Schwartz (Eds.), *Well-Being: The foundations of hedonic psychology* (pp. 3-25). New York: Russell Sage Foundation.

Kammann, R. (1982). *Personal circumstances and life events as poor predictors of happiness*. Annual Convention of the American Psychological Association, Washington, D.C., 1982.

Kammann, R. (1983). Objective circumstances, life satisfactions and sense of well-being: Consistencies across time and place. *New Zealand Psychologist*, *12*, 14-22.

Kammann, R., Christie, D., Irwin, R., & Dixon, G. (1979). Properties of an inventory to measure happiness (and psychological health). *New Zealand Psychologist*, *8*, 1-9.

Karasek, R. A. (1976). *The impact of the work environment on life outside the job*. Unpublished doctoral dissertation, Massachusetts Institute of Technology.

Kasser, T. (1997). Two versions of the American dream: Which goals and values make for a high quality of life? Paper presented at the International Society for Quality-of-Life Studies Conference, Charlotte, North Carolina, November 20-22, 1997.

Kasser, T. & Ryan, R. M. (1993). The dark side of the American Dream: Differential correlates of financial success as a central life aspiration. *Journal of Personality and Social Psychology, 65*, 410-422.

Kasser, T., & Ryan, R. M. (1996). Further examining the American dream: Differential correlates of intrinsic and extrinsic goals. *Personality and Social Psychology Bulletin, 22*, 280-287.

Kasser, T., & Ryan, R. M. (1998). Be careful what you wish for: Optimal functioning and the relative attainment of intrinsic and extrinsic goals. Working paper.

Kasser, T., Ryan, R. M., Zax, M., & Sameroff, A. J. (1995). The relations of maternal and social environments to late adolescents' materialistic and prosocial values. *Developmental Psychology, 31*, 907-914.

Kavanagh, M. J., & Halpern, M. (1977). The impact of job level sex differences on the relationship between life and job satisfaction. *Academy of Management Journal, 20*, 66-73.

Kekes, J. (1982). Happiness. *Mind, 91*, 358-376.

Kekes, J. (1988). *The examined life.* Lewisburg, Bucknell University Press.

Kekes, J. (1992). Happiness. In L. C. Becker and C. B. Becker (Eds.), *Encyclopedia of ethics* (pp. 430-435). New York: Russell Sage Foundation.

Kenny, A. (1966). Happiness. *Proceedings of the Aristotelian Society, 66*, 93-102.

Kette, G. (1991). *Haft: Eine socialpsychologgische analyse* (Prison: A social psychological analysis). Gottingen: Hogrefe.

Kim, K. A. & Mueller, D. J. (2001). To balance or not balance: confirmatory factor analysis of theAffect-Balance Scale. *Journal of Happiness Studies, 2*, 289-306.

Kitayama, S. & Markus, H. R. (2000). The pursuit of happiness and the realization of sympathy: Cultural patterns of self, social relations, and well-being. In E. Diener and E. M. Suh (Eds.), *Culture and Subjective Well-being* (pp. 113-161). Cambridge, MA: The MIT Press,

Kosenko, R., Sirgy, M. J., & Efraty, D. (1990). A life satisfaction measure based on need hierarchy theory. In H. L. Meadow & M. J. Sirgy (Eds.), *Quality-of-life studies in marketing and management* (pp. 657-667). Blacksburg, VA: Virginia Tech, Center for Strategy and Marketing Stduies.

Kozma, A. (1996). Top-down and bottom-up approaches to an understanding of subjective well-being. World Conference on Quality of Life, University of Northern British Columbia, Prince George, (August 22-25).

Kozma, A., & Stones, M.J. (1992). Longitudinal findings on a componential model of happiness. In M. J. Sirgy, H. L. Meadow, D. Rahtz, & A. C. Samli (Eds.), *Developments in Quality-of-Life Studies in Marketing*, volume 4 (pp. 139-142). Blacksburg, Virginia: Academy of Marketing Science.

Kozma, A., Stone, S., Stones, M. J., Hannah, T. E., & McNeil, K. (1990). Long- and short-term affective states in happiness: Model, paradigm and experimental evidence. *Social Indicators Research, 22*, 119-138.

Kraut, R. (1979). Two conceptions of happiness. *The Philosophical Review*, 138, 167-197.

Kremer, Y., & Harpaz, I. (1982). Leisure patterns among retired workers: Spillover or compensatory trends. *Journal of Vocational Behaviour, 21*, 183-195.

Krieger, L. S., Reynolds, E. & Neill, L. (1997). *World history: Perspectives on the past*. Evenston, IL: McDougal Little.

Kruglanski, A. W. & Mayseless, O. (1990). Classic and current social comparison research: Expanding the perspective. *Psychological Bulletin, 108*, 195-208.

Kubey, R., & Csikszentmihalyi, M. (1990). *Television and the quality of life: How viewing shapes everyday experience*. Hillsdale, NJ: Lawrence Erlbaum.

Kuiper, N. A., Olinger, L. J., MacDonald, M. R., & Shaw, B. F. (1985). Self-schema processing of depressed and nondepressed content: The effects of vulnerability on depression. *Social Cognition, 3*, 77-93.

LaBarbera, P. A., & Gurhan, Z. (1997). The role of materialism, religiosity, and demographics in subjective well-being. *Psychology & Marketing, 14*, 71-97.

Lacy, W. B., Hougland, J. G., & Shepard, J. M. (1982). Relationship between work and nonwork satisfaction: Is it changing and does occupational prestige make a difference? *Sociological Spectrum, 2*, 157-171.

Laing, R. D., Phillipson, H., & Lee, A. R. (1966). *Interpersonal perception: A theory and method of research*. New York: Springer Publishing.

Lance, C. E., Mallard, A. G. C., & Michalos, A. C. (1995). Tests of causal directions of global-life facet satisfaction relationships. *Social Indicators Research, 34*, 69-92.

Lane, R. E. (1991). *The market experience*. Cambridge: Cambridge University Press.

Lane, R. E. (2000). *The loss of happiness in market democracies*. New Haven, CT: Yale University Press.

Larsen, R. J. (1978). Thirty years of research on the subjective well being of older Americans. *Journal of Gerontology, 33*, 109-125.

Larsen, R. J., Diener, E., Cropanzano, R. S. (1987). Cognitive operations associated with individual differences in affect intensity. *Journal of Personality and Social Psychology, 53*, 767-774.

Larsen, R. J., Diener, E., & Emmons, R. A. (1985). An evaluation of subjective well-being measures. *Social Indicators Research, 17*, 1-18.

Lee, G. R., Seccombe, K., & Shehan, C. L. (1991). Marital status and personal happiness: An analysis of trend data. *Journal of Marriage and the Family, 53*, 839-844.

Leelakulthanit, O., Day, R., & Walters, R. (1991). Investigating the relationship between marketing and overall satisfaction with life in a developing country. *Journal of Macromarketing*, (Spring), 3-23.

Leiter, M. P., & Durup, M. J. (1996). Work, home, and in-between: A longitudinal study of spillover. *Journal of Applied Behavioral Science, 32*(1), 29-47.

Lepper, H. (1996). In pursuit of happiness and satisfaction in later life: A study of competing theories of subjective well-being. Ph.D. dissertation, University of California, Riverside.

Levitin, T. E., & Quinn, R. P. (1974). Changes in sex roles and attitude toward work. Paper presented at the 1974 Conference of the American Association for Public Research.

Levinson, H., Price, C. R., Munden, K. J., Mandl, H. J., & Solley, C. M. (1962). *Men, management and mental health*. Cambridge, MA: Harvard University Press.

Lewellyn, P. A., & Wibker, E. A. (1990). Significance of quality of life on turnover intentions of Certified Public Accountants. In H. L. Meadow & M. J. Sirgy (Eds.), *Quality-of-life studies in marketing and management* (pp.182-193). Blacksburg, VA: Virginia Tech, Cneter for Strategy and Marketing Studies.

Lewicki, P. (1984). Self-schema and social information processing. *Journal of Personality and Social Psychology, 47*, 1177-1190.

Lewin, K. (1951). *Field theory in social science*. New York: Harper & Row.

Lewinsohn, P. M., Redner, J. E., & Seeley, J. R. (1991). The relationship between life satisfaction and psychosocial variables. In F. Strack, M. Argyle, & N. Schwarz (Eds.), *Subjective well-being* (pp. 141-169). Oxford, UK: Pergamon Press.

Linderman, M. & Verkasalo, M. (1996). Meaning in life. *Journal of Social Psychology, 136*, 657.

Lipkus, I., Dalbert, C., & Siegler, I. (1996). The importance of distinguishing the belief in a just world for self versus others. *Personality and Social Psychology Bulletin, 22,* 666.

Lipset, S. M., Trow, M. A., & Coleman, J. S. (1956). *Union democracy: The internal politics of the international typographical union.* Glencoe: The Free Press.

Loewenstein, G. & Frederick, S. (in press). Hedonic adaptation: From the bright side to the dark. In D. Kahneman, E. Diener, & N. Schwartz (Eds.), *Understanding quality of life: Scientific perspectives on enjoyment and suffering.* New York: Russell-Sage.

Loscocco, K. A. (1989). The interplay of personal and job characteristics in determining work commitment. *Social Science Research, 18,* 370-394.

Lucas, R. E., Diener, E., & Suh, E. (1996). Discriminant validity of well-being measures. *Journal of Personality and Social Psychology, 71,* 616-628.

Luper, S. (1996). *Invulnerability: On securing happiness.* Chicago: Open Court.

Lyubomirsky, S. (1994). The hedonistic consequences of social comparison: Implications for enduring happiness and transient mood. Ph.D. dissertation, Stanford University, Palo Alto, California.

Lyubomirsky, S., & Ross, L. (1997). Hedonic consequences of social comparison: A contrast of happy and unhappy people. *Journal of Personality and Social Psychology, 73,* 1141-1157.

Lykken, D. (1999). *Happiness: The nature and nurture of joy and contentment.* New York: St. Martin's Griffin.

Lykken, D. & Tellegen, A. (1996). Happiness is a stochastic phenomenon. *Psychological Science, 7,* 186-189.

Magen, Zipora (1996). Commitment beyond self and adolescence: The issue of happiness. *Social Indicators Research, 37,* 235-267.

Malatesta, C. Z., Grigoryev, P., Lamb, C., Albin, M., & Culver, C. (1986). Emotion socialization and expressive development in preterm and full-term infants. *Child Development, 57,* 316-330.

Markus, H. (1977). Self-schemata and the processing of information about the self. *Journal of Personality and Social Psychology, 35,* 63-78.

Maslow, A. H. (1954, 1970). *Motivation and personality.* New York: Harper.

Massimini, F., Csikszentmihalyi, M., & Carli, M. (1987). The monitoring of optimal experience: A tool for psychiatric rehabilitation. *Journal of Nervous and Mental Disease, 175*(9), 545-549.

Massimini, F., Csikszentmihalyi, M., & Delle Fave, A. (1988). Flow and biocultural evolution. In M. Csikszentmihalyi & I. Csikszentmihalyi (eds.), *Optimal experience: Psychological studies of flow of consciousness.* New York: Cambridge University Press.

Masters, J. C., Furman, W., & Barden, R. (1977). Effects of achievement standards, tangible rewards and self-dispensed achievement evaluations on children's task mastery. *Child Development, 48*, 217-224.

Matlin, M. W. & Gawron, V. J. (1979). Individual differences in pollyannaism. *Journal of Personality Assessment, 43*, 411-412.

Mayerfield, J. (1996). The moral symmetry of happiness and suffering. *Southern Journal of Philosophy, 34*, 317-338.

Mayerfield, J. (1999). *Suffering and moral responsibility.* New York: oxford University Press.

McClelland, D. C. (1961). *The achieving society.* New York: The Free Press.

McGregor, I. & Little, B. (1998). Personal projects, happiness, and meaning: On doing well and being yourself. *Journal of Personality and Social Psychology, 74*, 494.

McCall, G. J. and J. L. Simmons (1978). *Identities and Interactions: An Examination of Human Associations in Everyday Life.* New York: Free Press.

McCrae, R. R., & Costa, P. T. (1986). Personality coping, and coping effectiveness in an adult sample. *Journal of Personality, 54*, 385-405.

McFall,L. (1989). *Happiness.* New York: Peter Lang.

McKennell, A. C. (1978), Cognition and affect in perceptions of well-being. *Social Indicators Research, 5*, 389-426.

McKennell, A. C., & Andrews, F. M. (1980). Models of cognition and affect in perceptions of well-being. *Social Indicators Research, 8*, 257-298.

Meadow, H. L. (1988). The satisfaction attitude hierarchy: Does marketing contribute? In S. Shapiro and others(Eds.), *Proceedings of the 1988 American Marketing Association Winter Educators' Conference* (pp. 482-483). Chicago, IL: American Marketing Association.

Meadow, H. L., & Cooper, P. D. (1990). Finding useful marketing measures for the future: Life satisfaction preparation for a marketing view. In H. L. Meadow and M. J. Sirgy (Eds.), *Quality-of-Life Studies in Marketing and Management* (pp. 645-656). Blacksburg, VA: Virginia Tech, Center for Strategy and Marketing Studies.

Meadow, H. L., Mentzer, J. J., Rahtz, D. R., & Sirgy, M. J. (1992). A life satisfaction measure based on judgment theory. *Social Indicators Research, 26*(1), 23-59.

Mechanic, D. (1979). Development of psychological distress among young adults. *Archives of General Psychiatry, 36*, 1233-1239.

Meissner, M. (1971). The long arm of the job: A study of work and leisure. *Industrial Relations, 10*, 239-260.

Michalos, A. C. (1980). Satisfaction and happiness. *Social Indicators Research, 8*, 385-422.

Michalos, A. C. (1985). Multiple discrepancies theory (MDT). *Social Indicators Research, 16*, 347-413.

Michalos, A. C. (1991). *Global on student well-being. Volume 1: Life satisfaction and happiness.* New York: Springer Verlag.

Michalos, A. C. (1993). *Global report on student well-being. Volume IV: Religion, education, recreation, and health.* New York: Springer Verlag.

Mill, J. S. (1979). *Utilitarianism.* Indianapolis: Hackett.

Miller, D. T., & Ross, M. (1975). Self-serving biases in attribution of causality: fact or fiction? *Psychological Bulletin, 82*, 213-225.

Miller, L. & Weiss, R. (1982). The work-leisure relationship: Evidence for the compensatory. *Human Relations, 35*, 763-771.

Montague, R. (1967). Happiness. *Proceedings of the Aritotelian Society, 67*, 87-102.

Munkel, T., Strack, F., & Schwarz, N. (1987). *Der EinfluB der experimentellen Honorierrung aufStimmung und Wolhbefinden: Macht Schokolade glucklich?* 29th Tagung Experimentell Arbeitender Psychologen, Aachen, FRG.

Murray, C. & Peacock, M. J. (1996). A model-free approach to the study of subjective well-being. In *Mental health of Black America.* Thousand Oaks, California: Sage Publications.

Murray, H. A. (1938). *Explorations in personality.* New York: Oxford University Press.

Myers, D. G. (1992). *The pursuit of happiness: Who is happy--and why.* New York: William Morrow.

Myers, D. G. (1993). *The pursuit of happiness.* New York: Avon Books.

Myers, D. G. (1999). Close relationships and quality of life. In D. Kahneman, E. Diener, & N. Schwartz (Eds.), *Well-being: The foundations of hedonic psychology* (pp. 374-391). New York: Russell Sage.

Neal, J., Sirgy, M. J., & Uysal, M. (1999). The role of satisfaction with leisure travel/tourism services and experiences in satisfaction with leisure life and overall life. *Journal of Business Research, 44* (March), 153-163.

Near, J. P. (1986). Work and nonwork attitudes among Japanese and American workers. In R. N. Farmer (Ed.), *Advances in international comparative management*, vol. 2 (pp. 57-67).

Near, J. P., Rice, R. W., & Hunt, R. G. (1980). The relationship between work and nonwork domains: A review of empirical research. *Academy of Management Review, 5*(3), 415-429.

Neugarten, B. L., Havighurst, R. J., & Tobin, S. S. (1961). The measurement of life satisfaction. *Journal of Gerontology, 16*, 134-143.

Neugarten, B. L., R. J. Havighurst, and S. S. Tobin (1961). "The Measurement of Life Satisfaction." *Journal of Gerontology, 16*, 134-143.

Niven, D. (2000). *The 100 simple secrets of happy people: What scientists have learned and how you can use it.* New York: Harper San Francisco.

Nozick, R. (1989). *The examined life.* New York: Simon and Schuster.

O'Brien, G. E. (1986). *Psychology of work and unemployment.* New York: Wiley.

Oishi, S., Diener, E., Suh, E., & Lucas, R. E. (1999). The value as a moderator model in subjective well being. *Journal of Personality. 67,* 157-183.

Okun, M. A., Stock, W. A., Haring, M. J., & Witter, R. A. (1984). Health and subjective well being: A meta-analysis. *International Journal of Aging and Human Development, 19,* 111-132.

Omodei, M. M., & Wearing, A. J. (1990). Need satisfaction and involvement in personal projects: Toward an integrative model of subjective well being. *Journal of Personality and Social Psychology, 59*(4), 762-769.

Organ, D. W., & Near, J. P. (1985). Cognition vs. affect in measures of job satisfaction. *International Journal of Psychology, 20,* 241-253.

Orpen, C. (1978). Work and nonwork satisfaction: A causal correlational analysis. *Journal of Applied Psychology, 63,* 530-532.

Panos, K. (1997). Linking: Exploration of related constructs and effects on happiness. Master's thesis, American University, Washington, D.C.

Parducci, A. (1968). The relativism of absolute judgements. *Scientific American, 219,* 84-90.

Parducci, A. (1984). Value judgements: Toward a relational theory of happiness. In J. R. Eiser (Ed.), *Attitudinal Judgement.* New York: Springer-Verlag.

Parducci, A. (1995). *Happiness, pleasure, and judgement: The contextual theory and its applications.* Mahwah, New Jersey: Lawrence Erlbaum Associates.

Pelham, B. W., & Wachsmuth, J. D. (1995). The waxing and waning of the social self: Assimilation and contrast in social comparison. *Journal of Personality and Social Psychology, 69,* 825-838.

Plato. (1892). *The dialogues of Plato* (B. Jowett, Translator), New York: Random House (original work published 360 BC).

Pollner, M. (1989). Divine relations, social relations, and well-being. *Journal of Health and Social Behavior, 30,* 92-104.

Pomerantz, E. M., Saxon, J. L., & Oishi, S. (1998). The psychological tradeoffs of making it personally important: Implications for anxiety and depressive symptoms. Manuscript submitted for publication, University of Illinois.

Porter, J. R. & Washington, R. E. (1979). Black identity and self-esteem. *Annual Review of Sociology*, *5*, 53-74.

Pyszczynski, T. (1982). Cognitive strategies for coping with uncertain outcomes. *Journal of Research in Personality*, *16*, 386-399.

Rabinowitz, S. & Hall, D. T. (1977). Organizational research on job involvement. *Psychological Bulletin*, *84*, 265-288.

Rapoport, R., Rapoport, R., & Thiessen, V. (1974). Couple symmetry and enjoyment. *Journal of Marriage and the Family*, *36*, 588-591.

Rawls, J. (1971). *A theory of justice*. Cambridge, Mass.: Harvard University Press.

Rehberg, K-S. (2000). The fear of happiness: anthropological motives. *Journal of Happiness Studies*, *1*, 479-500.

Reich, J. W., & Zautra, A. (1981). Life events and personal causation: Some relationships with satisfaction and distress. *Journal of Personality and Social Psychology*, *41*, 1002-1012.

Reif, K. & Inglehart, R. (Eds.) (1991). *Eurobarometer: The dynamics of European public opinion*. Houndsmill, Basingstoke, & London: Macmillan.

Rescher, N. (1972). *Welfare: the social issues in philosophical perspective*. Pittsburgh: Pittsburgh University Press.

Reynolds, T. J. & Guttman, J. (1988). Laddering theory, method, analysis, and interpretation. *Journal of Advertising Research*, *28*(February-March), 11-31.

Rice, R. W., Near, J. P., & Hunt, R. G. (1980). The job- satisfaction/life-satisfaction relationship: A review of empirical research. *Basic and Applied Social Psychology* , *1*, 37-64.

Rice, R. W., McFarlin, D. B., Hunt, R. G., & Near, J. P. (1985). Organisational work and the perceived quality of life: Toward a conceptual model. *Academy of Management Review*, *10*, 296-310.

Rice, R. W., Near, J. P., & Hunt, R. G. (1980). The job satisfaction-life satisfaction relationship: A review of empirical research. *Basic and Applied Social Psychology*, *1*, 37-64.

Rice, R. W., Phillips, S. M., & McFarlin, D. B. (1990). Multiple discrepancies and pay satisfaction. *Journal of Applied Psychology*, *75*, ARti-93.

Roberts, K. H. & Glick, W. (1981). The job characteristics approach to task design: A critical review. *Journal of Applied Psychology*, *66*, 193-217.

Roese, N. J. (1997). Counterfactual thinking. *Psychological Bulletin*, *121*, 133-148.

Roese, N. J., & Olson, J. M. (Eds.). (1995a). *What might have been: The social psychology of counterfactual thinking*. Mahwah, N.J.: Erlbaum.

Roese, N. J., & Olson, J. M. (1995b). Counterfactual thinking: A critical review. In N. J. Roese and J. M. Olson (Eds.), *What might have been: The social psychology of counterfactual thinking* (pp. 1-55). Mahwah, N.J.: Erlbaum.

Rogers, C. &Dymond, R. (Eds.). (1954). *Psychotherapy and personality changes.* Chicago, IL: University of Chicago Press.

Rokeach, M. (1973). *The nature of human values.* New York: The Free Press.

Rosenberg, M. (1979). *Conceiving the self.* New York: Basic Books.

Rosenberg, M. & Simmons, R. G. (1972). *Black and white self-esteem: The urban school child.* Washington, DC: American Sociological Association, Rose Monograph Series.

Rosenman, R. H., Friedman, M., Straus, R., Wurm, M., Jenkins, C. D., Messinger, H. B., Kositchek, R., Hahn, W., & Werthessen, N. T. (1966). Coronary heart disease in the Western Collaborative Group Study. *Journal of the American Medical Association, 195,* 86-92.

Ross, M., Eyman, A., & Kishchuck, N. (1986). Determinants of subjective well being. In J. M. Olson, C. P. Herman, and M. Zanna (Eds.), *Relative deprivation and social comparison* (pp. 78-103). Hillsdale, N.J.: Erlbaum.

Ross, M., & Fletcher, G. J. O. (1985). Attribution and social perception. In G. Lindzey & E. Aronson (Eds.), *The handbook of social psychology* (3rd ed., pp. 73-122). Reading, MA: Addison-Wesley.

Roth, S., & Cohen, L. J. (1986). Approach, avoidance, and coping with stress. *American Psychologist, 41,* 813-819.

Rozin, P., & Vollmecke, T. A. (1986). Food likes and dislikes. *Annual Review of Nutrition,* 6, 433-456.

Russell, B. (1975). *The conquest of happiness.* London: Unwin. (original work published 1930)

Safilios-Rothschild, C. (1970). The influence of the wife's degree of work commitment upon some aspects of family organization and dynamics. *Journal of Marriage and the Family, 32,* 681-691.

Salancik, G. R., & Pfeffer, J. (1977). An examination of need-satisfaction models of job attitudes. *Administrative Science Quarterly,* 23, 224-253.

Saris, W. E. (2001). What influence subjective well-being in Russia? *Journal of Happiness Studies, 2,* 137-146.

Saris, W. E. & Andreenkova, A. (2001). Following changes in living conditions and happiness in post communist Russia: the Russet panel. *Journal of Happiness Studies, 2,* 95-109.

Saris, W., & Kasse, M. (1997). The Eurobarometer--a tool for comparative survey research. In W. Saris & M. Kasse (Eds.), *Eurobarometer:*

Measurement instruments for opinions in Europe. Mannheim, Germany: ZUMA.

Scheck, C. L., Kinicki, A. J., & Davy, J. A. (1997). Testing the mediating processes between work stressors and subjective well being. *Journal of Vocational Behaviour, 50*, 96-123.

Scheier, M. F., & Carver, C. S. (1985). Optimism, coping, and health: Assessment and implications of generalized outcome expectancies. *Health Psychology, 4*, 219-247.

Scheier, M. F., & Carver, C. S. (1993). On the power of positive thinking. *Current Directions in Psychological Science, 2*, 26-30.

Schkade, D. A., & Kahneman, D. (1998). Does living in California make people happy? A focusing illusion in judgements of life satisfaction. *Psychological Science, 9*, 340-346.

Schmitt, N., & Bedian, A. G. (1982). A comparison of LISREL and two-stage least squares analysis of a hypothesized life-job satisfaction reciprocal relationship. *Journal of Applied Psychology, 67*, 806-817.

Schmitt, N., & Mellon, P. A. (1980). Life and job satisfaction: Is the job central? *Journal of Vocational Behaviour, 16*, 51-58.

Schuman, H., & Presser, S. (1981). *Questions and answers in attitude surveys: Experiments on question form, wording and context.* New York: Academic Press.

Schwarz, N. (1983). Stimmung als Information: Zum Einfluß von Stimmungen auf die Beurteilung des eigenen Lebens. In G. Luer (ed.), *Bericht uber den 33, Kongreß der Deutschen Gesellschaft fur Psychologie in Manz 1982.* Gottingen: Hogrefe.

Schwarz, N. (1988). Was Befragte aus Antwortvorgaben lenen: Zur information Funktion von Antwortvorgraben bei Verhaltensberichten. *Planung und Analyse, 15*, 103-107.

Schwarz, N., & Clore, G. L. (1983). Mood, misattribution, and judgments of well-being: Informative and directive functions of affective states. *Journal of personality and Social Psychology, 45*, 513-523.

Schwarz, N., & Hippler, H. J. (1987). What response scales may tell your respondents. In H. J. Hippler, N. Schwarz, & S. Sudman (eds.), *Social information processing and survey methodology.* New York: Springer Verlag.

Schwarz, N., & Strack, F. (1991). Evaluating one's life: A judgement model of subjective well-being. In F. Strack, M. Argyle, & N. Schwarz (Eds.), *Subjective well-being* (pp. 27-47). Oxford, UK: Pergamon Press,

Schwarz, N, & Strack, F. (1999). Reports of subjective well-being: Judgmental processes and their methodological implications. In D.

Kahneman, E. Diener, & N. Schwarz (Eds.), *Well-being: The foundations of hedonic psychology* (pp.61-84). New York: Russell Sage Foundation.

Schwarz, N., Strack, F., Kommer, D., & Wagner, D. (1987). Soccer, rooms, and the quality of your life: Mood effects on judgements of satisfaction with life in general and with specific life domains. *European Journal of Social Psychology, 17*, 69-79.

Schyns, P. (1998). Cross-national differences in happiness: Economic and cultural factors explored. *Social Indicators Research, 43*, 3-26.h

Scitovsky, T. (1976). *The joyless economy: The psychology of human satisfaction*. New York: Oxford University Press.

Scott, V. P. & McIntosh, W. D. (1999). The development of a trait measure of ruminative thought. *Personality & Individual Differences, 26*, 1045.

Scott, W. A., & Stumpf, J. (1984). Personal satisfaction and role-performance: subjective and social aspects of adaptation. *Journal of Personality and Social Psychology, 47*, 812-827.

Scrutton, R. (1975). Reason and happiness. In R. S. Peters (Ed.), *Nature and conduct* (pp. 139-161). New York: Macmillan.

Seeman, M. (1967). On the personal consequence of alienation and job satisfaction. *Industrial and Labor Review, 23*, 207-219.

Seidlitz, L., & Diener, E. (1993). Memory for positive versus negative life events: Theories for the differences between happy and unhappy persons. *Journal of Personality and Social Psychology, 64*, 654-664.

Sen, A. (1987). *Commodities and capabilities*. New York: oxford University Press.

Shamir, B. (1986). Unemployment and nonwork activities among persons with higher education. *Journal of Applied Behavioral Science, 22*(4), 459-475.

Shea, J. R., Spitz, R. S., & Zeller, F. A. (1970). *Dual careers: A longtitudinal study of labor market experience of women,* Vol. 1, Manpower Research Monograph No. 21 (Washington, D.C.: U.S. Government Printing Office).

Sheldon, K. M., & Kasser, T. (1995). Coherence and congruence: Two aspects of personality integration. *Journal of Personality and Social Psychology, 68*, 531-543.

Shepard, J. M. (1974). A status recognition model of work-leisure relationships. *Journal of Leisure Research, 6*, 58-63.

Shostak, A. B. (1987). Singlehood. In M. B. Sussman & S. K. Steinmetz (Eds.), *Handbook of marriage and the family* (pp. 355-367). New York: Plenum.

Simpson, R. (1975). Happiness. *American Philosophical Quarterly, 12*, 169-176.

Simpson, R. (1990). Conflict styles and social network relations as predictors of marital happiness. Ph.D. dissertation, University of Michigan, Ann Arbor, Michigan.

Sirgy, M. J. (1982). Self-concept in consumer behavior: A critical review. *Journal of Consumer Research, 9*(December), 287-300.

Sirgy, M. J. (1986). *Self-congruity: Toward a theory of personality and cybernetics.* New York: Praeger Publishers.

Sirgy, M. J. (1998). Materialism and quality of life. *Social Indicators Research, 43*, 227-260.

Sirgy, M. J. (2001). *Handbook of quality-of-life research: An ethical marketing perspective.* The Netherlands: Kluwer Academic Publishers.

Sirgy, M. J., Cole, D., Kosenko, R., Meadow, H. L., Rahtz, R. D., Cicic, M., Jin, G. X., Yarsuvat, D., Blenkhorn, D., Nagpal, N. (1995a). A life Satisfaction measure: Additional validational data for the Congruity Life Satisfaction measure. *Social Indicators Research, 34*, 237-259.

Sirgy, M. J., Cole, D., Kosenko, R., Meadow, H. L., Rahtz, D., Cicic, M., Jin, G. X., Yarsuvat, D., Blenkhorn, D. L., & Nagpal, N. (1995b). Developing a life satisfaction measure based on need hierarchy theory. In M. J. Sirgy and A. C. Samli (Eds.), *New dimensions of marketing and quality of life* (pp. 3-26). Westport, CT: Greenwood Press.

Sirgy, M. J., Hansen, D. E., & Littlefield, J. E. (1994). Does hospital satisfaction affect life satisfaction? *Journal of Macromarketing, 14* (Fall), 36-46.

Sirgy, M. J., Lee, D-J., Kosenko, R., Meadow, H. L., Rahtz, D., Cicic, M., Jin, G. X., Yarsuvat, D., Blenkhorn, D., & Wright, N. (1998a). Does television viewership play a role in the perception of quality of life? *Journal of Advertising, 27* (Spring), 125-142.

Sirgy, M. J., Lee, D-J., Larsen, V., & Wright, N. (1998b). Satisfaction with material possessions and general well being: The role of materialism. *Journal of Consumer Satisfaction/Dissatisfaction and Complaining Behavior, 11*, 103-118.

Sirgy, M. J., Mentzer, J. T., Rahtz, D., & Meadow, H. L. (1991). Satisfaction with healthcare marketing services consumption and life satisfaction among the elderly. *Journal of Macromarketing, 11* (Spring), 24-39.

Sirgy, M. J., Rahtz, D. R., Cicic, M., & Underwood, R. (2000). A method for assessing residents' satisfaction with community-based services: A quality-of-life perspective. *Social Indicators Research, 49*, 279-316.

Smith, T. W. (1979). Happiness. *Social Psychology Quarterly*, 42, 18-30.

Solomon, R. L. (1980). The opponent-process theory of acquired motivation: The costs of pleasure and the benefits of pain. *American Psychologist, 35*, 691-712.

Spreitzer, E., & Snyder, E. (1974). Correlates of life satisfaction among the elderly. *Journal of Gerontology, 29*, 454-458.

Staats, S., Armstrong-Stassen, M., & Partillo, C. (1995). Student well-being: Are they better off now? *Social Indicators Research, 34*, 93.

Staines, G. L. (1980). Spillover versus compensation: A review of the literature on the relationship between work and nonwork. *Human Relations, 33*, 111-129.

Staines, G. L., & Pagnucco, D. (1977). Work and nonwork: Part II—An empirical study. In Survey Research Center, *Effectiveness in Work Roles: Employee Responses to Work Environments* (Vol. 1).

Steiner, D. D., & Truxillo, D. M. (1989). An improved test of the disaggregation hypothesis of job and life satisfaction. *Journal of Occupational Psychology, 62*, 33-39.

Stouffer, S. A. Ed. (1949). *The American soldier: Adjustment during wartime life.* Vol. 1. Princeton, New Jersey: Princeton University Press.

Strack, F., Martin, L. L., & Schwarz, N. (1987). The context paradox in attitude surveys: Assimilation or contrast. *ZUMA Arbeitsbericht, 7.*

Strack, F., Martin, L. L., & Schwarz, N. (1988). Priming and communication: Social determinants of information use in judgements of life satisfaction. *European Journal of Social Psychology, 18*, 429-442.

Strack, F., Schwarz, N., & Gschneidinger, E. (1985). Happiness and reminiscing: The role of time perspective, mood, and mode of thinking. *Journal of Personality and Social Psychology, 49*, 1460-1469.

Strauman, T. J. (1989). Self-discrepancies in clinical depression and social phobia: Cognitive structures that underlie emotional disturbances. *Journal of Abnormal Psychology, 98*, 14-22.

Strauman, T. J., & Higgins, E. T. (1987). Autonomic activation of self-discrepancies and emotional syndromes: When cognitive structures influence affect. *Journal of Personality and Social Psychology, 53*, 1004-1014.

Stryker, S. (1968). Identity salience and role performance: The relevance of symbolic interaction theory for family research. *Journal of Marriage and the Family, 30*, 558-564.

Sumner, L. W. (1996). *Welfare, happiness, and ethics.* New York: Oxford University Press.

Swann, W. B., Jr. (1983). Self-verification: Bringing social reality into harmony with the self. In J. Suls & A. G. Greenwald (Eds.), *Social psychology perspectives,* Vol. 2 (pp. 33-66). Hillsdale, NJ: Erlbaum.

Swann, W. B., Jr., & Hill, C. A. (1982). When our identities are mistaken: Reaffirming self-conceptions through social interactions. *Journal of Personality and Social Psychology, 43*, 59-66.

Swann, W. B., Jr., & Read, S. J. (1981a). Acquiring self-knowledge: The search for feedback that fits. *Journal of Personality and Social Psychology*, 41, 1119-1128.

Swann, W. B., Jr., & Read, S. J. (1981b). Self-verification processes: How we sustain our self-conceptions. *Journal of Experimental Social Psychology*, *17*, 351-370.

Sweeney, P. D., Schaeffer, D. E., & Golin, S. (1982). Pleasant events, unpleasant events, and depression. *Journal of Personality and Social Psychology*, *43*, 136-144.

Swinyard, W. R., Kau, A-K, & Phua, H-Y. (2001). Happiness, materialism, and religious experience in the US and Singapore. *Journal of Happiness Studies*, *2*, 13-32.

Tait, M., Padgett, M. Y., & Baldwin, T.T. (1989). Job satisfaction and life satisfaction: A reexamination of the strength of the relationship and gender effects as a function of the date of the study. *Journal of Applied Psychology*, *74*, 502-507.

Tanaka, J. S., & Huba, G. J. (1984). Confirmatory hierarchical factor analyses of psychological distress measures. *Journal of Personality and Social Psychology*, *43*(3), 621-635.

Tannen, D. (1994). *Talking from 9 to 5: How women's and men's conversational styles affect who gets heard, who gets credit, and what gets done at work.* New York: William Morrow.

Tatarkiewicz, W. (1976). *Analysis of happiness* (translated by Rothert, Edward and Zielinskin, Danutt). The Hague: Martinus Nijhoff.

Taylor, M. C. & Walsh, E. J. (1979). Explanations of Black self-esteem: Some empirical tests. *Social Psychology Quarterly*, *42*, 242-253.

Taylor, S. E. (1983). Adjustments to threatening events: A theory of cognitive adaptation. *American Psychologist*, 38, 1161-1173.

Taylor, S. E. & Brown, J. D. (1988). Illusion and well-being: A social psychological perspective on mental health. *Psychological Bulletin*, *103*(2), 193-210.

Taylor, S. E., Lichtman, R. R., & Wood, J. V. (1984). Attributions, beliefs about control, and adjustment to breast cancer. *Journal of Personality and Social Psychology*, *46*, 489-502.

Tedeschi, J. T. & Riess, M. (1981a). Predicaments and verbal tactics of impression management. In C. Antaki (Ed.), *Ordinary language explanations of social behaviour.* London: Academic Press.

Tedeschi, J. T. & Riess, M. (1981b). Identities, the phenomenal self, and laboratory research. In J. T. Tedeschi (Ed.), *Impression Management Theory and Social Psychological Research* (pp. 3-32). New York: Academic Press,.

Tellegen, A., Lykken, D. T., Bouchard, T. J., Wilcox, K.J., Segal, N.L., & Rich, S. (1988). Personality similarity in twins and reared apart and together. *Journal of Personality and Social Psychology, 54*, 1031-1039

Tesser, A. (1980). Self-esteem maintenance in family dynamics. *Journal of Personality and Social Psychology, 39*, 77-91.

Tesser, A., & Campbell, J. (1980). Self-definition: The impact of relative performance and similarity of others. *Social Psychology Quarterly*, 43, 341-347.

Tesser, A., Campbell, J., & Smith, M. (1984). Friendship, choice and performance: Self-evaluation maintenance in children. *Journal of Personality and Social Psychology, 46*, 561-574.

Tesser, A., & Paulhus, D. (1983). The definition of self: Private and public self-evaluation management strategies. *Journal of Personality and Social Psychology, 44*, 672-682.

Tesser, A., Pilkington, C. J., & McIntosh, W. D. (1989). Self-evaluation maintenance and the mediational role of emotion: The perception of friends and strangers. *Journal of Personality and Social Psychology, 57*, 442-456.

Thomas, D. A. L. (1968). Happiness. *Philosophical Quarterly, 18*, 97-113.

Thompson, R. F., & Spencer, W. A. (1966). Habituation: A model phenomenon for the study of neuronal sustrates of behavior. *Psychological Review, 73*(1), 16-43.

Thorne, B. (1992). Feminism and the family: Two decades of thought. In B. Thorne (with M. Yalom; Eds). *Rethinking the family: Some feminist questions* (pp. 3-30). Boston: Northeaster University Press.

Thurman, C. (1981). Personality correlates of the type A behaviour pattern. Ph.D. dissertation, University of Georgia, Athens, Georgia.

Turner, C. (1994). Follow through in conflict resolution as a factor in marital satisfaction and personal happiness. Master's thesis, University of Nevada, Las Vegas, Nevada.

Tversky, A., & Griffin, D. (1991). Endowment and contrast in judgements of well-being. In F. Strack, M. Argyle, and N. Schwartz (Eds.), *Subjective well-being: An interdisciplinary perspective* (pp. 101-118). Oxford: Pergamon Press.

Vallacher, R. R., & Wegner, D. M. (1989). Levels of personal agency: Individual variation in action identification. *Journal of Personality and Social Psychology, 57*, 660-671.

Van de Stadt, H., Kapteyn, A., & van de Geer, S. (1985). The relativity of utility: Evidence from panel data. *The Review of Economics and Statistics, 67*(2), 179-187.

Van Hook, E., & Higgins, E. T. (1988). Self-related problems beyond the self-concept: The motivational consequences of discrepant self-guides. *Journal of Personality and Social Psychology*, 55, 625-633.

Van Praag, B. M. S. (1971). The individual welfare function of income in Belgium: An empirical investigation. *European Economic Review*, 2, 337-369.

Von Wright, G. H. (1963). *The varieties of goodness*. London: Routledge & Keegan Paul.

Veenhoven, R. (1984a). *Conditions of happiness*. Boston: Reidel.

Veenhoven, R. (1984b). *Data book on happiness*. Boston: Reidel.

Veenhoven, R. (1991). Is happiness relative? *Social Indicators Research*, 24, 1-34.

Veenhoven, R. (1991). Question on happiness: Classical topics, modern answers, and blind spots. In F. Strack, M. Argyle, & N. Schwarz (eds.), *Subjective well-being: An interdisciplinary perspective* (pp. 7-26). Oxford, U.K.: Pergamon Press.

Veenhoven, R. (2000). The four qualities of life. *Journal of Happiness Studies*, *1*, 1-39.

Veenhoven, R. and coworkers (1994*). World database of happiness: Correlates of happiness*. Rotterdam: Erasmus University.

Walker, K. & Gauger, W. (1973). Time and its dollar value in household work. *Family Economics Review*, Fall, 8-13.

Walker, K. & Woods, M. (1976). *Time use: A measure of household production of family goods and services*. Washington, D.C.: American Home Economics Association.

Warner, R. (1987). *Freedom, enjoyment, and happiness: an essay on moral psychology*. Ithaca: Cornell University Press.

Watson, D., & Clark, L. A. (1984). Negative affectivity: The disposition to experience negative affective states. *Psychological Bulletin*, *96*, 465-490.

Watson, D., Clark, L. A., & Tellegen, A. (1988). Development and validation of brief measures of positive and negative affect: The PANAS scales. *Journal of Personality and Social Psychology*, *54*, 1063-1070.

Watson, D., & Pennebaker, J. W. (1989). Health complaints, stress, and distress: Exploring the central role of negative affectivity. *Psychological Review*, *96*, 234-254.

Wilensky, H. (1960). Work, careers, and social integration. *International Social Science Journal*, *12*, 543-560.

Williams, D. G. (1988). Gender, marriage, and social class. In R. Staples (Ed.), *The Black family: Essays and studies* (2nd ed., pp. 236-243). Belmont, CA: Wadsworth.

Wilson, J. (1968). Happiness. *Analysis*, *29*, 13-21.

Wilson, J. (1980). Sociology of leisure. *Annual Review of Sociology*, *6*, 21-40.

Wilson, S., Henry, C., & Peterson, G. (1997). Life satisfaction among low-income rural youth in Appalachia. *Journal of Adolescence*, *20*, 443.

Wilson, T. (2000). Why happiness is like food. Presentation at the Second Annual Positive Psychology Summit, October 13-15, 2000, Washington, DC.

Wolf, S. (1997). Happiness and meaning: two aspects of the good life. *Social Philosophy and Policy*, *14*, 207-225.

Wood, J. V., Taylor, S. E., & Lichtman, R. R. (1985). Social comparison in adjustment to breast cancer. *Journal of Personality and Social Psychology*, *49*, 1169-1183.

Wood, V., Wylie, M., & Sheafer, B. (1969). An analysis of a short self-report measure of life satisfaction: Correlation with rater judgments. *Journal of Gerontology*, *24*, 465-469.

Wood, W., Rhodes, N., & Whelan, M. (1989). Sex differences in positive well-being: A consideration of emotional style and marital status. *Psychological Bulletin*, *106*, 249-264.

Wright, N. & Larsen, V. (1993). Materialism and life satisfaction: A meta-analysis." *Journal of Consumer Satisfaction, Dissatisfaction, and Complaining Behavior*, *6* 158-165.

Yancey, W. L., Rigsby, L., & McCarthy, J. D. (1972). Social position and self-evaluation: The relative importance of race. *American Journal of Sociology*, *78*, 338-359.

Zuckerman, M. (1979). Attribution of success and failure revisited, or: The motivational bias is alive and well in attribution theory. *Journal of Personality*, *47*, 245-287.

APPENDIX

STRATEGIES AND PRINCIPLES OF QUALITY-OF-LIFE ENHANCEMENT

The Bottom-Up Spillover Strategy

o   *The Bottom-Up Spillover Principle: Subjective well being can be increased by allowing positive life domains to spill over positive affect unto the most superordinate domain (overall life). The positive affect accumulates in life domains as a direct function of satisfaction of human development needs*

o   *The Means-End Chain Principle of Bottom-up Spillover: Establishing meaningful connections between life events, life domains, and overall life can facilitate bottom-up spillover. Subjective well being can be enhanced by making meaningful connections with positive life events--events that can be evaluated positively. A life event is positive when it generates positive affect as a result of satisfaction of one or more human developmental needs. Conversely, an event is negative when it generates negative affect as a result of failing to satisfy one or more needs.*

o   *The Multi-domain Satisfaction Principle of Bottom-up Spillover: Subjective well being can be enhanced by increasing the salience of positive life domains, decreasing the salience of negative domains, increasing positive affect in positive domains, and/or decreasing negative affect in negative domains. A life domain is positive when it contains significantly more positive than negative affect generated from satisfaction of human developmental needs. Conversely, a life domainis negative when it contains significantly more negative than positive affect.*

o   *The Abstractness of Life Domain Principle of Bottom-up Spillover: Subjective well being can be enhanced by evaluating abstract life domains, if these evaluations are anticipated to be positive. If the evaluations are anticipated to be negative, then the damage to subjective well being can be minimized by diverting the evaluation to concrete domains.*

o   *The Self-proximity Principle of Bottom-up Spillover: Subjective well being can be enhanced by evaluating life domains proximal to the self, if these evaluations are antiicipated to be positive. If the evaluations are anticipated to be negative, then the damage to subjective well being can be minimized by evaluating domains distal to the self.*

The Top-Down Spillover Strategy

o   *The Principle of Top-Down Spillover: Subjective well being can be increased by allowing spillover of positive affect from overall life to important life domains. This should increase positive affect (or decrease negative affect) in these life domains. Positive affect is generated as a direct function of satisfaction of human developmental needs.*

o   *The Personality Principle of Top-down Spillover: Top-down spillover of positive affect from overall life to various life domains is likely to occur more readily for people who are extraverts, optimistic, have high self-esteem, have high expectancies of control, have the Pollyanna syndrome, or have a genetic predisposition to be happy. Conversely, top-down spillover of negative affect from overall life to various life domains is likely to occur more readily for people who are introverts, pessimistic, have low self-esteem, have low expectancies of control, do not have the Pollyanna syndrome, or do not have a genetic predisposition to be happy.*

o   *The Very Happy and the Depressed Principle of Top-down Spillover: Top-down spillover of positive affect from overall life to various life domains is likely to occur more readily for people who are very happy. Conversely, top-down spillover of negative affect from overall life to various life domains is likely to occur more readily for people who are very depressed.*

The Horizontal Spillover Strategy

o   *The Horizontal-Spillover Principle: Subjective well being can be enhanced by inducing positive affect in a particular life domain to horizontally spill over to neighbouring important domains. Doing so increases the positive valence of the neighbouring domains (or decreases negative valence). This, in turn, should enhance subjective well being through a bottom-up spillover of positive affect from the neighbouring domain to overall life.*

o   *The Overlap Principle of Horizontal Spillover: Horizontal spillover is likely to occur when the individual is highly involved in the two life domains and these domains overlap in time, place, people, and/or activities.*

o   *The High Involvement Principle of Horizontal Spillover: Horizontal spillover between two life domains is more likely to occur if the individual is emotionally involved in both domains than if he or she is not emotionally involved.*

o   *The Skills Principle of Horizontal Spillover: Horizontal spillover is likely to occur if the individual uses skills learned in one life domain in the context of another domain.*

o   *The Cultural Pressures Principle of Horizontal Spillover: Horizontal spillover between two life domains is likely to occur if the individual feels cultural pressure arising from one of the domains (a high involvement domain) to be involved in the other domain.*

The Compensation Strategy

o   *The Compensation Principle: Increasing the salience of a domain having more positive than negative affect can enhance subjective well being. Conversely, decreasing the salience of a domain having more negative than positive affect can enhance subjective well being.*

o   *The Repeated Failure Principle of Compensation: Compensation between two life domains is likely to occur when failure is experienced repeatedly in one domain. The repeated failure causes the individual to decrease the importance of the failure domain and compensate by increasing the salience of a success domain. Doing so enhances subjective well being.*

o   *The Low-versus-High-Status Principle of Compensation:*
    Compensation between two life domains is likely to occur when the
    person recognises that he has high status in one domain but low in
    another.   Recognition of low status in one domain causes the
    individual to decrease the importance of that domain and
    compensate by increasing the salience of the high-status domain.

o   *The Personal Crisis Principle of Compensation:* *Compensation*
    between two life domains is likely to occur when the person
    experiences a crisis in one domain.   To deal with the crisis, the
    person decreases the importance of that domain and compensates
    by increasing the salience of another domain.

o   *The Public Condition Principle of Compensation:* *Compensation*
    between two life domains is more likely to occur when the person
    experiences failure in one domain in a public way (significant
    others have knowledge of the failure).   To deal with public
    humiliation, the person decreases the importance of that domain
    and compensates by increasing the salience of another domain.

o   *The Fixed-Sum-of-Resources Principle of Compensation:*
    Compensation between two life domains is likely to occur when
    satisfaction derived from these domains require significant
    resources and given that these resources cannot be provided.

o   *The Needs Principle of Compensation:* *Compensation can be*
    facilitated if the new salient domain can satisfy the same needs of
    the domain made less salient.

The Re-Evaluation Based on Personal History Strategy

o   *The Personal History Principle of Re-evaluation:* *Satisfaction*
    results when a life event or outcome is evaluated to equal or exceed
    one's expectations of that outcome based on what the person has
    grown accustomed to in the past. The better the outcome compared
    to what the person is accustomed to the higher the satisfaction.
    Dissatisfaction results when the outcome is evaluated to fall short
    from what the person has been accustomed to in the past.   The
    greater the discrepancy from what the person has been accustomed
    to the greater the dissatisfaction.

o *The Adaptation-Level Principle of Re-evaluation: Satisfaction experienced in a life domain can be increased (and dissatisfaction can be decreased) by comparing perceived events in that domain to referents having hedonic values lower than the hedonic value of the perceived events.*

o *The Range-Frequency Principle of Re-evaluation: Satisfaction of a life domain can be increased (and dissatisfaction can be decreased) by comparing perceived events in that domain to referents having hedonic values lower than the hedonic value of the current events in terms of not only the frequency of past outcomes but also the range of outcomes.*

o *The Adaptation-over-time Principle of Re-evaluation: Satisfaction resulting from a life event judged much better than what one has been accustomed to decreases toward neutrality over time. Conversely, dissatisfaction resulting from an event judged much worse than what one has been accustomed to decreases toward neutrality over time.*

o *The Sensitisation-over-time Principle of Re-evaluation: Satisfaction in a life domain increases by repeated exposure over time to the same stimuli associated with the life event that initially induced the positive feelings, given that the repeated exposure is experienced with a positive mood. Conversely, dissatisfaction in a life domain increases by repeated exposure over time to the same stimuli associated with the life event that initially induced the negative feelings, given that the repeated exposure is experienced with a negative mood.*

The Re-Evaluation Based on Self-Concept Strategy

o *The Self-concept Principle of Re-evaluation: People feel satisfied about themselves when they compare themselves against self-expectations and discover that their actual self is better or equal to what they expect of themselves. Conversely, they feel dissatisfied about themselves when they compare themselves against what they expect of themselves and find that they had performed less than what they expected. Positive self-evaluations boost subjective well being, while negative self-evaluations reduce subjective well being.*

o   *The Ideal Self Principle of Re-evaluation*: *Satisfaction in a life domain can be increased (and dissatisfaction can be decreased) by evaluating specific events in that domain against an ideal self that is likely to generate positive self-evaluations. Positive self-evaluations are experienced given the perception of low discrepancy between the actual and ideal self.*

o   *The Social Self Principle of Re-evaluation*: *Satisfaction in a life domain can be increased (and dissatisfaction can be decreased) by evaluating specific events in that domain against a social self that is likely to generate positive self-evaluations. Positive self-evaluations are experienced given the perception of low discrepancy between the actual and social self.*

o   *The Deserved-self Principle of Re-evaluation*: *Satisfaction in a life domain can be increased (and dissatisfaction can be decreased) by re-evaluating specific events in that domain against a deserved self that is likely to generate positive self-evaluations. Positive self-evaluations are experienced given the perception of low · discrepancy between the actual and deserved self.*

o   *The Minimum-needs Principle of Re-evaluation*: *Satisfaction in a life domain can be increased (and dissatisfaction can be decreased) by re-evaluating specific events in that domain against a minimum-needs self that is likely to generate positive self-evaluations.*

o   *The Predicted Self Principle of Re-evaluation*: *Satisfaction in a life domain can be increased (and dissatisfaction can be decreased) by re-evaluating specific events in that domain against a predicted self that is likely to generate positive self-evaluations.*

o   *The Competent Self Principle of Re-evaluation*: *Satisfaction in a life domain can be increased (and dissatisfaction can be decreased) by re-evaluating specific events in that domain against a competent self that is likely to generate positive self-evaluations evaluations when goals related to the competent self are attained (or at least progress towards the attainment of these achievement-related goals).*

o   *The Aspired Self-Principle of Re-evaluation*: *Satisfaction in a life domain can be increased (and dissatisfaction can be decreased) by re-evaluating specific events in that domain against an aspired self that is likely to generate positive self-evaluations.*

o *The Principle of Self-concept Integration of Re-evaluation:* Satisfaction in a life domain can be increased (and dissatisfaction can be decreased) by ensuring that self-evaluations are performed using self-concept standards likely to generate consistent positive self-evaluations.*

The Re-Evaluation Based on Social Comparison Strategy

o *The Principle of Social Comparison:* Satisfaction in a life domain can be increased (and dissatisfaction can be decreased) by evaluating life events in that domain to similar others (e.g., relative and friends, neighbours, professional associates and colleagues, people of the same age, same sex, same race or ethnic background, same handicap, same home place, and same social class).*

o *The Self-enhancement Principle of Re-evaluation:* People compare positive events in their life with others that have experienced similar but negative events. This downward social comparison generates satisfaction, which in turn enhances subjective well being. Downward social comparison serves to satisfy the self-enhancement motive by inducing positive self-evaluations.*

o *The Self-improvement Principle of Re-evaluation:* People compare negative events in their life with others that have experienced similar events with a positive outcome. This upward social comparison generates satisfaction, which in turn enhances subjective well being. Upward social comparison serves to satisfy the self-improvement motive by allowing the person to predict a positive future for one's condition based on the positive condition of the significant other.*

o *The Self-identification Principle of Re-evaluation:* People compare negative events in their life with others that have experienced similar eventswith a positive outcome. This upward social comparison generates satisfaction, which in turn enhances subjective well being. Upward social comparison serves to satisfy the self-identification motive by allowing the person to identify with those others who have experienced positive events. This self-*

identification with those positive others induces positive self-evaluations, which in turn enhances subjective well being.

o   *The Principle of What Might Have Been of Re-evaluation*: *Satisfaction of a life domain can be increased (or dissatisfaction can be decreased) by comparing one's situation against negative "what-might-have-been" fictitious occurrences.*

o   *The Principle of Integrated Social Comparisons: Subjective well being could be enhanced by making social comparison judgements that satisfy the needs of self-enhancement, self-identification, and self-improvement, simultaneously or conjointly.*

The Goal Selection Strategy

o   *The Goal Selection Principle: Subjective well being can be enhanced by being highly selective in pursuing the kind of goals in which goal attainment is likely to induce positive emotions, e.g., joy, affection, pride.*

o   *The Principle of Goal Meaningfulness of Goal Selection: Selecting meaningful goals in important life domains generates substantial satisfaction in these domains upon attainment. This satisfaction is likely to contribute significantly to subjective well being.*

o   *The Intrinsicness Principle of Goal Selection: Subjective well being can be increased (or dissatisfaction can be decreased) by selecting intrinsic than extrinsic goals in that domain. Attainment of intrinsic goals induces more positive affect in that domain than extrinsic goals.*

o   *The High-Level Principle of Goal Selection : Subjective well being can be increased (or dissatisfaction can be decreased) by selecting more high-level than low-level goals. Attainment of high-level goals induces more positive affect in that domain than low-level goals.*

o   *The Growth Needs Principle of Goal Selection: Subjective well being can be increased by selecting goals related to the satisfaction of growth needs (higher-order needs such as social, esteem, and self-actualisation). Dissatisfaction can be decreased through selection of goals related to the satisfaction of basic needs (lower-order needs such as biological and safety needs).*

o   *The Approach Principle of Goal Selection: Subjective well being can be increased (or dissatisfaction can be decreased) by taking action to approach and attain a desirable state of affairs rather than action to avoid an undesirable state of affairs.*

o   *The Frequency Principle of Goal Selection: Subjective well being can be enhanced by selecting goals that allow the person to experience positive affect repeatedly and in small doses rather than sparsely and in large doses.*

o   *The Cultural Norms Principle of Goal Selection: Selecting goals consistent with cultural norms can enhance subjective well being because achieving those goals brings about social recognition and therefore heightened satisfaction.   Achieving goals inconsistent with cultural norms, on the other hand, may not be as rewarding because of the lack of social recognition.*

o   *The Need Deprivation Principle of Goal Selection: Selecting goals that reflect deprived needs can enhance subjective well being.   The attainment of these goals induces intense positive affect because of heightened involvement in those life domains through which these needs are met.*

o   *The Achievement Principle in Goal Selection: Selecting achievement-oriented goals rather than non-achievement goals can enhance subjective well being.   The attainment of these goals induces intense positive affect because of heightened involvement in those life domains involving achievement goals.*

o   *The Autonomy Principle of Goal Selection: Selecting goals autonomously, i.e., without the interference or cajoling of others, can enhance subjective well being.   The attainment of autonomous goals induces intense positive affect because of heightened involvement in those life domains involving those goals.*

o   *The Flow Principle of Goal Selection: Subjective well being can be enhanced by selecting goals in life domains requiring a certain level of skill matching the person's skill level. Doing so enhances positive affect, which in turn contributes to subjective well being.*

o *The Skilful Winning Principle of Goal Selection: Subjective well being can be enhanced by winning competitive events requiring a certain level of skill matching the person's skill level. Doing so generates positive affect, which in turn contributes to subjective well being.*

o *The Adaptation Principle of Goal Selection: Selecting goals to reflect changes in circumstances can decrease dissatisfaction in a life domain. The new goals consistent with the new circumstances may also serve to increase satisfaction in the long run. Doing so should enhance subjective well being.*

o *The Feedfoward Principle of Goal Selection: Goals likely to be attained are selected by conjuring up scenarios visualising alternative ways to achieve those goals. Goals that are selected should reflect the person's confidence of goal attainment.*

o *The -Motive Congruence Principle of Goal Selection: Subjective well being can be increased (or dissatisfaction can be decreased) by selecting goals consistent with needs. Doing so increases the likelihood of goal attainmen and subjective well being.*

o *The Cultural Value Congruence Principle of Goal Selection: Subjective well being can be increased (or dissatisfaction can be decreased) by selecting goals consistent with cultural (and/or subcultural) values. Doing so increases the likelihood of goal attainment and subjective well being.*

o *The Resources Congruence Principle of Goal Selection: Subjective well being can be increased (or dissatisfaction can be decreased) by selecting goals consistent with available resources. Doing so increases the likelihood of goal attainment and subjective well being.*

o *The Realism Principle of Goal Selection: Subjective well being can be increased (or dissatisfaction can be decreased) by selecting realistic goals rather than unrealistic ones. Realistic goals are more likely to be attained, and therefore generate positive affect, than unrealistic goals. Doing so enhances subjective well being.*

o   <u>*The Conflict Principle of Goal Selection*</u>*: Subjective well-being can be increased (or dissatisfaction can be decreased) by selecting goalsin one or more life domains that do not conflict with one another. Doing so increases the likelihood of goal attainment and subjective well being.*

The Goal Implementation and Attainment Strategy

o   <u>*The Principle of Goal Implementation and Attainment*</u>*: Satisfaction in a life domain can be increased (or dissatisfaction can be decreased) by taking action to implement and achieve important goals set in that domain. Doing so contributes to subjective well being.*

o   <u>*The Principle of Recognition of Goal Attainment*</u>*: Focusing attention to one's accomplishments in a life domain can increase satisfaction in that domain. A good sense of appreciation of one's accomplishments can be a significant factor in enhancing subjective well being.*

o   <u>*The Concreteness Principle of Goal Attainment*</u>*: Abstract goals translated concretely in measurable terms are likely to result in greater domain satisfaction than abstract goals that are non-measurable. This is because satisfaction can only be experienced when the person recognises goal attainment. Recognition of goal attainment is facilitated by goal concreteness, thus contributing to subjective well being.*

o   <u>*The Progress Principle of Goal Attainment*</u>*: Action directed toward goal attainment within a life domain contributes to increases in satisfaction in that domain in two ways: (a) The action increases the likelihood of goal attainment inducing positive affect in that domain, which in turn contributes to subjective well being. (b) The action itself induces positive affect by prompting the anticipation of goal attainment, which in turn contributes to subjective well being.*

o   <u>*The Commitment Principle of Goal Implementation*</u>*: Action reflective of goal commitment (e.g., persistent efforteven in light of* *failure outcomes) in the context of a life domain contributes to subjective well being by enhancing the likelihood of goal attainment in that domain. Goal attainment is a major source of domain satisfaction and subjective well being.*

o   *The Feedback Principle of Goal Implemntation: Trial-and-error learning facilitates task completion and therefore the experience of satisfaction that follows from task completion and goal attainment. Trial-and-error learning entails trying out different ways to accomplish the task, those that lead to task completion are identified and reinforced.*

The Re-appraisal Strategy

o   *The Re-appraisal Principle: Re-interpreting significant negative events can convert negative affect associated with these events into positive affect. This should decrease dissatisfaction in the domain housing these events. Conversely, re-interpreting significant positive events can enhance the positive valence of the events, thereby increasing satisfaction in the domain housing these events. Doing so should help enhance subjective well being.*

o   *The Teaching Principle of Re-appraisal: Re-interpreting significant negative events in rational terms can convert negative affect associated with these events into positive affect. This should decrease dissatisfaction within the domain housing these events. A person (e.g., counselor) who assumes the role of the teacher can facilitate this re-interpretation. Doing so should enhance subjective well being.*

o   *The Spiritual Principle of Re-appraisal: Re-interpreting significant negative events in spiritual terms can convert negative affect associated with these events into positive affect. This should decrease dissatisfaction within the domain housing these events. Conversely, re-interpreting significant positive events in spiritual terms may enhance the positive valence of the events, thereby increasing satisfaction. Doing so should enhance subjective well being.*

o   *The Social Support Principle of Re-appraisal: Re-interpreting significant negative events with the assistance of significant others can reduce the valence of the negative affect associated with these events. This should decrease dissatisfaction within the domain housing these events. Doing so should enhance subjective well being.*

o   *The Time Principle of Re-appraisal: Dissatisfaction in a given domain arising from a significant negative event decreases over time. Thus, domain dissatisfaction can be reduced by allowing time to pass without thinking and dwelling on the negative event. Doing so enhance subjective well being.*

The Balance Strategy

o   *The Principle of Balance Within Life Domains: Balance within a life domain contributes to the enhancement of subjective well being. Balance within a life domain involves action designed to balance positive and negative events within that domain.*

o   *The Principle of Balance Between Life Domains: Balance between life domains serve to enhance subjective well being. Balance involves increasing the salience of negative and positive life domains. Increasing the salience of a negative domain serves to heighten motivation to take future action to increase satisfaction in that domain. In contrast, increasing the salience of positive life domains serves to generate more positive affect to compensate for the increased negative affect--resulting from the increased salience of the negative life domain.*

o   *The Quota Principle of Balance: Satisfaction from one life domain can contribute only a limited amount (a quota) to subjective well being. Conversely, dissatisfaction in one life domain can adversely affect subjective well being up to some threshold (or limit).*

o   *The Aggregation Principle of Balance: Aggregating various amounts of satisfaction from various life domains serves to enhance subjective well being. The more satisfaction is experienced from multiple life domains, the higher the subjective well being.*

o   *The Satisfaction Efficiency Principle of Balance: Satisfaction from a small set of important life domains generate higher levels of subjective well being than satisfaction from a larger set of domains that are equally important. This is due to the fact that the amount of satisfaction experienced is inversely related to the effort consumed to generate this satisfaction. Thus, satisfaction generated from a small set of domains is likely to involve less effort than satisfaction generated from a larger set of domains.*

INDEX

Abelson, 196, 244
Abramson, 176, 226
abstract attributes, 76
abstract goals, 195
accounts theory, 108
achievement principle, 178
Achievement Principle in Goal Selection, 178
achievement values, 79
active teaching, 116, 200, 207
activity pleasure, 181
actual-ideal discrepancies, 137, 143
actual-ought discrepancies, 137, 143
Adams, 34, 183, 226
adaptation level, 61, 114, 120, 121, 122, 126
adaptation principle, 183
Adaptation Principle of Goal Selection, 183
Adaptation-Level Principle of Re-evaluation, 122
adaptation-over-time principle, 127
Adaptation-over-time Principle of Re-evaluation, 127
Adelmann, 232
affective allostasis, 59
aggregation, 25, 212, 213, 221
Aggregation Principle, 221
Ahuvia, 176
Aiello, 226
Ajzen, 81, 238
Albin, 250
Alderfer, 51, 226
Aldous, 80, 174

Allardt, 98, 226
Allman, 60, 234
Alloy, 226
Almeder, 19, 226
Alsaker, 242
altruism, 7
Andreenkova, 22, 257
Andrews, 21, 22, 29, 33, 36, 41, 43, 48, 50, 226, 227, 244, 251
Andrisani, 62, 227
Annas, 19, 227
Antaki, 263
Antonucci, 232
Appley, 228
Argyle, 61, 126, 155, 180, 187, 189, 227, 236, 238, 240, 242, 249, 258, 264
Aristotle, 17, 18, 227
Armstrong-Stassen, 204, 261
aspiration level, 6, 147
aspired self, 13, 64, 114, 131, 136, 138, 147
Aspired Self-Principle of Re-evaluation, 147
Audrian, 246
Austin, 19, 227
autonomy principle, 179
Autonomy Principle of Goal Selection, 179
avoidance, 61, 115, 171, 172, 238, 243, 257
B.A.T. Exercise, 194
Baird, 166, 230
Baker, 170, 227
Balance, 5, 7, 66, 213, 214, 215, 216, 217, 218, 220, 221, 225, 247
balance principle, 212, 218
Balatasky, 227

Balatsky, 22
Baldwin, 74, 262
Barak, 35
Barden, 135, 251
basking in reflected glory, 158
Baumeister, 111, 227
Beck, 203, 228
Bedian, 62, 257
Benditt, 18, 228, 230
benevolence, 61, 204
Bentham, 17
Berlyne, 128, 228
Best, 106, 228
Bhargava, 217, 228
Biases related to interview or questionnaire format, 43
Biases related to mood, 43
Biases related to scaling effects, 43
Biases related to situational influences, 43
Biases related to social desirability, 43
Biases related to standard of comparison, 43
Blenkhorn, 260, 261
Bless, 210, 228
Bornstein, 129, 228
Botcheva, 90, 146, 241
Bottom-up spillover, 6, 63, 69
Bottom-Up Spillover Principle, 75
Bower, 129
Bradburn, 22, 23, 29, 228
Braungart, 228
Brebner, 204, 228
Brewer, 134, 228
Brickman, 126, 228, 229
Brief, 21, 29, 62, 229, 240
Brody, 229
Bromet, 62, 229
Brown, 33, 41, 42, 204, 229
Brunstein, 185, 197, 229
Buddha, 155, 198
Bukstel, 229

Bulman, 110, 229
Burke, 134, 229
Burroughs, 255
Buskel, 122
Buunk, 156, 229, 235
Cadotte, 229
Cameron, 22, 229
Campbell, 21, 29, 43, 50, 73, 126, 134, 135, 137, 141, 228, 230
Cantor, 166, 167, 171, 178, 186, 187, 189, 193, 230
Cantril, 21, 33, 34, 184, 230
Capwell, 243
Carli, 180, 250
Carlson, 182
Carson, 18, 228, 230
Carver, 90, 145, 166, 167, 171, 203, 230, 231, 257
Centers, 157, 231
Cesa, 227
Chamberlain, 21, 23, 25, 231
Chason, 109, 244
Chassin, 134, 241
Chen, 204, 217, 231, 249
Cheng, 204, 231
Cheung, 198, 238
Christie, 245
Cialdini, 158, 231
Cicic, 260, 261
Clark, 23, 29, 90, 106, 112, 141, 182, 231, 239, 265
classical conditioning,, 186
Clore, 47, 210, 228, 232, 239, 258
Coates, 126, 229
cognitive evaluation theory, 108
cognitive map, 76
Cohen, 136, 171, 232, 257
Cole, 237, 260
Coleman, 98, 232, 249
collective cultures, 173
Collins, 156, 229
Colvin, 60, 234

compensation, 7, 11, 12, 16, 63, 64, 67, 68, 83, 93, 103, 104, 106, 107, 108, 111, 112, 213, 228, 261

Compensation, 5, 6, 69, 103, 105, 107, 108, 109, 110, 111, 112, 113

compensatory   self-inflation theory, 111

competence, 61, 78

competent self, 13, 64, 114, 131, 136, 138, 146, 147

Competent Self Principle of Re-evaluation, 146

ComQuality of life-A5, 19, 33, 39

concrete attributes, 76

concrete goals, 195

concrete thinking, 195

Concreteness Principle, 195

Congruity Life Satisfaction, 33, 37, 135, 260

contextual theory of happiness, 123

Converse, 50, 73, 134, 135, 230

Cooper, 34

Coopersmith, 136, 232

coping, 171, 172, 203, 209, 229, 231, 235, 239, 251, 255, 257

Costa, 90, 170, 203, 208, 232, 251

Cotgrove, 106, 232

Cottingham, 19, 232

Coyne, 170, 234

crime, 9, 208

Crist-Houran, 165, 232

Crohan, 62, 232

Crooker, 21, 29, 232

Croponzano, 203

Crosby, 154, 233

Crouter, 62, 98, 233

Crowe, 243

Csikszentmihalyi, 180, 233, 247, 250

cultural norm principle, 175

cultural norms, 99, 115, 173, 175, 186, 187

Cultural Norms Principle of Goal Selection, 175

Cultural Pressures Principle of Horizontal Spillover, 102

cultural value, 115, 173, 182, 186, 187

Culver, 250

Cummins, 19, 33, 39, 59, 60, 61, 106, 154, 188, 228, 233

Czepiel, 226

Dakof, 156, 170, 229, 234

Dalbert, 208, 249

Danna, 53

Dattilio, 239

David, 210, 222, 223, 224, 237

Davidson, 232

Davis, 18, 234

Davy, 209, 257

Day, 74, 226, 234, 248

Dea, 108, 234

Deci, 166, 234

DeFries, 228

Delighted-Terrible (D-T) Scale, 33, 36

Delle Fave, 180, 250

DeLongis, 170, 234

Denton, 255

Depressed people, 203

depression, 11, 15, 23, 24, 25, 28, 29, 30, 46, 49, 61, 62, 91, 92, 103, 125, 137, 143, 190, 203, 226, 239, 240, 243, 262

Derryberry, 234

deserved self, 13, 64, 114, 131, 135, 138, 140, 142, 144, 147, 148

deserved-self principle, 142

Deserved-self Principle of Re-evaluation, 141

Deutsch, 46

developmental needs, 11, 15, 50, 51, 52, 221, 225
Dew, 62, 229
Diener, 6, 8, 21, 22, 23, 24, 25, 29, 33, 37, 43, 47, 48, 54, 60, 73, 79, 80, 90, 91, 97, 124, 126, 137, 141, 146, 147, 152, 153, 154, 156, 166, 170, 172, 173, 175, 186, 187, 203, 204, 227, 230, 234, 235, 236, 237, 238, 239, 240, 243, 245, 247, 248, 249, 250, 253, 258, 259, 262
Dixon, 245
domain hierarchy, 12, 55, 56, 63, 67, 70, 85, 94
domain importance, 106
domain salience, 50, 56, 57, 67, 75, 78, 80, 81, 83
Donahue, 148, 236
downward comparison, 152, 153
Drakopoulos, 141, 236
Dubin, 57, 101, 226, 237
Duncan, 126, 237
Dunnette, 237
Dunning, 90, 156, 237
Durup, 62, 248
Dutton, 204, 229
Dymond, 136, 256
Easterlin, 154, 237
Edwards, 19, 237
Efraty, 40, 73, 237
Eichhorn, 106, 241
Eiser, 254
Elder, 46, 125, 237
Elkman, 232
Ellis, 205, 206, 207, 237
Ellison, 203, 238
Emmons, 23, 29, 43, 60, 147, 170, 171, 190, 198, 208, 235, 238, 248
Emotion-focused re-appraisal, 209
endowment effect, 73
endowment/contrast model, 127
Enneavor, 182

Epstein, 155, 238
Eurobarometer, 33, 36
expectancies of control, 90, 91, 146
expectancy of control, 90
extraversion, 54, 90, 170, 232, 240
Eyman, 45, 256
Farmer, 253
Federick, 127
feedback, 116, 184, 191, 199
Feedback, 184, 199
feedforward principle, 184
feedfoward, 184
Feedfoward Principle of Goal Selection, 184
Fein, 239
Ferrans, 33, 38
fictitious occurrences, 115, 149, 158, 159
financial satisfaction, 80
financial well being, 74
Fishbein, 81, 238
Fisher, 238
Flammer, 242
flow, 87, 91, 115, 180, 181, 182, 233, 251
flow principle, 180, 181, 182
Flow Principle of Goal Selection, 181
focusing illusion effect, 127
Fogarty, 106, 239
Folkman, 170, 208, 234, 239
Formative indicators of subjective well being, 42
Forrester, 239
Frederick, 126, 128, 184, 239, 249
Freeman, 232, 239
frequency principle, 173
Frequency Principle of Goal Selection, 173
Frey, 111, 239
Friedman, 22, 100, 176, 239, 243, 256

friendships, 40, 75, 107, 218
Frijda, 239
Frisch, 4, 21, 33, 39, 81, 84, 107, 142, 166, 194, 195, 205, 217, 239, 240
Frone, 98, 240
Fujita, 22, 23, 29, 90, 147, 152, 166, 187, 235, 236, 240, 250, 262
Fulker, 228
functional consequences, 76
Furman, 135, 251
Furnham, 98, 106, 204, 231, 240
Ganey, 80, 174
Garza, 134, 240
Gatz, 227
Gauger, 107, 264
Gauthier, 18, 240
Gawron, 90, 251
Gecas, 106, 109, 112, 135, 231, 240
Gelya, 182
gender socialisation, 174
genetic predisposition to be happy, 90, 91
George, 62, 73, 240, 241, 247
Gerson, 174, 241
Gert, 19, 241
Gerwood, 208, 241
Gibbons, 235
Glatzer, 47, 241
Glick, 51, 256
goal approach, 171, 172
Goal Approach Principle of Goal Selection, 172
goal commitment, 116, 191, 197, 198
Goal Commitment Principle, 198
goal concreteness, 116, 193, 195, 196
Goal Conflict Principle of Goal Selection, 190

goal implementation and attainment, 7, 12, 13, 16, 63, 65, 114, 115, 191, 194
Goal implementation and attainment, 7, 191
goal intrinsicness, 167
Goal Intrinsicness Principle of Goal Selection, 167
goal realism principle, 189
Goal Realism Principle of Goal Selection, 189
goal selection, 7, 12, 13, 16, 63, 65, 114, 115, 161, 162, 164, 185
Goal selection, 7, 164
Goal Selection Principle, 164
Goal-Cultural Value Congruence Principle of Goal Selection, 186
goal-motive congruence principle, 185
Goal-Motive Congruence Principle of Goal Selection, 185
Goal-Resources Congruence Principle of Goal Selection, 188
Goldstein, 19, 106, 241
Golin, 91, 262
Golisano, 210, 228
Gollwitzer, 171, 241
Gordon, 241
Grant, 137, 143, 243
Grassman, 185, 229
Greenberg, 33, 41, 42, 111, 241
Greenglass, 174, 244
Greenley, 33, 41, 42
Griffin, 18, 53, 73, 127, 134, 235, 241, 264
Grigoryev, 250
Grob, 90, 146, 241
Grodsky, 227
Gross, 204, 242
Groves, 128
growth factors, 169, 170

Growth Needs Principle of Goal Selection, 170
Gschneidinger, 44, 46, 124, 262
Gullone, 19, 33, 39, 233
Gurhan, 79, 248
Guttman, 75, 242, 255
Haavio-Mannila, 106, 242
Hagerty, 124, 242
Hahn, 100, 256
Hall, 57, 229, 255
Haller, 106, 242
Halpern, 62, 246
Hannah, 247
Hansen, 73, 260
happiness, 6, 7, 8, 9, 10, 11, 14, 15, 17, 18, 19, 20, 21, 22, 23, 24, 25, 28, 29, 30, 32, 38, 39, 44, 47, 48, 50, 51, 53, 59, 61, 70, 75, 86, 89, 90, 92, 108, 122, 123, 124, 125, 126, 127, 142, 146, 152, 153, 156, 164, 165, 166, 167, 171, 174, 175, 176, 177, 182, 188, 194, 205, 208, 209, 212, 217, 218, 219, 221, 226, 227, 228, 231, 234, 237, 238, 240, 242, 244, 245, 247, 248, 249, 250, 251, 252, 254, 255, 257, 259, 260, 262, 263, 264, 265
happiness pie exercise, 218
happy people, 8, 89, 91, 203, 204, 211, 253
Haring, 74, 154, 242, 253
Harpaz, 98, 247
Hartley, 231
hassles, 170, 234
Have-relevant others discrepancy, 154
Havighurst, 253
Haviland, 229
Haw, 146, 242
Haybron, 18, 19, 20, 242
Headey, 23, 29, 61, 90, 126, 154, 170, 242, 243
Headley, 57, 237

Heckhausen, 59, 243
hedonic treadmill, 126
Helson, 120, 121, 122, 125, 243
Henry, 189, 197, 243, 265
Herman, 256
Herringer, 134, 240
Herzberg, 30, 51, 169, 243
Hewstone, 241
hierarchy of gender identities, 174
Higgins, 137, 143, 144, 146, 148, 171, 243, 258, 262, 264
High-Level Goal Principle of Goal Selection, 168
high-level goals, 168, 195
Hill, 19, 230, 244
Hippler, 46, 258
Hoelter, 134, 244
Holzberg, 156, 237
homeostasis, 59
Horizontal spillover, 6, 12, 64, 67, 69, 93, 100, 101, 102
Horizontal-Spillover Principle, 99
Horwitz, 170, 235
Hougland, 98, 248
Hovland, 232
Hsee, 196, 244
Huba, 24, 62, 263
Hulin, 244
Hunt, 50, 53, 57, 62, 74, 253, 255
Hunter, 210, 244
hygiene factors, 169
Hyland, 172
Hymes, 243
ideal self, 13, 64, 114, 131, 135, 136, 137, 138, 142, 143, 145, 147
Ideal Self Principle of Re-evaluation, 138
imbalanced, 218, 219, 220
imitation, 186
income, 22, 23, 29, 70, 74, 79, 80, 86, 121, 124, 126, 137, 141, 143,

144, 152, 154, 155, 156, 174, 187, 188, 231, 233, 236, 264, 265
Index of Overall Life Quality, 36
individualist cultures, 173
Inglehart, 23, 33, 36, 124, 176, 226, 244
Inglis, 174, 244
instrumental learning, 186
instrumental values, 8, 9, 76
intrinsic and extrinsic goals, 166, 246
irrational thinking, 206, 207
irrationality, 205
Irwin, 147, 244, 245
Jackson, 4, 22
Jacobs, 19, 244
Jacques, 109, 244
James, 135, 244
Janis, 232
Janoff-Bulman, 61, 126, 229, 244
Jenkins, 100, 229, 256
Jin, 4, 260, 261
job satisfaction, 53, 74, 80, 89, 98, 141, 155, 169, 245, 246, 254, 255, 257, 258, 259
John, 96, 97, 236
Jones, 111, 227
Judge, 89, 244, 245
Kaase, 36
Kabanoff, 62, 245
Kahneman, 28, 44, 127, 227, 230, 235, 236, 239, 243, 245, 249, 253, 257, 258
Kaiser, 171, 238
Kammann, 48, 245
Kapteyn, 124, 245, 264
Karasek, 98, 245
Kasser, 166, 190, 245, 246, 259
Kau, 209, 262
Kavanagh, 62, 246
Kavanaugh, 239
Kean, 246

Kekes, 19, 246
Kelley, 243
Kelly, 23, 29
Keltner, 246
Kenny, 19, 246
Ketelaar, 248
Kette, 90, 247
Kilman, 122
Kilmann, 229
Kim, 23, 247
King, 190, 238
Kinicki, 209, 257
Kishchuck, 45, 256
Kitayama, 139, 216, 247
Kommer, 45, 47, 258
Kosenko, 40, 260, 261
Kositchek, 100, 256
Kostin, 229
Kozma, 22, 24, 26, 247
Kraut, 19, 247
Kremer, 98, 247
Krieger, 198, 247
Kruglanski, 156, 247, 258
Kubey, 180, 233, 247
LaBarbera, 79, 248
Lacy, 98, 248
Lamb, 250
Lance, 137, 141, 143, 144, 152, 154
Landerman, 73, 241
Lane, 20
Larsen, 23, 34, 43, 60, 97, 126, 203, 220, 235, 238, 248, 261, 265
Larson, 73
Lawrence, 230, 240, 248, 254
Lazarus, 170, 234, 239
LeBlanc, 208, 241
Lee, 4, 174, 248, 261
Leelakulthanit, 74, 248
LeFevre, 233
Leiter, 62, 248
Lepper, 165, 248
Leuenberger, 90, 237

Levine, 60, 235, 238
Levinson, 249
Levison, 102
Levitin, 62, 248
Lewellyn, 38
Lewin, 53, 249
Lewinsohn, 24, 62, 249
Lewis, 229
Liao, 210, 244
life satisfaction, 6, 10, 11, 15, 17, 21, 22, 23, 24, 29, 30, 32, 33, 34, 35, 36, 37, 39, 41, 42, 44, 48, 51, 53, 54, 59, 60, 61, 62, 63, 69, 70, 71, 73, 74, 76, 78, 80, 81, 89, 90, 91, 94, 99, 100, 106, 124, 135, 137, 141, 143, 144, 152, 154, 161, 165, 171, 173, 176, 183, 184, 189, 193, 204, 208, 210, 217, 218, 219, 220, 221, 222, 228, 229, 233, 234, 235, 237, 238, 239, 240, 242, 245, 249, 251, 253, 255, 257, 260, 261, 262, 265
Life Satisfaction Index-A, 34
Life Satisfaction Index-B, 34
Life Satisfaction Rating, 33, 34
Lindeman, 195
Linderman, 249
Lipkus, 208, 249
Lipset, 98, 249
Little, 196, 247, 251
Littlefield, 73, 260
Lo, 97, 106, 228
Locke, 89, 245, 246
Loewenstein, 126, 127, 184, 239, 249
Loewnstein, 128
Loscocco, 62, 249
Lovelace, 197, 243
Lucas, 22, 23, 29, 79, 91, 170, 173, 186, 235, 236, 249, 253
Luer, 258
Luper, 19, 249
Lykken, 90, 250, 263
Lyubomirsky, 156, 203, 250

Macek, 90, 146, 241
Magen, 7, 250
Magnus, 250
Malatesta, 186, 250
Mallard, 137, 141, 143, 144, 152, 154
Mandl, 102, 249
marital conflict, 171, 198
marital satisfaction, 75, 263
Markel, 98, 240
Markus, 134, 139, 216, 247, 250
marriage, 80, 97, 98, 112, 125, 128, 174, 188, 205, 224, 244, 260, 265
Martin, 44, 45, 61, 220, 227, 230, 238, 262
Maruish, 240
Maslow, 8, 40, 51, 169, 219, 250
Massimini, 180, 250
Masters, 135, 178, 251
material consumption, 9
materialism, 9, 176, 220, 248, 255, 261, 262
materialistic, 57, 79, 246
Matlin, 90, 251
Mausner, 243
Mayerfeld, 18
Mayerfield, 251
Mayseless, 156, 247
McCabe, 19, 33, 39, 233
McCall, 56, 134, 251
McCarthy, 266
McClelland, 51, 251
McCrae, 90, 170, 203, 208, 251
McFall, 19, 251
McFarlin, 50, 53, 137, 255
McGregor, 196, 251
McIntosh, 204, 220, 259
McKennell, 21, 29, 226, 251
McNeil, 247
McRae, 232
Meadow, 33, 34, 37, 135, 153, 232, 247, 251, 260, 261

Mealsky, 226
meaningfulness, 61, 115, 164, 165
Means-End Chain Principle of Bottom-up Spillover, 77
means-ends chain, 75
Measurement caveats, 43
Mechanic, 24, 62, 252
Meissner, 101, 112, 252
Mellon, 62, 258
Memory biases, 43
Mentzer, 251, 261
mere exposure theory, 128
Messinger, 100, 256
metropolitan residents, 106
Meyerowitz, 156, 237
Michalos, 4, 21, 22, 124, 135, 137, 141, 143, 144, 152, 154, 252
Mill, 19, 252
Miller, 105, 227, 244, 246, 252
minimum tolerable self, 131, 135, 138
minimum-need expectations, 142
Minimum-needs Principle of Re-evaluation, 143
moderately balanced, 219, 222, 223
Monat, 239
Montague, 18, 252
mood, 31, 34, 45, 46, 49, 98, 129, 130, 170, 234, 250, 262
Moore, 252
Moschis, 252
motive-incongruent goals, 185
Mueller, 23, 247
multiattribute attitude, 81, 83, 84
Multiattribute Attitude Principle of Bottom-up Spillover, 83
multiple discrepancies theory, 124, 135, 137, 141, 143, 144, 154
Munden, 102, 249
Munkel, 47, 252
Murray, 166, 181, 252

Myers, 74, 203, 210, 252, 253
Nagpal, 260
Nakamura, 134, 228
Neal, 73, 253
Near, 21, 29, 50, 53, 62, 74, 102, 232, 253, 254, 255
need deprivation, 154, 176, 177
Need Deprivation Principle of Goal Selection, 177
Need Hierarchy Measure of Life Satisfaction, 33, 40
needs principle, 113, 143, 146, 171
Neill, 198, 247
Neugarten, 33, 34, 253
neuroticism, 54, 90, 190, 232, 240, 250
Newcomb, 231
Niven, 122, 152, 183, 190, 207, 209, 220, 253
Nolen-Hoeksema, 253
Norris, 232
Nozick, 18, 253
Nye, 112, 231
O'Brien, 51, 253
Oishi, 79, 91, 173, 186, 222, 235, 236, 253, 254
Okun, 74, 154, 242, 253
Oliver, 139, 254
Olson, 159, 256
Omodei, 181, 254
opponent-process theory, 60, 261
optimism, 49, 61, 66, 90, 145, 188, 194
optimistic, 86, 90, 203
Organ, 21, 29, 254
Orpen, 62, 254
Ortony, 239
Oswald, 141, 231
Overlap Principle of Horizontal Spillover, 100
Padgett, 74, 262
Pagnucco, 98, 261

Panos, 204, 254
Parducci, 18, 28, 44, 61, 122, 123, 125, 254
Parkinson, 62, 229
Partillo, 204, 261
past self, 124, 135, 144
Patterson, 182
Paul, 227, 244, 264
Pavot, 60, 90, 172, 234, 236, 250
Peacock, 166, 252
Pederson, 243
Pelham, 156, 254
Pennebaker, 170, 265
perceived quality of life, 6, 10, 17, 32, 50, 134, 255, 282
perfectionist happiness, 18, 19, 20
personal crises, 68, 107, 110, 210
personal crisis principle, 110
personal history principle, 120
Personality   Principle   of Horizontal Spillover, 100
Personality Principle of Top-down Spillover, 90
Peterson, 189, 265
Pfeffer, 51, 257
Phillips, 137, 255
Phua, 209, 262
Piazza, 208, 241
Plato, 17, 254
Plomin, 228
Pollner, 203, 254
pollyannaism, 90, 251
Pomerantz, 222
Pomrantz, 254
Porter, 109, 254
positive and negative affect, 10, 11, 14, 15, 17, 23, 24, 29, 30, 32, 48, 52, 54, 66, 126, 169, 170, 212, 213, 227, 231, 235, 265
Powers, 33, 38
predicted self, 115, 131, 136, 144, 145, 146

Predicted Self Principle of Re-evaluation, 145
predictive expectations, 144, 181
Presser, 45, 258
Price, 102, 249
principle   of   fixed   sum   of resources, 112
Principle of Goal Implementation and Attainment, 193, 195, 196, 198, 199
Principle of Goal Meaningfulness of Goal Selection, 165
principle of *range and frequency*, 124, 125
Principle of Recognition of Goal Implementation and Attainment, 194
Principle   of   Self-concept Integration, 148
principle of skilful winning, 181, 182
Principle of Social Comparison, 152
Principle of Top-Down Spillover, 89
Principle of What Might Have Been of Re-evaluation, 159
problem-focused   re-appraisals, 209
progress principle, 197
progress toward goal attainment, 13, 114, 116, 193, 196
prosocial behaviour, 7
prudential happiness, 18, 19
psychological happiness, 18, 19, 20
public condition principle, 111
Pyszczynski, 108, 111, 241, 255
QOL, 20, 153, 282
quality of life, 1, 6, 8, 9, 10, 11, 14, 15, 17, 19, 21, 36, 39, 40, 41, 50, 73, 76, 93, 107, 109, 110, 146,

157, 161, 164, 165, 171, 200, 205, 213, 230, 233, 240, 241, 243, 244, 245, 247, 249, 253, 260, 261, 282
Quality of life, 9, 19, 40, 240
quality of rural and metropolitan life, 106, 228
Quality-of-Life Index, 33, 38
Quality-of-Life Inventory, 33, 39, 239
Quality-of-Life Questionnaire, 33, 41, 42
quantity of life, 9
Quinn, 62, 248
Quota Principle, 220
Rabier, 23, 124, 244
Rabinowitz, 57, 255
Rahtz, 35, 237, 240, 247, 251, 260, 261
Range-Frequency Principle of Re-evaluation, 125
range-frequency theory, 18, 61
Rapoport, 106, 239, 255
rational thought, 205
Rational-emotive psychotherapy, 205
Rational-emotive therapy, 207
Rawls, 19, 255
Re-appraisal, 5, 7, 65, 200, 202, 205, 208, 209, 210, 211
re-appraisals, 204, 209
recognition of goal attainment, 116, 193, 194
Reddner, 62
Reder, 237
Redner, 24, 249
Reed, 234
re-evaluation based on personal history, 7, 11, 13, 16, 63, 64, 114, 117
Re-evaluation based on personal history, 6
re-evaluation based on self-concept, 13, 63, 64, 114, 131

re-evaluation based on social comparison, 7, 12, 13, 16, 63, 65, 115, 149
Re-evaluation based on social comparison, 7
Re-evaluation based on the self-concept, 6
Reflective Life Satisfaction (RLS) measure, 33, 35
Rehberg, 23, 255
Reich, 24, 62, 255
religion, 18, 64, 152, 198, 208, 209, 210, 238
religiosity, 198, 209, 248
religious people, 203
Repeated Failure Principle, 108
Rescher, 18, 255
resources, 38, 65, 68, 103, 107, 112, 115, 147, 166, 182, 183, 187, 188, 197, 213, 234, 241, 243
retired people, 98, 165
Reynolds, 75, 198, 247, 255
Rice, 50, 53, 57, 62, 74, 137, 253, 255
Ridenfleisch, 255
Riess, 108, 263
Rigsby, 266
Roberson, 21, 29, 229
Roberts, 51, 236, 256
Robins, 236
Robinson, 21, 43, 226
Roborgh, 256
Rodgers, 50, 73, 134, 135, 230
Roese, 159, 256
Rogers, 136, 256
Rokeach, 8, 256
Romeo, 19, 33, 39
Roney, 243
Rosenberg, 56, 109, 136, 226, 256
Rosenman, 100, 256
Rosenmayr, 106, 242
Ross, 45, 156, 203, 250, 256

Roth, 171, 257
Rozin, 129, 257
Russell, 17, 227, 230, 235, 236, 239, 243, 245, 246, 249, 253, 257, 258
Rusting, 253
Ryan, 108, 166, 234, 246
Sabatier, 90, 146, 241
Safilios-Rothschild, 98, 257
Salancik, 257
Salanick, 51
Sameroff, 246
Samli, 234, 247, 260
Sanderson, 166, 167, 171, 178, 186, 187, 189, 230
Sandvik, 43, 60, 126, 172, 236
Saris, 22, 36, 152, 257
satisfaction efficiency, 212, 213, 223, 225
satisfaction quota, 212
Satisfaction with Life Scale, 33, 37, 235
Saxon, 222, 254
Schaeffer, 262
Schaffer, 91
Scheck, 209, 257
Scheier, 90, 145, 167, 171, 203, 230, 231, 257
Schkade, 127, 257
Schmitt, 62, 257, 258
Schultheiss, 185, 229
Schultz, 59, 243
Schuman, 45, 258
Schwartz, 44, 227, 230, 235, 236, 239, 243, 245, 249, 253, 264
Schwarz, 43, 44, 45, 46, 47, 124, 153, 210, 227, 228, 236, 238, 240, 242, 249, 252, 258, 259, 262, 264
Schwarzer, 234
Schyns, 124, 154, 259
Scitovsky, 126, 164, 259
Scott, 106, 134, 135, 204, 259
Scruton, 19
Scrutton, 259

Seccombe, 248
Seeley, 24, 62, 249
Seeman, 51, 53, 259
Seidlitz, 43, 204, 236, 259
self-assessment, 153
self-concept differentiation, 147, 236
self-concept integration, 115, 131, 148
self-concept principle, 134
Self-concept Principle of Re-evaluation, 134
self-efficacy, 49, 139
self-enhancement, 115, 149, 153, 154, 155, 156, 158
Self-enhancement Principle of Re-evaluation, 155
self-esteem, 20, 22, 40, 49, 73, 80, 90, 91, 108, 109, 112, 136, 137, 139, 153, 155, 156, 173, 187, 188, 194, 218, 232, 235, 254, 256, 263
self-identification, 115, 149, 153, 158
Self-identification Principle of Re-evaluation, 158
self-improvement, 115, 149, 153, 156, 157
Self-improvement Principle of Re-evaluation, 157
Seligman, 226
Sen, 18, 259
sensitisation, 114, 117, 128, 129
Sensitisation-over-time Pinciple of Re-evaluation, 129
Seppanen, 98
Shaefer, 33, 35
Shah, 137, 143, 243
Shamir, 98, 259
Shao, 236
Shapiro, 62, 227, 251
Shaver, 226
Shea, 106, 259
Shehan, 248

Sheldon, 166, 190, 259
Shepard, 98, 105, 171, 248, 259
Shepherd, 238
Sherman, 90, 237
Short, 240
Shostak, 174, 260
Siegel, 73, 237
Siegler, 208, 249
Silver, 260
Simmons, 56, 109, 134, 251, 256
Simpson, 19, 171, 260
Sirgy, 1, 14, 20, 33, 37, 40, 73, 135, 136, 137, 138, 153, 166, 189, 232, 237, 247, 251, 253, 260, 261
Skilful Winning Principle of Goal Selection, 182
Skills Principle of Horizontal Spillover, 101
Smith, 23, 29, 45, 47, 236, 261
Snyder, 33, 35
social comparison, 115, 149, 152, 153, 155, 157, 158, 175, 229, 235, 247, 250, 254, 256
social comparisons, 13, 45, 114, 135, 149, 154, 155, 156
social self, 13, 64, 114, 131, 132, 135, 138, 139, 140, 144, 147, 254
Social Self Principle of Re-evaluation, 140
Social Support Principle, 210
social values, 79
social/psychological consequences, 76
social-self principle, 140
Socrates, 17
Solley, 102, 249
Solomon, 60, 261
Sonnemans, 239
spiritual beliefs, 208
Spiritual Principle, 209
Spitz, 106, 259
Spreitzer, 33, 35

Srull, 228
Staats, 204, 261
Stacey, 256
Staines, 62, 98, 99, 100, 101, 106, 261
status principle, 109
Steiner, 62, 80, 261
Steinmetz, 260
Stetsenko, 90, 146
Stock, 54, 74, 154, 242, 253
Stone, 247
Stones, 24, 26, 247
Stouffer, 154, 262
Strack, 43, 44, 45, 46, 47, 124, 153, 227, 236, 238, 240, 242, 249, 252, 258, 259, 262, 264
Strauman, 137, 143, 262
Straus, 100, 256
stress diary technique., 205
Stroebe, 241
Stryker, 56, 262
Sttsenko, 241
Stumpf, 106, 134, 135, 259
subjective well being, 6, 7, 8, 10, 11, 12, 13, 14, 15, 17, 20, 21, 22, 23, 24, 25, 28, 29, 30, 32, 33, 34, 36, 40, 41, 42, 43, 44, 45, 46, 47, 48, 50, 51, 54, 55, 60, 62, 63, 64, 65, 66, 67, 69, 70, 73, 74, 75, 76, 79, 80, 83, 84, 85, 87, 89, 90, 91, 93, 94, 97, 98, 99, 100, 102, 103, 106, 107, 108, 110, 112, 114, 115, 117, 124, 125, 127, 131, 134, 137, 141, 142, 143, 144, 145, 146, 147, 148, 149, 152, 153, 154, 155, 156, 157, 158, 159, 161, 164, 165, 166, 169, 171, 172, 173, 175, 177, 178, 179, 180, 181, 182, 183, 185, 186, 187, 188, 189, 190, 191, 193, 194, 195, 197, 198, 203, 207, 208, 209, 210, 211, 212, 213, 216, 217, 219, 220, 221, 223, 225, 226, 235, 236, 242, 248, 253, 254, 256, 257
success log, 195

Sudman, 258
Suedfeld, 121
Suh, 22, 23, 29, 48, 79, 91, 173, 186, 235, 236, 247, 249, 253, 262
Sumner, 18, 262
Sussman, 260
Sweeney, 91, 262
Swinyard, 209, 262
Tait, 74, 262
Tanaka, 24, 62, 263
Tannen, 174, 263
Tatarkiewicz, 19, 263
Taveggia, 237
Taylor, 109, 110, 156, 228, 229, 263
teaching-appraisal principle, 208
Teasdale, 226
Tedeschi, 108, 263
Tehrani, 198, 238
Telfer, 18
Tellegen, 23, 29, 90, 250, 263, 265
Temporal stability problems, 43
terminal values, 8, 76
Tesser, 230
Theodossiou, 141, 236
Thiessen, 106, 255
Thomas, 19, 263
Thompson, 128
Thorne, 174, 263
Thurman, 194, 263
time, 25, 27, 28, 30, 35, 38, 41, 43, 44, 47, 75, 86, 91, 97, 99, 100, 107, 110, 112, 113, 114, 116, 117, 120, 121, 126, 127, 128, 129, 137, 140, 143, 148, 157, 173, 174, 183, 190, 193, 196, 198, 200, 207, 210, 211, 218, 222, 223, 234, 242, 244, 245, 262
Time Principle, 211
Titus, 229
Tobin, 253
Top-down spillover, 6, 12, 63, 67, 69, 85, 90, 92

Traveggia, 57
travel, 10, 79, 86, 159, 186, 253
Trial-and-ErrorLearning Principle, 199
Trow, 98, 249
Truxillo, 62, 80, 261
Tully, 134, 229
Turner, 197, 240, 263
Tversky, 73, 127, 264
two-factor theory, 169, 227
Tykocinski, 144, 146, 243
Type A personality, 100
Underwood, 261
unemployment, 98, 231, 253
unhappy people, 30, 89, 92, 203, 204, 232, 250
uplifts, 170, 234
utilitarianism, 17
Uysal, 73, 253
Vallacher, 189
values, 6, 8, 9, 18, 20, 22, 28, 39, 44, 47, 76, 79, 122, 123, 125, 134, 139, 173, 186, 241, 244, 245, 246, 256
van de Geer, 124, 264
van de Stadt, 124
Van de Stadt, 264
Van Hook, 148, 264
van Praag, 264
Van Praag, 124
Van Yperen, 156, 229
Van Zandt, 246
Veenhoven, 8, 19, 21, 22, 47, 74, 141, 154, 264
Verkasalo, 195, 249
Very Happy and the Depressed Principle of Top-down Spillover, 92
victimisation, 208
Victorian Quality-of-Life Study, 54, 126
vision quest technique, 218

Vollmecke, 129, 257
volunteering, 165
Von Wright, 18, 264
Vookles, 144, 146, 243
Wachsmuth, 156, 254
Wackman, 265
Wagner, 45, 47, 258
Walker, 107, 264
Walsh, 109, 263
Walters, 74, 248
Wang, 249
Wansbeek, 245
Wantanbe, 89
Ward, 265
Warner, 19, 265
Washington, 109, 228, 234, 242, 245, 254, 256, 259, 264, 265
Watanabe, 245
Watson, 23, 29, 90, 170, 265
Wearing, 23, 29, 54, 61, 90, 126, 154, 170, 181, 242, 243, 254
Wegner, 189
Wei, 249
Weintraub, 171, 231
Weiss, 105, 252
Werthessen, 100, 256
what might have been, 158, 159
what-might-have-been principle, 159
Wibker, 38
Wilensky, 62, 93, 103, 265
Wilkie, 252
Williams, 80, 265
Wilson, 6, 18, 59, 98, 189, 265

Withey, 21, 22, 33, 36, 41, 48, 50, 227
Witter, 74, 253
Wolf, 18, 265
Wong, 180
Wood, 33, 34, 35, 174, 265
Woodruff, 229
Woods, 107, 264
work involvement, 80, 106, 231
work satisfaction, 12, 64, 67, 74, 93, 98
world illusions, 61
worthiness, 61
Wortman, 110, 229
Wright, 220, 226, 261, 265
Wrightsman, 226
Wurm, 100, 256
Wyer, 228
Wylie, 33, 35
Xiao, 249
Yancey, 109, 266
Yardley, 98, 240
Yarsuvat, 260, 261
Ying and Yang, 139, 216
Young, 134, 241, 249
Zajonc, 128
Zanna, 256
Zautra, 24, 62, 255
Zax, 246
Zeller, 107, 259
Zemke, 182
Zhang, 249
Zheng, 249
Zimmerberg, 239
Zumbo, 233

.

ABOUT THE AUTHOR

M. JOSEPH SIRGY is a social/industrial psychologist (Ph.D., U/Massachusetts, 1979), Professor of Marketing and Virginia Real Estate Research Fellow at Virginia Polytechnic Institute and State University (Virginia Tech). He has published extensively in the area of quality-of-life (QOL) research and has been invited frequently by academic institutions and conferences as a distinguished scholar to speak on quality-of-life issues in relation to business, philosophy, measurement, and public policy. He has published over 200 books, journal articles, book chapters, and other scholarly work related to quality-of-life issues. Among his books related to QOL are *New Dimensions of Quality-of-Life/Marketing Research* (Greenwood Press, 1995) and *Handbook of Quality-of-Life Research* (Kluwer Academic Publishers, 2001). He is considered to be one of the leading scholars at the forefront of the QOL movement. Much of his work has focused on measuring perceived quality of life, consumer well being, leisure well being, work quality of life, community quality of life, and community health-related quality of life, and corporate social performance. He co-organized at least seven conferences related to quality of life (1985, 1989, 1992, 1995, 1997, 1998, 2000, and 2001). He edited several conference proceedings related to quality of life and authored several monographs including: *Quality of Life Studies and Social Indicators Research* (ISQOLS, 1998) and *Classic Works, Literature Reviews, and Other Important References in QOL Research in QOL Research* (ISQOLS, 1998). He has been (still is) the editor of the Quality-of-Life/Marketing section of the *Journal of Macromarketing* for many years. He is the founding father of the International Society for Quality-of-Life Studies (established in 1995) and remains its Executive Director since its inception. He is also the founding father of the Management Institute for Quality-of-Life Studies (a social science research thinktank helping organizations adopt QOL measures to assess organizational performance). He has directed the Office of Quality-of-Life Measurement since the early 1980s at Virginia Tech through which many QOL studies were conducted to benefit the business community as well as government. He is also the president-elect of the Academy of Marketing Science, the largest academic association of marketing professors worldwide. In a recent survey of scholarly productivity in business ethics, he was ranked as 82nd among 2,371 business ethics scholars worldwide.

Social Indicators Research Series

1. V. Møller (ed.): *Quality of Life in South Africa*. 1997   ISBN 0-7923-4797-8
2. G. Baechler: *Violence Through Environmental Discrimination*. Causes, Rwanda Arena, and Conflict Model. 1999   ISBN 0-7923-5495-8
3. P. Bowles and L.T. Woods (eds.): *Japan after the Economic Miracle*. In Search of New Directories. 1999   ISBN 0-7923-6031-1
4. E. Diener and D.R. Rahtz (eds.): *Advances in Quality of Life Theory and Research*. Volume I. 1999   ISBN 0-7923-6060-5
5. Kwong-leung Tang (ed.): *Social Development in Asia*. 2000   ISBN 0-7923-6256-X
6. M.M. Beyerlein (ed.): *Work Teams: Past, Present and Future*. 2000
        ISBN 0-7923-6699-9
7. A. Ben-Arieh, N.H. Kaufman, A.B. Andrews, R. Goerge, B.J. Lee, J.L. Aber (eds.): *Measuring and Monitoring Children's Well-Being*. 2001   ISBN 0-7923-6789-8
8. M.J. Sirgy: *Handbook of Quality-of-Life Research. An Ethical Marketing Perspective*. 2001   ISBN 1-4020-0172-X
9. G. Preyer and M. Bös (eds.): *Borderlines in a Globalized World*. New Perspectives in a Sociology of the World-System. 2002   ISBN 1-4020-0515-6
10. V. Nikolic-Ristanovic: *Social Change, Gender and Violence: Post-communist and war affected societies*. 2002   ISBN 1-4020-0726-4
11. M.R. Hagerty, J. Vogel and V. Møller: *Assessing Quality of Life and Living Conditions to Guide National Policy*. 2002   ISBN 1-4020-0727-2
12. M.J. Sirgy: *The Psychology of Quality of Life*. 2002   ISBN 1-4020-0800-7

KLUWER ACADEMIC PUBLISHERS – DORDRECHT / LONDON / BOSTON